Early Medieval Kingship

Early Medieval Kingship

edited by
P. H. SAWYER AND I. N. WOOD

Published under the auspices of
The School of History
University of Leeds

© The University of Leeds and Contributors

ISBN 0 906200 00 8

First published in 1977 by the editors under the auspices of
The School of History, The University of Leeds, Leeds LS2 9JT

Reprinted 1979

Printed in Great Britain by the University Printing Service at the University of Leeds

Preface

This book is based on a series of six lectures that were arranged by the editors and delivered in the University of Leeds in the summer term of 1977. We were encouraged to publish them, and hope to be excused for any shortcomings that result from our attempt to do as quickly and inexpensively as possible. The main shortcoming of which we are aware is in the bibliography, which includes some inconsistencies and duplication, caused by minor differences in the methods of different contributors. We very much regret that we have not been able to include an additional contribution on the terminology of kingship that was specially written for this volume by David Dumville. The text was lost in the post and unavoidable circumstances have made it impossible to obtain a second copy in time to avoid a protracted delay in publication. We have therefore very reluctantly decided to omit it, although the bibliography includes its references.

All the contributors have benefited greatly from the discussions, both formal and informal, that followed the lectures and thanks are due to all the participants. We also wish to express our gratitude to the School of History in the University of Leeds for facilitating the lectures and giving generous financial support to the publication, to the Leeds Philosophical and Literary Society for their contribution to the cost, to Deborah Baboolal for her help with the typing, and to the University Printing Service for the efficiency and speed with which they have made this book.

P.H.S.
I.N.W.

Contents

	Preface	v
	Introduction IAN WOOD	1
1	Kings, Kingdoms and Consent IAN WOOD	6
2	Julian of Toledo and the Royal Succession in Late Seventh-Century Spain ROGER COLLINS	30
3	Inauguration Rituals JANET L. NELSON	50
4	Kingship, Genealogies and Regnal Lists DAVID N. DUMVILLE	72
5	*Lex Scripta* and *Verbum Regis*: Legislation and Germanic Kingship, from Euric to Cnut PATRICK WORMALD	105
6	Kings and Merchants P. H. SAWYER	139
	Bibliography	159
	Index	181

Introduction

Early Medieval Kingship is an elusive topic. The evidence relating to kings is vast and yet few Dark Age writers stopped to theorize about royal office, at least before the ninth century. At the same time the importance of kings was such that anyone seeking to understand this early period must try to understand its kingship. Doubtless for this reason much has been written on this subject and some of the best work is to be found in English;[1] a rare pleasure. The publication of this group of lectures therefore does not open up a new topic to students of the Dark Ages: rather the contributors to this series have used their specialist knowledge of particular aspects of royal office in the period either to explore and chart more fully paths already indicated, or to suggest new directions of approach.

In the Preface to his Ford lectures, Professor Wallace-Hadrill remarked on the connections between his own work and that of Professor Ullmann; "Our approach is rather different but we move in the same world."[2] Indeed both of these scholars move in a world of Dark Age writers and theologians; of men who, although they rarely explained what kingship meant to them, at least thought carefully about what they wrote and, if only spasmodically, provided insights into royal power, which was formed, in time, into fully fledged political thought. In general these writers had what Professor Wallace-Hadrill has termed elsewhere "nobility of mind."[3] Early medieval thinkers were learned men and they were especially learned when it came to a knowledge of the Bible. They could provide apt quotations for most political developments. It is not surprising, therefore, that the work of Professor Wallace-Hadrill and of Professor Ullmann is full of references to the Bible and to the church canons.

But the Bible and the canons feature rarely in these lectures; part of the reason for this lies in the very fact of the stress laid on these elements already.[4] To say more about these foundations of royal power would require another lecture devoted entirely to the Bible and its influence on kingship and the lecture would be the harder because of the subtlety of argument required. It is not always easy to discern whether kings acted in a particular way because of the Bible or whether

---

[1] Above all Wallace-Hadrill 1971. Also Binchy 1970 and Ullmann 1969.
[2] Wallace-Hadrill 1971, p. viii. As Professor Wallace-Hadrill here acknowledges, his ideas were also greatly influenced by the seminal paper of Ewig 1956.
[3] Wallace-Hadrill 1975 pp. 1–18 esp. p. 18.
[4] See also Ewig 1956 and Ullmann 1963.

priests described what kings were doing in Biblical terms, because the Bible provided appropriate language. The Vulgate and its Latin precursors were concerned, after all, with a society both Mediterranean and tribal and described them in prose as influential in the development of Latin as the Authorised Version was for the English language. In fact the problem of the relationship between the Bible and kingship is illustrated by three of the lectures printed here. Roger Collins faces the question of a Biblical inspiration behind royal unction in Visigothic Spain and stresses the lack of evidence for this theory.[5] Janet Nelson, whilst emphasising the Old Testament model behind Pippin's anointing, finds it necessary to ask what part of that model was appropriate.[6] Patrick Wormald traces the influences of biblical models on the barbarian laws.[6a] Clearly, any further study of the Biblical foundations of early medieval kingship will require great precision. Moreover such a study will have to take account of the relative dearth of Biblical parallels used by churchmen in the fifth and sixth centuries when compared with the eighth and ninth.[7]

On the whole there is little evidence to help the historian reconstruct the political theory of the early barbarian successor states. Cassiodorus, Avitus and Theudebert were concerned primarily with the relationship between Germanic kings and the Emperor.[8] Where there are traceable sources for their ideas, it is the *Panegyrici Latini* and late Roman rhetoric which figure most prominently. However none of these lectures considered kingship as a philosophical abstraction. The concern of the individual papers was with specific issues and areas of evidence; king-making, unction, genealogy, law and trade. Inevitably, one result of dividing kingship into various aspects is that emphases fall differently than in a broader survey. Above all by limiting oneself to a particular kind of evidence, the central questions that emerge are concerned with why such evidence was written and what are its limits? The result of this is a growing stress on the context of individual ideas or events at the expense of the more coherent and abstract account of kingship in its many aspects over several centuries, which earlier scholars have supplied.

To some extent this stress on particular context is also relevant to a second issue; the coherence of the picture offered by the papers. It would be wrong to assert that all the contributors were in total agreement. There are moments of conflict in the papers as published; there were also moments of disagreement in the discussions which followed the lectures. But there is a broader coherence, stemming partly from the emphasis on the precise circumstances of political development and the specific contexts in which documents were drawn up. King-making proved to be a central

---

[5] See below pp. 43–4. See also King 1972 pp. 48–9 n. 5 for further difficulties in using Biblical reminiscences to date the origins of unction in Visigothic Spain.

[6] See below p. 58.

[6a] See below pp. 131–32.

[7] In considering the reason for the land division of 511 (see below) I have not considered any possible Biblical inspiration, perhaps wrongly. But as Gregory of Tours provides no Biblical allusion I have preferred to leave the issue aside.

[8] Epistolae Austrasiacae 19, 20.

issue for four of us. The person of a king, his pedigree, the ease with which he took the throne and the ways in which authority was conferred on him were all important factors and they all require precise treatment. The impression resulting from the studies of these individual aspects is one of political activity. The same impression might be gathered from two of the papers in this series which were concerned with particular types of evidence; the genealogies and the laws. A fundamental theme in both papers was the danger of extracting material from these documents, without first considering the context in which they were drawn up. Again, this context might be called political. Given this particular emphasis, what emerges is a picture of a world in which political activity was still important. It is also a sub-Roman world, where the importance of Rome may be measured not only in the areas where continuing Roman influence can be studied, but also in the contrast with those areas which had always been outside the Empire, as Peter Sawyer points out.[10]

Thus these papers have a sense of politics and of Roman influence in common. But this does not mean that the early medieval period has been remade to an anachronistic model, for another point which emerges in several of these papers is the influence of social anthropologists on the writing of Dark Age history. Inaugurations, law, trade and stability itself are all issues in which the historian has learnt from the anthropologist; a timely reminder that however Roman the Dark Ages were, they were tribal and not Roman in any classical sense. Besides, direct Roman influence can be overstressed. It was important for the Merovingians and for the Visigoths; but as Roman influence and Germanic power coalesced in the seventh century a rather different picture was seen. Whatever the origins of those Frankish inauguration rites which legitimized Pippin, they were neither clearly Germanic nor clearly Roman and the church was already beginning to transform them. This transformation was slow and tentative, as Janet Nelson shows, and continued into the tenth century and beyond.

It may be that the clerics of the ninth century started to direct kingship along new paths, that the royalty of Charles the Bald and of Otto I had few links with the kingship of Clovis. Within the immediate circle of the king men like Hincmar were making their influence felt even if no totally coherent political philosophy emerged.[11] But there was no absolute break with the past. Merovingian traditions lie behind some aspects of Carolingian kingship.[12] But if the seventh and the ninth centuries can be profitably compared, it is also important to remember the continuities up into the tenth and eleventh centuries. Here the paper by Peter Sawyer provides some interesting insights into the continuity of early medieval kingship beyond the tenth century and into some of the reasons for its later transformation. The transition of the kingship of the early middle ages into that of the twelfth century is a problem which might now profitably be studied further.

[9] See Wormald 1976 esp. pp. 224f.
[10] See below pp. 142–44.
[11] See Nelson 1977.
[12] See Nelson 1977 (b).

Any such series as this is bound to leave gaps. War-leadership, the royal activity with which barbarian kings were most often occupied does not feature here. There is almost no consideration of the archaeological evidence for kingship. The tombs of Tournai and Sutton Hoo are neglected,[13] as are the royal burial churches and palaces.[14] Further, there is no consideration of coinage which can often be used to highlight developments in kingship as well as lines of contact in significant ways.[15]

Nor are the gaps in this volume merely gaps of topic; despite the large geographical area covered complete nations are omitted. The Lombards, for instance, appear only fleetingly, yet in many ways they complete and refine a study of Germanic kingship. Evidence about Lombard kings begins with those awkward and semi-legendary records of Paul the Deacon; the interregnum, however, emphasises the precarious nature of royal power, against which the later history of the Lombard kings should probably be measured. With the revival of the royal office, new issues are raised. From the start there is a problem in the precise relationship of the Lombards and the Merovingians, the latter both as enemies and as relatives. The Frankish threat seems to have revived the kingship; but queen Theudelinda was a Frank through her Bavarian blood. Even with the successful promotion of an image of royalty by the Lombard kings, there are problems. On the one hand Paul the Deacon provides a picture of a court centred in Pavia, Monza and Milan, a court whose palaces, churches and regalia were clearly impressive. On the other hand it is curious how infrequently we see the Lombard monarchy in action; outside tales of campaigns and rebellions, Paul's knowledge is sketchy at best. The royal charters provide some glimpses of the kings at work; however, the papal material does not add greatly to the evidence. The independence of Spoleto and Benevento is a much stressed fact, but how important were the Lombard kings even in the north? How far was the glitter of the palace and the majesty of Lombard law a magnificent statement of the power of the Lombard kings, which had rather less foundation in reality? The possible limitations of royal power in Italy may have its parallels in Visigothic Spain if not in Merovingian Gaul.[16]

And the Lombards provide one other point of entry into Dark Age Kingship. For the Merovingians we still await a reliable edition of the royal charters; what work has been done on their authenticity is still scattered in various studies of individual monasteries and dioceses. For the Anglo-Saxons we are much better off; many of the charters have been or are being re-edited and there is at least a hand-list to provide some guide to the authenticity of individual documents.[17] But there is still no

---

[13] Wallace-Hadrill 1960. See now Wallace-Hadrill 1975 pp. 53–56. If Sutton Hoo is seen as aristocratic, there is the problem of where else can we find an aristocrat with such wealth; a point made to me by Jean le Patourel.

[14] See Krüger 1971, Erlande-Brandenburg 1975 and Brühl 1975.

[15] Hillgarth 1966.

[16] See below, Roger Collins pp. 32–4. On the problems of Lombard kingship I have learnt much from Chris Wickham in numerous conversations.

[17] Sawyer 1968.

coherent attempt to assess the significance of royal power as revealed in the charters. As regards the Lombards, these requirements have been filled largely through the work of Professor Brühl.[18]

A further gap apparent in this collection of lectures and perhaps the most significant is Byzantium. Despite its imperial traditions it provides some parallels to the West, during its own Dark Age. The problem of some Byzantine law-giving has recently been studied in a way readily intelligible to historians of the early medieval West. Leo VI's 'dossier' on the *dunatoi* has been set in a precise political context.[19] But even if it is legitimate to isolate the internal problems of Byzantine authority and claim that they belong to a history of empire not of kingship, there remains the question of Byzantine influence on the Western successor states. How far did the West derive the style and regalia of kingship from the East? How much was late Roman? These issues are important but difficult. The real problem may well turn out to be the paucity of Byzantine influence. Why did the West not draw more from the East?[20]

Finally there is another Empire which is largely disregarded here; that of the Ottonians. Again it might be argued that theories of Empire do not belong to the history of early medieval kingship. However in its origins the Ottonian empire was no more than a Carolingian successor state. From the evidence of Widukind on the inauguration of Otto I we know that the Ottonians were part of the transformation of royal ritual which can be traced from Pippin III to Edgar.[21] But they may deserve a more prominent position.

Some of the lacunae in this book have already been fully discussed elsewhere. Others will need further research before they can be adequately treated. But this was not intended to be a comprehensive survey of early medieval kingship. It can be read as a group of separate essays illuminating various aspects of a subject already treated by major scholars in this country and on the continent. It may be, however, that the reader will agree that there is a wider coherence in the papers included in this book than mere unity of subject. After one of the lectures a member of the audience commented that it had removed some of the mystique but had increased the complexity of early medieval kingship. It is to be hoped that all the papers in this volume achieve the same result.

IAN WOOD

---

[18] Brühl 1970 and Brühl 1973.
[19] Morris 1976.
[20] This was a point made by Rosemary Morris in the discussion after one of the lectures.
[21] See Janet Nelson, below p. 68.

1

Kings, Kingdoms and Consent
IAN WOOD

In the last months of 511, Clovis lay dying in Paris. No doubt there gathered at his bedside numerous interested parties.[1] There was Theuderic, his eldest son, by a concubine. He was probably twenty-six and already had a son of his own, who could be described as *elegans* and *utilis*.[2] Then there were Clovis' three sons by his Burgundian wife, Chrodechildis, the eldest of whom, Chlodomer, can have been little more than fourteen.[3] There must have been other notable Franks present, though probably not of royal birth.[4] But for this period the Frankish aristocracy is hard to trace. More certainly there was the influential Chrodechildis herself, whose political influence had by no means ended.[5] Granted the youth of her children, her likely allies were the bishops, with whom she had long associated herself.[6] Only four or five months before, bishops above all from Aquitaine, the most Romanised area of Clovis' newly expanded kingdom, had gathered at Orleans for the first Merovingian Church Council. There, at least, they had had a taste of policy-making in the newly catholic kingdom.

After his death, Clovis was buried in his own foundation, the Church of the Holy Apostles in Paris.[7] His kingdom was divided into four, each of his sons receiving an equal share.[8] This division of 511 is one of the central factors of Frankish history, dominating the later patterns of political organisation. But, why Clovis' kingdom was divided remains a puzzle.[9] Although Lex Salica implies that allodial lands should be divided between all the male heirs, it does not necessarily solve the problem. First, it cannot be proved that the Merovingians regarded the kingdom as allodial. Second, other nations made similar provisions for family estates but did not

---

[1] I am indebted to all my fellow contributors for their comments and advice; in particular I was saved from many errors by David Dumville and Patrick Wormald. I have also profited from the comments and criticism of John Gillingham. Finally I would like to thank Maureen Hastie for her considerable help in typing this piece.

[2] Gregory Hist. II 43; III 1. See Ewig 1974 p. 37.

[3] Ewig 1974 p. 38.

[4] Gregory Hist. II 42. But see the claims of Sigivald and Munderic, Hist. III 13, 14. These may have been related by the female line.

[5] Gregory Hist. III 6.

[6] For Remigius, Gregory Hist. II 31. For Theodore, Proculus and Dinifius at Tours, Hist. X 31. For Lupus see Hericus De Miraculis S. Germani I Ch. 4 (39); P.L. 124 col. 1226.

[7] Gregory Hist. II 43.

[8] Gregory Hist. III 1. The meaning of *aeque lantia* is not altogether clear. See Ewig 1952 esp. p. 10.

[9] But see Zöllner 1970 pp. 74—5

apply them to the inheritance of the kingdom.[10] Nor is there any evidence to suggest that earlier Frankish kings had divided their petty kingdoms in this way, although it is interesting to note that only one heir is recorded for each of these these.[11] Moreover the earlier kingdoms, even that of Childeric at Tournai, are not comparable in kind with that left by Clovis. This latter was sizeable and it was, in many respects, Roman. The Roman aristocracy, especially the bishops, were influential and doubtless Clovis relied upon them.

It is the purpose of this paper, therefore, to investigate those elements in early medieval kingship, which may clarify the events of 511. Of these, the first issue which requires consideration is the structure and the activity of royal dynasties. The second concerns the nature of the division of kingdoms between rulers. The final consideration is that of Clovis' authority; wherein lay its origins and what made it effective? Although this discussion must inevitably revolve around the Frankish evidence, the issues involved are not merely those of Frankish history.

A history of the royal dynasties of early medieval Europe is not easily begun, for it seems clear that, before the migrations, most nations had several aristocratic families from whom a king might be chosen. Effectively these families were potential royalty. But not all nations chose to live constantly under kings, if we are to assess kings by their function, that is as supreme rulers, rather than by any nomenclature used in the texts. Although the pre-migration Visigoths appear to have regarded their aristocracy as royal, they only elected Athanaric to the supreme post of command, the judgeship, during a period of crisis.[12] The temporary nature of this command might seem to correspond to the Germanic Kingship depicted by classical historians;[13] it can also be paralleled by Bede's description of the continental Saxons, who were usually ruled by satraps, but who elected a *dux* in time of war.[14] No doubt these men were likely to dedicate themselves to their war god for the time of the campaign. And even if this sacrality was purely temporary, the control of cults exercised by these men as aristocrats, to judge by the Visigothic evidence, must have facilitated the assumption of sacrality by the chosen leader, for the length of the war.[15]

This picture, however, ceased to be true for most of the Germanic tribes during the period of migrations. It may well be that we should associate the change in kingship with the social and territorial dislocation of this period. Perhaps the prolonged period of crisis caused by migration facilitated the emergence of royal

---

[10] Inheritance by all sons is to be assumed from Pactus Legis Salicae LIX, Lex Salica XCI, Lex Burgundionum XIV, 2, Leges Visigothorum IV 2(1), (11) and the Edict of Rothari CL III. See Additional Note 1.

[11] Gregory Hist. II 9. See also the evidence for the other Frankish kingdoms of Clovis' time, Hist. II 40—42. See also Hübrich 1975, p. 5.

[12] Central here is Wolfram 1975.

[13] Wolfram 1975 pp. 272ff. See also Wallace-Hadrill 1971 pp. 5—7 for kings whose power was not so limited.

[14] Bede H. E. V 10.

[15] Thompson 1966 pp. 66—7. See Additional Note 2.

dynasties. At all costs, those kings who did lead their peoples successfully into the empire, tended to leave a now permanent kingship to their heirs.

The histories written for these momentarily successful families suggest a very different picture. These liked to make extravagant claims for their predecessors, not all of which can be accepted. The genealogy of the Amal kings of the Ostrogoths includes *non puros homines, sed semideos id est Ansis*.[16] Demigods are a signal for caution. Nevertheless from the arrival of the Ostrogoths in Italy until the last years of the kingdom, the Amals did monopolise the royal power. But it is clear, even from their genealogy, that before this time kings had been taken from other families.[17] Later, in the acute crisis of the Gothic wars the army was prepared to look elsewhere for a king, once again.[18] For a while, however, the kingship had seemed hereditary and in the later years of this hereditary period it had been possible, retrospectively, to incorporate demigods into the family. The Franks did the same with the sea-monster, Merovech's father; the Anglo-Saxons had a habit of finding Woden in their family trees.[19] It may also be that this same retrospective sleight of hand was capable of upgrading members of the family who had never held the supreme kingship, such as it existed before the migration.

With the exception of the Vandals, this picture of royal families establishing themselves during their entry into the empire and later stressing their earlier royal pre-eminence, holds good for the leading Germanic tribes. The problem posed by the Vandalic evidence stems from the apparent division of the nation into two peoples; one of which, the Hasdings, carried the same name as the royal dynasty.[20] Nor do later traditions help us identify the lineage of the pre-migration kings. The Visigoths, on the other hand, provide an exact parallel with the Ostrogothic Amals. In the sixth century, Jordanes asserted that they had been ruled by one family only, the Balts,[21] but this had not been the case before Alaric led his people across Italy, nor was it the case after 531. In that year the tradition of hereditary monarchy ended with the murder of Amalaric. Despite the attempts of some later individuals to found royal dynasties, the kingship of the Visigoths remained primarily elective.[22]

The Lombards, in their own rather untidy way, repeated the formula. Paul the Deacon believed that for seven generations, before entry into the lands of the

---

[16] Jordanes Getica XIII 78. This and related evidence is discussed in Grierson 1941 esp. pp. 5ff.

[17] But Getica V 42 implies that the Amals were the only royal dynasty.

[18] Procopius Wars V XI 5 (election of Wittigis), VI XXIX 18–19 (offer of royal power to Belisarius).

[19] Fredegar II 9. For the Anglo-Saxons Sisam 1953 p. 288. The texts of the genealogies are to be found in Dumville 1976 pp. 30–37. Granted the continental parallels one might wonder whether on occasion the Anglo-Saxons have not tidied rather complex patterns of royal succession into the neatness of a royal dynasty. This raises the question of the reality of descent from a dynastic founder like Cerdic. It was possible to add and to excise figures from a genealogy. On this and the circumstances behind such action see David Dumville below.

[20] Courtois 1955 pp. 31, 237.

[21] Jordanes, Getica V 42. See, however, Grierson 1941 pp. 11–13.

[22] The elective nature of Visigothic kingship has been most fully studied in Claude 1971.

Empire, the kingship had been monopolised by the descendants of Leth.[23] Later, after the settlement in Italy, the royal office was interrupted by an interregnum, when the warleaders decided to live without a king.[24] But in time the family did return to power and retained its influence, remarkably, for the best part of a century, through the influence of two queens, Theudelinda and her daughter, Gundiperga. Both these ladies, it seems, were widowed, but were allowed to choose another husband, who was also to succeed to the kingship.[25] Amalasuntha had done as much for the Ostrogoths.[26] Later the crown of the Lombards did pass out of the hands of the Lething dynasty. No other family managed to assert a monopoly for any length of time.

If any historian had pronounced on the nature of barbarian kingship in 520, he would have been justified in announcing that it was always hereditary. In every barbarian kingdom there was a royal dynasty and most of these royal dynasties were suggesting that they had monopolised the kingship even before the barbarian migrations. Sixty years later the evidence suggested a very different picture. The Hasdings had not been superceded, but they and their people had been destroyed. So too had the Burgundians, another Germanic tribe, whose claim to be ruled by one dynasty, the Gibichungs, is well attested.[27] The Amals had lost hold of the Ostrogothic crown, before their people had been destroyed. The Visigoths had survived, but their royal dynasty, the Balts had fallen. The Lombard interregnum had begun. On the continent the Franks alone had kept the same line of kings; looking back we tend to regard the Merovingians as holding the only hereditary title outside Anglo-Saxon England.

Even the Franks may have conformed to the model of pre-migration royal aristocracies and a post-migration kingship, although they never experienced migration as did the majority of Germanic tribes. To Gregory of Tours' consternation Sulpicius Alexander calls the leaders Sunno and Marcomer *regales*, not *reges*.[28] Gregory's own picture of numerous kings over small bands of warriors does

---

[23] Paul the Deacon "Historia Langobardorum" I 21. See also Grierson 1941 pp. 15ff.

[24] Paul, Hist. II 31.

[25] Paul Hist. III 35. The evidence for Gundiperga is less certain; Fredegar IV 70. Further, as Chris Wickham has pointed out to me, no early source stresses Theudelindas descent from Leth.

[26] Jordanes Romana 368, Getica LIX 306. See Grierson 1941 p. 9.

[27] Lex Burgundionum III. Sisam 1953 p. 323 may seem to cast doubt on this family tree. But *regiae memoriae auctores nostros* must mean "ancestors". It is hard to believe that Gundobad associated himself with the singularly unsuccessful Gundaharius without due reason. In the light of later Dark Age genealogies, the wonder is that Gibichungs were so faithful in recording their ancestry. As for the claims of Gregory Hist. II 28 that Gundioc was of the house of Athanaric, this does not seem to mean that a Visigothic dynasty was imported. Intermarriage is a possible solution. But Gregory may be wishing to link the Gibichungs with an arch-persecutor and no more.

[28] Gregory Hist. II 9. Regales could mean men of royal status and thus might suggest that these were men from whom kings were chosen. Ammianus XVI 12 (26), however, suggests that regales were subkings. I am indebted to John Hind who drew my attention to the importance of Ammianus' evidence on the Alamans.

not conflict with this. Some of these petty kings were inter-related.[29] Towards the end of his life Clovis spent a good deal of energy destroying these rival dynasties.[30] This deliberate extermination of the other Frankish royal families marks the end of the royal aristocracies in Gaul. Henceforth there was but one ruling line. Clovis' actions must have strengthened Merovingian security, although had the family of Ragnachar survived, it too might have claimed to be the offspring of the sea-monster's son, Merovech.

That Ragnachar was a kinsman of Clovis raises a significant issue. The triumph of one family in retaining the kingship, was not necessarily a solution to the problem of royal inheritance. Just as the process of royal election could be a force working for unity in a kingdom; hereditary kingship could be a force leading to division. It did not help that there was no clear rule to govern succession within a royal family. Gaiseric, for instance, appears to have intended that all his sons should succeed in turn before the crown passed to the third generation. Not surprisingly other paternal interests came to the fore in the next generation. Huneric began a relentless persecution of those relatives of his who might have succeeded before his own son. But there may also have been some political wisdom in Huneric's savagery. The rivalries within the family which Gaiseric's will would have been likely to promote, might have been even more divisive than his son's political expedients.[31]

But direct filial inheritance did not necessarily avoid conflict. Because there was no tradition of primogeniture or indeed any written rule to state how the claims of more than one son were to be made good, inheritance was likely to be complicated by the numbers of male heirs surviving. This was the particular problem faced by the Merovingians. The general pattern of Merovingian royal inheritance is as follows: the sons of kings, if they lived long enough, became kings themselves. If their father died while they were minors, they would still be regarded as kings, but would only take over the kingship ceremonially at a later date, sometimes, though not always, when they reached the *legitima aetas* of fifteen.[32] Circumstances could make princes into warleaders at a younger age. However princes did not always succeed their fathers. Even in the earlier Merovingian period kings intervened against the children of their dead brothers. In this respect the acquiescence of established authority was necessary. The most notable case of such intervention is the murder of two of the sons of Chlodomer by Childebert and Chlothar. The only surviving son, Chlodovald, was content to become a monk.[33] Childebert and Chlothar also

---

[29] Hübrich 1975 pp. 4–5.

[30] Gregory Hist. II 40–42. See Additional Note 3.

[31] Courtois 1955 pp. 238–42. Courtois names this system as tanistry. However tanistry, as understood in an Irish context seems rather different from the agnatic succession of Gaiseric's will. For the Irish *tánaise* see Binchy 1956 pp. 221–2 and Charles-Edwards 1971.

[32] Ewig 1974 esp. pp. 22ff.

[33] Gregory Hist. III 18. On Chlodovald see also the late Vita Chlodovaldi, 7ff. For a similar incident see the fate of Merovech, son of Theuderic II; Fredegar IV 42 and Jonas Vita Columbani II 25. On the identification see Eckhardt 1975 p. 119.

attempted to disinherit Theudebert, the son of their half-brother, Theuderic, but Theudebert had the support of his *leudes* and possession of his father's treasure.[34] The presence of the *leudes* suggests that there were already powerful groups whose backing could represent a substantial challenge to the word of a king. Theudebert had had ample time to cultivate such support, for he was already a warleader of note and may even have been older than his uncles.[35] His survival led to a series of political realignments. In both these stories Childebert and Chlothar appear as unpleasant and immoral uncles, depriving their kin of rightful inheritance. But there is nothing at this stage in Frankish history, to imply that the sons of Chlodomer and Theuderic had to inherit the throne. So far as we know the 511 land division was the only clear precedent for the inheritance of all the male heirs of a king. If 511 was only the compromise of one generation, the problem of providing for the next generation had still to be faced. It may be that Theudebert's success helped to create a tradition here. If this is so, what looks to us like Frankish tradition may only have been formed by the political compromises of the first half of the sixth century. One result of such a suggestion must be that in 511 Chrodechildis could not have been certain that her sons, young as they were, would survive. Nor was there much certainty in the later part of the century. After the murder of Sigibert in 575, Gundovald took the young prince, Childebert, out of harm's way; then having collected Sigibert's *gentes*, he had Childebert installed as king. The son of Brunichildis might never have become king without the connivance of Gundovald.[36] Similarly Chlothar II, the son of Fredegundis and Chilperic, was protected and made king by Ansovald in 584.[37] In both cases the opposition seems to have been headed by other members of the royal family.

Nor were uncles and nephews the only enemies amongst the Merovingians. There are also cases of fathers ordering the death of sons. Occasionally the sons of long-lived kings decided that they ought to be given greater powers. The case of Chramn, son of Chlothar I, is revealing here. He was set over the Auvergne by his father; Gregory of Tours describes his power there as royal; he is called *rex*.[38] He then proceeded to expand his lordship over neighbouring areas by making a royal progress, although he did concede that he would reign with his father's consent, when his half-brothers were sent against him.[39] Nevertheless he later sided with one of his uncles, Childebert, against his father. Eventually he was defeated in battle, strangled and burnt. His career reveals the problems of independent minded princes as well as the possibility of support from other royal figures. The career of Merovech, son of Chilperic, is similar. Merovech never aspired to royal power so

---

[34] Gregory Hist. III 23. His gift giving suggests control of his father's treasure.
[35] Gregory Hist. III 7, 21. On his age, Ewig 1974 p. 37.
[36] Gregory Hist. V 1.
[37] Gregory Hist. VII 7.
[38] Gregory Hist. IV 9, 13.
[39] Gregory Hist. IV 16. See Hübrich 1975 p. 41.

explicitly as Chramn. His most daring action was to marry his aunt, the widowed queen Brunichildis.[40] Like him, his brother, Chlodovech, met an unhappy end. This last prince was foolish enough to look forward to the inheritance of the whole of his father's kingdom, although his father and his step-mother, Fredegundis, were still alive. Not surprisingly Fredegundis encompassed his execution.[41]

It was not only in Frankia that sons threatened their fathers. The most dangerous of all such challenges came, indeed, in Visigothic Spain. Hermenegild's rebellion against his father Leovigild was made more terrible by his conversion from Arianism to Catholicism, thus adding a doctrinal appeal to a family struggle. Hermenegild's position was not unlike that of Chramn, for Leovigild provided his sons with capitals, from which they might rule, no doubt as sub-kings.[42] Such provision for mature princes within the political structure of a kingdom could never have become an established tradition, not least because kings often died before their sons reached maturity. But on occasion early medieval kings did provide a position of some authority for their adult sons.

The Merovingians, however, made little use of any office of sub-king, before 622. Numerous factors militated against such an office; the youth of most princes, the fact that the kingdom was already divided and perhaps even memory of the career of Chramn. It was not until Chlothar had reunified the kingdom in 613, that the question of a subordinate kingdom arose. In 622 he associated his son, Dagobert, with the kingship, effectively along lines which meant the redivision of the kingdom; Chlothar was to rule Neustria and Burgundy, whilst Dagobert was placed over Austrasia, which he ruled with the aid of two of the leading Austrasian magnates, Arnulf of Metz and Pippin I.[43] Charibert II, Chlothar's second son was apparently ignored. Even when the old king died in 629, Dagobert claimed the whole kingdom. Charibert rebelled, supported by his uncle Brodulf. In the end he was palmed off with the lands around Gascony and the Pyrenees.[44] He died in 630 and his young son Chilperic was killed soon after, probably on Dagobert's orders.[45] Two years later the kingdom was redivided, this time on the advice of the great men and bishops. Dagobert placed his son, Sigibert III, on the throne of Austrasia, with his capital at Metz. He was left under the protection of bishop Chunibert of Cologne and Duke Adalgisel.[46] But when he created a sub-kingdom for Sigibert, Dagobert was not providing office for a son of mature age. The child was only three and the division was made explicitly on the advice of the magnates of Austrasia.

---

[40] Gregory Hist. V 3.

[41] Gregory Hist. V. 39. Fredegundis was also prepared to sacrifice her own child, Hist. V 22, but this reflects on the queen's personality more than on kingship.

[42] Gregory Hist. V 38. On Reccopolis see John of Biclaro Chron. 578, 4. (MGH AA XI p. 215).

[43] Fredegar IV 47, 58.

[44] Fredegar IV 56–7.

[45] Fredegar IV 67.

[46] Fredegar IV 75.

The case of Charibert II and his son highlights the continuity of Merovingian practice; it was still necessary for a Merovingian prince to have the support of an established ruler, if he wanted to achieve the kingship. On the other hand the appointment of Sigibert makes more explicit the influence of the aristocracy in the appointment of kings. The non-royal support on which Theudebert, Childebert and Chlothar II had depended for their survival has already been noted. By the seventh century this influence had grown. In many ways, indeed, the seventh century reveals a new departure in the pattern of royal succession, with the last years of Queen Brunichildis marking the watershed.

The political circumstances which preceded the fall of the old queen demand some attention, since the events of 613 were as influential for the history of the seventh century Merovingian kingdom as the events of 511 had been for the sixth. Brunichildis had little love for her grandson, Theudebert II, King of Austrasia. Accordingly she incited her other grandson, Theuderic II, King of Burgundy, against him. The latter defeated and killed his brother and his brother's children; he then turned against Chlothar II, King of Neustria. But the triumph of Brunichildis' policy was shortlived, for Theuderic died of dysentry before the year was out.[47] He left his four children at Metz in the hands of their great-grandmother. Instead of raising them all to the kingship, Brunichildis acclaimed Sigibert II alone as Theuderic's successor. No doubt political acumen prompted her decision; left with very little support, which, in the event, she over-estimated, she was more likely to secure the succession for one of her great-grandchildren than for all. As it was, she failed and she and her line, with the exception of Chlothar II's godson, Merovech, were exterminated.[48] Chlothar II's opposition to the son of Theuderic II is merely one more example of the importance of the acquiescence of a reigning king. Brunichildis' action is more unusual. It shows that in a state of crisis the tradition of inheritance by all the male heirs could be discarded and that another solution could be put forward.

There is only one later example of a king with more than one son, leaving his kingdom to all his known male heirs. Dagobert I left Neustria and Burgundy to Clovis II and Austrasia to Sigibert. But Fredegar's description of this sounds more like a compromise between Dagobert, Sigibert and the Neustrians, than any return to tradition.[49] Even the great Balthildis, Clovis II's wife, saw only one of her sons inherit in the first instance. The Franks chose her eldest son, Chlothar III, as king, albeit leaving the queen-mother as regent.[50]

---

[47] Fredegar IV 36ff.
[48] Fredegar IV 42. On the repercussions caused by Childebert's escape see Vita Rusticulae 9.
[49] Fredegar IV 76.
[50] Fredegar Cont. 1 and L.H.F. 44. The succession of Chlothar III's brother is also described as being the result of the political activity of the aristocracy in Fredegar Cont. 2. It is difficult to assess how far Balthildis herself was in agreement with these developments. But see Ewig 1973 pp. 106–114 for an assessment of the queen's influence.

A survey of the succession of the Merovingian Kings does not, therefore, reveal a hard and fast rule by which all male heirs of kings succeeded to the kingship. Rather, it suggests that although any prince had a claim to the throne, he needed to make good that claim with the support of some portion of the aristocracy or by gaining the approval of one of the kings already in power. In many ways succession was a matter of individual political events rather than a tradition. The Merovingian dynasty was not one happy family, whose activities tended to draw power into a united source of authority. There was not that much brotherly love and the resulting divisions provided every opportunity for aristocratic and urban factions to find a royal sponsor. On the other hand it may be that these divisions helped to keep the Regnum Francorum united under one family. Social anthropologists have taught us that conflict has a part to play in producing a wider social order. Perhaps the Merovingians held Frankia together for so long precisely because they were divided among themselves.[51]

Doubtless there were numerous personal reasons for the frequent hatred shown by one member of the family towards another. But there were other factors which must have exacerbated any rivalries. Not the least of these was concubinage, for the Merovingians practised concubinage with zest.[52] One result of this was the presence of bad-feeling between princes and their step-mothers.[53] But there were other effects on the succession, even if Gregory of Tours did not acknowledge the problems. When Sagittarius of Embrun said that Guntram's children could never take over royal power, because their mother had been a serving lady in Magnachar's household, Gregory commented that Sagittarius' opinion was wrong. According to the bishop of Tours, the offspring of kings were called kings' sons;[54] that is the status of their mother in no way affected their own status or rights. But it may be that all was not as cut and dried as Gregory thought. Certainly the evidence we have considered so far does not allow us to conclude that king's sons could easily assert rights of inheritance.

From a period early in the sixth century, the one requirement demanded of a Frankish king was that he should be a Merovingian.[55] Even those figures that are regarded as pretenders, attempted to show that they were members of the royal family. Munderic, for instance, asserted that he was a relative of Clovis' sons, *parens regium*. He decided to gather his people together and take an oath from

---

[51] Gluckman 1970 pp. 44–5.

[52] On concubinage, Ewig 1974 pp. 39ff.

[53] The relations between Fredegundis and Chlodovech, Gregory Hist. V 39 and with Merovech, Hist. V 14, provide clear examples.

[54] Gregory Hist. V 20.

[55] See the later assumptions in Fredegar II 9 and L.H.F. 5. There is a seventh century exception. Whether it is Alethius or Bertetrudis who is to be regarded as *regio genere de Burgundionibus*, direct Merovingian paternity seems out of the question. Nevertheless a hard-pressed propagandist might have made much of the intermarriage of Merovingians and Gibichungs. Both Chrotechildis and Sigismund's daughter (?Suavegotha), Gregory Hist. III 5, married Frankish kings. But if Alethius represented Burgundian separatist tendencies it is possible that Gibichung blood was enough.

them so that Theuderic should know that they were both kings.[56] Despite Clovis' attempts to exterminate his relatives,[57] it is not impossible that Munderic was related. Theuderic acknowledged Sigivald as his *parens*.[58] But it is Gundovald who provides the best example of a pretender claiming to be a Merovingian. He went to Childebert and asserted that he was the son of Chlothar I. The latter, like Sigibert I, refused to recognise him as such.[59] After living in Italy and Constantinople, Gundovald returned, still making the same claims. He said that he too was a *rex*, like Guntram, and told his hearers that if they wanted confirmation of his story, they should ask Radegundis at Poitiers or Ingitrudis at Tours.[60] As corroborative witness these ladies would have been most impressive; Radegundis had been Chlothar's queen and Ingitrudis was the kinswoman of his son, Guntram.[61] Moreover they were also the leading ascetics in the family. It may be rash to reject Gundovald's claims. But this much, at least, is certain; where royal concubinage was practised and where all the offspring of a king were to be accepted as heirs, Gundovald's claims would have been very hard to dismiss.

Nor was he the only man to pose as a son of Chlothar. Rauching made the same claim.[62] The latter's aspirations are less clear than those of Gundovald. He conspired to kill king Childebert and to become regent for the young Theudebert II; a slight ambition in view of his purported royal blood. Gregory, however, does seem to hint at darker hopes; the regency was to include the government of the *regnum Campaniae*; he vaunted his *gloria regalis sceptri*; his possessions eclipsed the royal treasury. All this from a self-styled member of the royal family might easily have led to usurpation.

The marital practices of the Merovingians, therefore, did not help clarify the royal lineage. Such dynastic confusion might be exploited to personal advantage. But even if the mother were known to be a royal concubine or a queen, it was not always certain that the child would be accepted as the offspring of a king. The suggestion that a prince was not of royal blood could have political repercussions. When Guntram was angry at Fredegundis' failure to appear before him with her son Chlothar II, he questioned Chlothar's legitimacy. He said that the boy was the son of one of his own *leudes*.[63] This challenge was serious enough to require a public

---

[56] Gregory Hist. III 14.
[57] Gregory Hist. II 42.
[58] Gregory Hist. III 13, although the connection may not have been on the male line.
[59] Gregory Hist. VI 24. But it was possible for princes to vanish cf. n 48 above.
[60] Gregory Hist. VII 36.
[61] Gregory Hist. IX 33.
[62] Gregory Hist. IX 9. This passage seems to be at odds with the dictum of Hist. V 20. That Gregory records these traditions about Rauching without comment may suggest that he was recording hostile propaganda.
[63] Gregory Hist. VIII 9. Guntram had already been surprised by Fredegundis' pregnant condition after Chilperic I's death. Hist. VII 7.

response. The queen gathered three bishops and three hundred leading men, who swore that the child was the true son of Chilperic. Similarly, in order to incite Theuderic against his brother, Brunichildis claimed that Theudebert was not Childebert's offspring, but the son of a gardener.[64] Theuderic, it seems, believed his grandmother's story or at least found it convenient, when he attacked his brother.

The attack on concubinage, when it came, was a moral one. Columbanus faced Brunichildis as very few others dared, refusing to bless her great-grandchildren. He claimed, almost as Sagittarius had claimed, that they would never hold royal power, having been born in adultery.[65] The prophesy naturally came true. This did not prevent Dagobert from continuing the Merovingian tradition a generation later. Fredegar lamented his debauchery, claiming that Dagobert had so many mistresses that to name them all would be tedious.[66] But by the seventh century the succession pattern of the Merovingian dynasty had changed; the *Teilreiche* had become rather more fixed units; new divisions were rarely made. This effectively stabilised the number of kings.[67] There was no repeat of the Gundovald affair. Instead the next political conflict caused by concubinage belongs to the history of the Carolingian mayors of the palace. Pippin II had a son, Charles, by his second wife Alpaida, whilst his first wife, Plectrudis was still alive; the word *uxor* is used for both.[68] When Pippin died, Plectrudis was one of the leading opponents of her stepson. By this time the Merovingians were little more than figure heads to whom rival parties might turn.[69]

Despite Clovis' assault on his relatives, the Merovingian family tree had not remained a very tidy one. We know little about the outer branches and about the fate of most Merovingian women. Clearly some of the mayors of the palace were pleased to marry members of the royal kin.[70] Some such marriage must lie behind the Merovingian name given to Grimoald's son Childebert, thus providing some Merovingian claim for Childebert's usurpation.[71] The family was, therefore, a far

---

[64] Fredegar IV 27.

[65] Jonas Vita Columbani I 19, Fredegar IV 36. Brunichildis might have been expected to criticise concubinage herself, after the treatment of her sister. Gregory Hist. IV 28.

[66] Fredegar IV 60.

[67] On the politics of seventh century Gaul, see Ewig 1953 esp. pp. 105ff.

[68] Fredegar Cont. 5, 6.

[69] Fredegar Cont. 9, 10 for Chilperic (Daniel) and Theuderic IV.

[70] On Merovingian princesses see Ewig 1974 pp. 46–9. Floachad married a niece of Nantechildis; Fredegar IV 89. Erchinoald was related to Dagobert's mother; Fredegar IV 84.

[71] This has been studied most recently in Eckhardt 1975. Eckhardt pp. 186–214 argues that Grimoald, the half-brother of Theudelinda, was the son of king Theudebald and that he was the maternal grandfather of the mayor of the palace called Grimoald. This is an attractive thesis and is not impossible in view of the known exclusion of other Merovingian princes. On the other hand Eckhardt is reduced to some weak arguments to uphold his case (p. 203). *Ex genere francorum*, Fredegar IV 34, must include Theudelinda and if Zöllner 1951 is right all the Agilulfings might be regarded as Franks. Grimoald and Gundoald could be straightforward Agilulfings. Similarly it is far fetched to suggest that *germana* means half-sister. Nevertheless Eckhardt's stress on the position of Wuldetrada is important. As for the connection between Merovingian and Carolingian families, Professor Wallace-Hadrill kindly drew my attention to the presence of Merovingian names in Charlemagne's family.

larger group than appears in the sources. Nor can the marital practices of the Merovingians have helped to unify it as a group. There was nothing to ensure that the family would act unanimously in any situation; there were numerous reasons why they should conflict and ample opportunities for them to do so. Not surprisingly the question of royal succession was one where clashes occurred. Even if a prince's royal paternity was unquestioned, he needed the consent of the other members of the dynasty or the support of a section of the Frankish aristocracy. Thus even the greatest of the dark age dynasties was not defined with total clarity, nor could its members be assured of power.

To turn from the kings to their kingdoms is to raise a new set of issues. But in the context of the 511 land division, one question is central. Did the division of the kingship in early medieval society lead to a territorial division of the kingdom?

Pairs of kings can be traced in the semi-legendary past of many Germanic tribes, but the problems of these Dioscuran twins do not belong here.[72] The historic period, however, boasts many examples of joint-rule. The pages of Ammianus Marcellinus provide some glimpses of this for the period before the barbarians entered the Empire. In one series of campaigns the Alamans boasted numerous kings; of these, two are mentioned *potestate excelsiores ante alios reges*.[73] These were both members of one family. What the extent of their power was and how they shared it, is not made clear. Among the lesser kings there were two brothers, Gundomarus and Vadomarus. When the former was killed the latter was left in sole command of their tribe.[74]

Of the instances of joint kingship amongst the barbarian successor states, one of the earliest, leaving aside the Merovingian evidence, is to be found in Liuva's decision to divide the Visigothic kingdom with his brother Leovigild. Liuva first came to power in Septimania, that is the Gothic lands of South-Western France. The later rebellion of the Paul in the same area may suggest a certain regional independence.[75] Liuva does not seem to have been active outside the province. In time the Visigothic territories were reunited under Leovigild. But he, in his turn, decided to hand over some authority to his sons, Hermenegild and Reccared, granting them both capitals. Although Hermenegild's rebellion ended part of this experiment in government, Leovigild appears to have begun something of a tradition in associating Reccared with himself in the kingship. Henceforward this type of

---

[72] On Hengest and Horsa, for example, see Wallace-Hadrill 1971 p. 22.
[73] Ammianus XVI 12, 23–6.
[74] Ammianus XVI 12, 17. These brothers appear to be separate from the kings of XVI 12, 26. Gundomarus is said to have ruled a *plebs*. Whether there is a distinction to be made between a *plebs* and a *pagus* is uncertain. Was each *pagus* ruled over by a dynasty? Ammianus XVII 10, 5 shows one king attacking the *pagus* of another.
[75] On Liuva, John of Biclaro, Chronicle 569? section 4. in MGH AA 11 p. 212. On the bitterness between Spain and Gallia Narbonensis see Thompson 1969 pp. 227f.

association became one of the ploys used by Visigothic kings to ensure an hereditary succession. Swinthila attempted to associate his son, Ricimer with himself as king and Chindaswinth did the same with his son Recceswinth.[76] In none of these cases is there evidence to suggest that the Visigothic kingdom was divided territorially to accommodate the heir apparent. There is, however, some late evidence to suggest that when Egica associated his son, Witiza, with him in the kingship, he set him over Galicia with his capital at Tuy.[77] But another example of association of the heir apparent in the kingship, from Anglo-Saxon England, does not suggest any territorial division. Ecgfrith attested charters from 787 as *rex*, long before the death of his father, Offa.[78]

The practise of designating an heir is not always evidence of dynastic ambition. As in the Roman empire such a method was used by childless rulers to indicate their successors. The clearest cases of this both belong to crises caused by the sickness of the ruler. The first is not to be found in the West, but in Byzantium. Justin II, increasingly affected by madness, associated Tiberius with himself as Caesar.[79] In the East association of this kind had a long history before and after the sixth century. Such designations are to be found in the days of Diocletian and earlier and it may be that the early Germanic kings had noted the precedent.[80] The case of Justin II was almost repeated when Liutprand fell ill in 735. His nephew Hildeprand became *consors regis*. Fortunately for the Lombards Liutprand recovered. But it appears that Hildeprand remained as Liutprand's associate and eventually succeeded him, none too successfully.[81]

With few exceptions these royal associations seem not to have entailed the division of the kingdom. Power was shared; there is nothing to suggest that it was divided territorially. Nor is it certain that the inheritance of a kingdom by two heirs automatically led to such a division. Paul the Deacon tells how Aripert left the kingdom to his two sons, Godepert and Perctarit. Each had his own capital; Godepert at Pavia and Perctarit at Milan.[82] But individual capitals might mean no more than separate

---

[76] Grierson 1941. p. 14.

[77] This is suggested by the Cronica Albeldense; *Witiza regnavit anni X*, to which is added in two manuscripts, *Iste in vita patris in Tudense urbe Galleciae resedit*. See also Epitome Oventensis MGH AA XI p. 374. The same point is made in the Cronica Rotense; *sed ante uxoris dimissionem abebat ex ea filium adulescentem nomine Vitizanem quem rex in vita sua in regno participem fecit et cum in Tudensum civitare avitare precepit, ut pater teneret regnum gotorum et filius suevorum*. This evidence is to be found in Gómez-Moreno 1932 pp. 601, 611. I am indebted to Roger Collins for calling my attention to this material. Livermore 1971 pp. 257–8 discusses the evidence of the Epitome Ovetensis.

[78] See Birch 253, 255, 271. I am grateful to David Dumville who drew my attention to the Anglo-Saxon parallel.

[79] Gregory Hist. IV 40.

[80] The Burgundian evidence may suggest this. Avitus uses the word *Caesar* in ep 77 (=Chevalier 68). He was skilled in diplomatic protocol.

[81] See the Continuatio Romano to Paul the Deacon in M.G.H. Scriptores Rerum Langobardicarum et Italicarum p. 200. Also Hodgkin 1894 pp. 472–3.

[82] Paul Historia Langobardorum IV 51.

royal households. It is almost certain, however, that this particular instance is not even a case of joint-kingship; but rather evidence of a disputed succession.[83]

Compared with the scarcity of examples of joint-rule amongst the Lombards and Visigoths, the evidence from Anglo-Saxon history is plentiful. But it also has its pecularities. For instance Oswiu, king of Northumbria had a *consors regiae dignitatis*, Oswine.[84] But the temporary co-existence of these two kings resulted from a long-standing division between two districts of Northumbria; Bernicia, with which Oswiu's family was associated, and Deira, the homeland of Oswine. The kingdoms seem to have remained distinct under Oswiu and his son Alhfrith.[85] This tendency for kingdoms to retain some territorial distinction, even after they had been subsumed into larger units is a common feature in Anglo-Saxon England. It can be detected in the subscriptions of kings and sub-kings to the charters of Offa.[86]

Nevertheless there are cases where the evidence is neither so clear, nor so simple. The early history of Wessex is beset with difficulties, but joint-kingship is well attested. Moreover by the time of Ine there was some territorial division of the kingdom apparent in the West Saxon shire system.[87] Whether these divisions represent a parcelling-out of the kingdom amongst members of the royal family is uncertain; the charter evidence is suspicious.[88] As for Bede and the Anglo-Saxon Chronicle, there are discrepancies. According to the latter Edwin killed five kings of Wessex in one campaign in 626.[89] Even so, two kings, Cynegils and Cwichelm were still alive in 628. Clearly there was a multiplicity of kings. But Bede, also describing the 626 campaign, does not enumerate royalty among the dead; only conspirators.[90] It is possible, therefore, that we are dealing with a group of principalities in Wessex, whose rulers were not regarded as kings by all writers. From one point of view a leader might be regarded as a king, while from another his status was less elevated;

---

[83] Bognetti 1966 II p. 334 suggested a disputed succession, arguing this unconvincingly on the basis of a theological distinction, Arian Pavia versus Catholic Milan. But more important is the mention of the time *quando Godebert invasionem fecit* in a charter of Perctarit ed Bognetti 1966 I pp. 234–9. I owe these points entirely to Chris Wickham.

[84] Bede H.E. III 14.

[85] The joint-kingship of the two suggests this. Bede H.E. III 25. But as David Dumville has reminded me, there is a change; both Oswiu and Alhfrith belonged to the same dynasty.

[86] Stenton 1971 pp. 210f.

[87] Chadwick 1905 pp. 282–290. For a fuller consideration of the West Saxon evidence see David Dumville's discussion below.

[88] Chadwick 1905 pp. 288f. But the crucial charters concerning Hean and his family are not well regarded. This is true especially for Birch 101, see comments in Sawyer 1968 No. 241. See too Birch 100, Sawyer 239; Birch 108, Sawyer 245. Another charter central to Chadwick's study is Birch 142, Sawyer 250, which is widely regarded as spurious. Clearly the sub-kings of Wessex need more cautious treatment than that of Chadwick; however it is interesting that forgers had no qualms about the presence of sub-kings.

[89] The evidence is in the E. text; perhaps it should be treated with caution.

[90] Bede H.E. II 9.

the title accorded to both the Bavarian and Frisian leaders flucutated between *rex* and *dux*.[91]

Such complications do not affect all the Anglo-Saxon kingdoms. For many of them joint-kingship is clear and frequent. Sometimes two or more kings are brothers or kinsmen; sometimes no relationship is recorded.[92] In two cases there may even be evidence of territorial division. The first of these is Essex, where Sighere and Sebbi rule together. But Sighere apostatized *cum sua parte populi*.[93] However, even if lordship over a certain section of the people does suggest that the kingdom was divided (and it need not), this is the only trace of it. Less debateable is the evidence for Kent. There Sigired is described as *rex dimidiae partis provinciae Cantuariorum*.[94] Nevertheless this description is unique and cannot describe a fixed state of affairs. First, although there was often more than one king, the number was not limited to two; Wihtred had three sons.[95] Second, King Eadberht and his son Eardwulf were active at the same time, in the same district of Kent, whilst Aethelberht was still reigning.[96]

Thus, leaving aside the evidence from Gaul, a brief survey of cases where a nation was ruled by more than one king does not permit the conclusion that the sharing of the royal office necessarily led to the territorial division of the kingdom. This negative conclusion is significant when we turn to the Burgundian evidence, for the kingdom of the Burgundians has been regarded as subject to territorial divisions.[97] Certainly it was ruled for a considerable period of time by more than one king; first by Gundioc and his brother Chilperic I, then by the former's sons.

The royal power of the first two is not easily assessed. Jordanes calls them kings, when he describes them as allies of the Visigoth Theodoric II.[98] But essentially their authority was Roman; they held power before the last emperor of the West had been deposed. According to a papal letter of 463 Gundioc intervened in an episcopal election, as *magister militium*[99] The activities of his brother, Chilperic, are better known, through the letters of Sidonius Apollinaris. He appears in residence at Lyons in 471—2. Although a heretic he was on good terms with the catholic bishop of the city. In 474 he was regarded as ruler of Germania Lugdunensis, in which capacity he

---

[91] Fredegar usually calls Radbod *dux* but Fredegar Cont. 31 mentions *reges*. See also Paul "Historia Langobardorum" VI 37. Fredegar calls Odovacrus *rex*, in the L.H.F. he is *dux*.

[92] Brothers, Bede H.E. II 5, III 18, IV 11, 13, V 23. Father and son II 9. Uncle and nephew IV 27. No relationship recorded III 30, IV 15.

[93] Bede H.E. III 30.

[94] Birch 194. I am indebted to Patrick Wormald for the evidence on Kent.

[95] Bede H.E. V 23. Wihtred had been co-ruler with Swæfheard, Bede H.E. V 8.

[96] Birch 173, 175, 190, 191 show the contemporary activity of these kings.

[97] Binding 1868 pp. 65, 73. was the most scholarly attempt to show this.

[98] Jordanes, Getica XLIV 231.

[99] Epistolae Arelatenses Genuinae 19.

heard treason accusations against a nobleman of Vaison.[100] Chilperic is also to be found as *patricius Galliae*, with his court in Geneva, probably in the year 467.[101] But because this activity seems to be that of a Roman official rather than of a barbarian king, no conclusion can be drawn about any territorial division of the Burgundian kingdom.

The four sons of Gundioc provide material for further investigation. Gregory of Tours gives their names; Gundobad, Godigisil, Chilperic and Godomar. But he does not say that they were all heirs of their father, nor does he use any word for king in this passage.[102] Scepticism on this issue is strengthened by the failure of the *Lex Burgundionum* to mention any except Gundobad as king.[103] Moreover, nothing is known of Godomar at all. Chilperic II is only remembered for his death, for Gundobad killed him and had his wife drowned. His two daughters, one of whom was Chrodechildis, later Clovis' queen, he exiled.[104] There is, then, nothing to suggest that the two younger brothers were connected with either the kingship or a district of the kingdom. The case for Godigisil, however, is not so clear. Gregory of Tours tells us that he and Gundobad held the kingdom which lay along the Rhône and the Saône and included the province of Marseilles.[105] After a while Godigisil sided with the Frankish king, Clovis, against his brother. Together they drove Gundobad south; Godigisil returned to Vienne, which he entered in triumph, as if he ruled the whole kingdom. As it was, Gundobad soon regained control and Godigisil died in the siege of the city.

None of this proves that the territory of the Burgundians was divided. But one piece of evidence suggests that Gundobad and Godigisil had capitals of their own. The Life of Saint Epiphanius of Pavia by Ennodius describes a diplomatic mission, which visited Gundobad at his court in Lyons and Godigisil in Geneva.[106] The mission dates to the year 496. There is another piece of evidence to link Godigisil to Geneva. A lady, Theodesinda, built a church dedicated to St. Vincent there in the time of rex Gundegisilus.[107] But Theodesinda is probably to be equated with Godigisil's queen, Theudelinda. It is probable that the two of them founded the monastery of St. Peter in Lyons.[108] This, however, shows them as being active in what ought to have been the centre of Gundobad's authority. Equally Gundobad's

---

[100] Sidonius Apollinaris ep VI 12, 3. V 6, 1. V 7, 7. The dates are from Loyen's edition. The implication of *Lugdunensis Germania* is presumably literary rather than administrative. All these letters seem to refer to the same man; Binding 1868 pp. 301–2 comes to different conclusions.

[101] Vita Patrum Jurensium. For the dating see Martine 1968 p. 337 fn 3.

[102] Gregory. Hist. II 28.

[103] Lex Burgundionum III

[104] Gregory Hist. II 28.

[105] Gregory Hist. II 32.

[106] Ennodius Vita Epiphani 174.

[107] Passio Ursi et Victoris 2. A.A.S.S. Sept. VIII p. 292. But see Fredegar IV 22.

[108] Coville 1928 pp. 262–4 summarizes the evidence with caution. I am not convinced that an Arian king could not help his catholic queen found a nunnery. The fact that the foundation was attributed to such insignificant royalty demands some consideration.

influence extended to Geneva in the period of the Epiphanius mission, for it was to Geneva that Gundobad sent his nieces after killing their father and it was from Geneva that Chrodechildis set out to marry Clovis not long before 496.[109] But this supremacy of Gundobad over Godigisel is actually confirmed by the source which mentions the latter's court in Geneva. Ennodius, Epiphanius' biographer and companion on the Burgundian mission, does not describe Godigisel as king, but as *germanus regis*.

The probability, then, is that there was never a total division of royal power in the Burgundian Kingdom. Even if Godigisil did rule over a province, which is not certain, it was only as a subordinate to his brother.[110] Nor does the evidence relating to a joint-kingship of Gundobad and his son Sigismund differ from this. Officially Sigismund was elevated to the kingship in 516, but he seems to have been regarded as *rex* and was even alluded to as *Caesar* before this date.[111] He was certainly of mature years long before his accession; his marriage to the daughter of Theodoric the Great may have taken place soon after 494.[112] If Sigismund had a capital of his own before 516, and there is some evidence to suggest that he did, it was probably Geneva.[113] It was in this region that he was most notably active while his father was alive. He founded the Monastery of Agaune at the other end of the Lac Léman. Moreover his full elevation to the kingship took place at the royal villa of Carouge in the suburbs of Geneva itself. Nevertheless it may be to this period that we should date Gundobad's restoration of the walls of the same city; Sigismund was not independent.[114]

But to return to Gundobad, the evidence does not suggest that he had a fixed capital. Rather it appears that the court was peripatetic. Avitus, bishop of Vienne, urged the king to pass the great ecclesiastical feasts in his cathedral city. But the king was as often in Lyons and Chalon-sur-Saône. Sigismund was often to be found with him.[115] As for Gundobad's law-giving, he legislated from his royal villa at Ambérieux as well as from Lyons.[116]

The Burgundian picture is an important one, not merely because it reveals the need for caution in considering royal practises, but also because, if Chrodechildis was used to any system of royal inheritance, it must have been that of her own nation. As

---

[109] On Chrodechildis in Geneva, Fredegar III 18. On Chrodechildis' marriage Ewig 1974 p. 38.

[110] N.B. however the importance of the province of Sapaudia in the Burgundian kingdom, perhaps governed from Geneva. The evidence on Sapaudia is summarized by Duparc 1958.

[111] Fredegar III 33. *Caesar*, Avitus ep 77 (Chevalier 68). He is regarded as second in the kingdom in Avitus Homily 25 (Chevalier 24).

[112] Anonymous Valesianus Continuation 63. c.f. Ewig 1974 p. 37.

[113] This inference is to be drawn from Avitus ep 8 (Chevalier 6 A), if it refers to Sigismund. Avitus Homily 19 might be the dedication homily. A general survey of the presence of the Burgundian royalty in Geneva is to be found in Blondel 1958. Some of the points made by Blondel are not above criticism.

[114] Notitia Galliarum in MGH AA IX p. 600. See D.A.C.L. VI (1) cols. 940–2 (Genève).

[115] See, for example, Avitus eps 76, 77, 79, 80, 81, 83 (Chevalier 50, 68, 72, 73, 74, 76).

[116] Ambérieux; Lex Burgundionum XLII

she considered the question of the succession in 511, she can have received no consolation from Burgundian history.

Thus far two general points concerning early medieval dynasties and their kingdoms have emerged. First, even in the most stable of royal families, no heir could be certain that his claim to the kingship would be made good. Many Merovingian princes did succeed, but Chlodomer's sons were killed; Theudebert had to rely on the support of his 'leudes'; Childebert II was saved by Gundovald and Chlothar II by Ansovald. All these examples come from the generations of Chrodechildis' grandsons and great grandsons. The second point is that even if all the heirs survived and the kingship was divided between them, the division did not have to be territorial. To investigate any further factors which might explain the Frankish solution of 511, it is necessary to return to the history of the Franks.

In a famous chapter Gregory of Tours excerpted the lost historians, Sulpicius Alexander and Renatus Profuturus Frigeridus. Then, recording the opinions of many he stated that the Franks left Pannonia, crossed the Rhine and the land of Thuringia and that they created long-haired kings for themselves there, *iuxta pagus vel civitates*, taking them from their most noble family. He goes on to say that this is proved by the victories of Clovis.[117] The significance of the phrase *iuxta pagus vel civitates* is not easily assessed. But in the account of Clovis' assault on his Frankish rivals which concludes Book Two of Gregory's history, it is interesting to note the urban settings. Sigibert the Lame did not fight with Clovis against the Goths at Vouillé; he had been wounded in a battle fought against the Alamanni at the oppidum of Zülpich. Later he was murdered whilst taking a stroll outside the city of Cologne. It appears that his treasure was kept in the city and it was there that his son's bid for the kingship failed. There too Clovis was raised on a shield in token of his election as king.[118] In similar fashion Ragnachar was killed outside Cambrai.[119] Nor is the presence of Frankish kings in Roman cities first apparent in the lifetime of Clovis. His father, Childeric, is to be connected above all with Tournai; it was there that he had his treasury, seemingly a continuation of an older Roman fisc, and it was there that he was buried.

The early presence of barbarians in cities need not surprise. In Procopius' "History of the Wars", the Herules are to be found in Singidunum in Dacia; that is, present-day Belgrade.[120] From the time of their entry into Italy the Lombards were concerned with cities and in the time of the interregnum every duke was associated

---

[117] Gregory Hist. II 9. Pagus in Ammianus seems generally to imply territory; XVII 10, 5. XXXI 3, 1. XXXI 10, 5. But in one case it seems to mean tribe XV 4, 1. For the later use of the word see Ewig 1957 p. 606.

[118] Gregory Hist. II 37, 40. See Hübrich 1975 p. 20ff. I do not see why Sigibert's combat at Zülpich should be linked with Clovis' victory over the Alamans in 506.

[119] Gregory Hist. II 42. On Cambrai see Hist. II 9. For Chararic see II 41. Dalton 1927 II p. 504. See also Wallace-Hadrill 1962 pp. 151–3 for this and Childeric.

[120] Procopius Wars VII, XXXIII (13).

with a civitas.¹²¹ Doubtless the cities fell into decay, but they were not abandoned; barbarian leaders did not avoid them.

By the end of his life Childeric's power was not confined to Tournai. His career had been uneven; although a son of Merovech he had been deposed by the Franks, who chose as their king — the word *rex* is used — the Roman *magister militum*, Aegidius. Merovingian blood was clearly not yet necessary; even Roman blood would do. A century later the Ostrogoths did much the same; they asked the enemy general, Belisarius, to take the kingship.¹²² But Childeric returned, perhaps with Byzantine support.¹²³

The full extent of Childeric's achievement can only be guessed at, for the first evidence to throw light on Clovis' power is not easily dated. Remigius, bishop of Rheims, acclaimed the new king's assumption of his inheritance in the context of his taking over the government of Belgica Secunda.¹²⁴ But until 486 the city of Soissons, which belonged to that province, was held by Aegidius' son Syagrius, who, although his jurisdiction had diminished, was remembered by Gregory of Tours as *Romanorum rex*.¹²⁵ But whether the Remigius letter is to be dated to 482 or 486, Clovis was regarded by the latter year as governor of a province which consisted of the cities of Rheims, Soissons, Chalons-sur-Marne, Noyon, Arras, Cambrai, Tournai, Senlis, Beauvais, Amiens, Thérouanne and Boulogne.¹²⁶ Among these cities are to be found the names of at least two, which were still ruled by other Frankish kings in the later part of Clovis' reign; Cambrai and Thérouanne.¹²⁷ Thus Clovis' early power was not merely a Germanic kingship over his own branch of Franks, but also a Roman territorial authority, which actually extended over lands held by other tribal groups. Remigius, for his part, was certain that Clovis had taken over governmental responsibilities; he advised him to follow the counsel of the bishops.¹²⁸

Indeed it was not foolish for a king, who was still a pagan, to turn to the Christian hierarchy. Although the main tenor of Remigius' advice concerns good works and pastoral care, a bishop's influence went far beyond this in the early medieval period. The activity of lay officials in the cities in this period is little known and it may be that it was more substantial than the evidence shows, but the extent of the activity of the bishops within the cities and their surrounding districts cannot be doubted. Their ecclesiastical position alone made them important men with control of the cultic and moral activity of the people of their *civitas*. During the barbarian migrations they had certainly added to their stature, helping organise urban defense

---

[121] Paul "Historia Langobardorum" II 32.
[122] Gregory Hist. II 11. Procopius Wars VI, XXIX (18–19)
[123] Wallace-Hadrill 1962 pp. 161–2.
[124] Epistolae Austrasiacae 2.
[125] Gregory Hist. II 27.
[126] Notitia Galliarum MGH AA IX pp. 590–2.
[127] See additional note 3. For Thérouanne see Dalton 1927 II p. 504 and Wallace-Hadrill 1962 pp. 151f.
[128] Wallace-Hadrill 1962 pp. 166-7.

or acting as ambassadors to Germanic kings. Finally they were aristocrats, more often then not with access to much influence and many contacts among the upper classes of Gaul. The admission of such men to his counsel must have facilitated the acceptance of Clovis by the Gallo-Romans. Territorially, the power of the bishops was based on the administrative units of the towns and their dependent countryside, that is, on the *civitates*. It was also *iuxta pagus vel civitates* that the Franks elected their kings. Some of the kings were to be found in the *civitates* of Belgica Secunda, Clovis' province. Despite the settlement of Franks in this area, there is no great evidence of discontinuity in the appointment of bishops.[129]

Clovis' power was, in effect, a double nature. He was a provincial governor in a late Roman tradition and he was a barbarian king. Other barbarians could boast the same dichotomy; the great Alaric had hoped for Roman office; Burgundian *reges* had been *magistri militum*; Odovacer and Theodoric, if they were not imperial officials, were at least kings who worked with the old administrative institutions of Italy.[130] In effect, as kings these men were national kings, but the full extent of their territorial power came from the Roman administration they had inherited. For Clovis, this distinction was significant, for he was not the only Frankish ruler to be found within the confines of Belgica Secunda.

Towards the end of his life, if we are to believe Gregory of Tours' chronology, Clovis embarked on a policy, the effect of which was to erode the distinction between his Roman and his Germanic power in North-East Gaul. Already he had conquered the Alamans to the South-East, the Burgundians to the South were subservient and he had annexed the country between the Loire and the Seine as well as Aquitaine. As a culmination of this activity he received the consulship at Tours from the Emperor Anastasius.[131] His success had been imperially recognised. Now, by a series of stratagems, he eliminated those other kings who lived, with their followers, round Cologne, Thérouanne and Cambrai. By the time of his death there was no territorial distinction between his Roman and his Germanic authority.

The Frankish kingship as it existed in 511 was, therefore, a new creation. Being new, the problem of the succession cannot have suggested any simple solution. Certainly Clovis had ensured that there were no rivals to his own family; a family whose lateral branches he had pruned brutally. But family feeling, even amongst brothers, was not tender enough to guarantee that all of the old kings' sons would inherit. Nor does it appear inevitable that the kingdom would be divided territorially. Neither the Frankish nor the Burgundian evidence suggests that this was traditional practice. On the other hand the oddities of the 511 division coincide exactly with the

---

[129] Arras and Cambrai were one see. Neither Thérouanne nor Boulogne were episcopal cities. The first recorded bishops for Noyon and Tournai come from about the time of Clovis. The same is true for Arras-Cambrai and Amiens, if one rejects the 346 council of Cologne. The episcopal lists for the other sees suggest continuity. See Duchesne 1915 III pp. 76–130. Also Wallace-Hadrill 1962, pp. 151ff.

[130] On Alaric, Zosimus V 48. On the Burgundians Epistolae Arelatenses Genuinae 19 and Avitus ep 93 (Chevalier 82). For Italy Jones 1962.

[131] Gregory Hist. II 38.

political situation at Clovis' death. First the position of Chrodechildis at court is likely to have been dominant. Second her allies are most likely to have been the catholic hierarchy.

The situation in which the queen found herself cannot have been easy. She was left a widow with three sons, the oldest of whom was probably fourteen. Clovis had another heir, considerably older, who already had a son approximately ten years old. Theuderic must have been the obvious successor. Granted Chrodechildis' concern to ensure that her grandchildren succeeded, when Chlodomer died, it is easy to assume that she had the same concern for her children. But if the kingship was to be divided between all four heirs, the question of how to effect this must have arisen. Theuderic's influence was likely to be preponderant; yet he alone was not the offspring of the queen. His power, if unchecked, might well have been a threat to Chrodechildis and her children. But such problems as might have arisen here, could be avoided by dividing the kingdom territorially. Such a division was likely to follow the lines of the old Roman *civitas* boundaries. The experts here were the bishops and the Gallo-Roman aristocracy. The division is inconceivable without their approval. This recreation of events is necessarily speculative, but it seems plausible to suggest that the famous division of the Frankish kingdom originated, not in tradition, but in a precise political compromise, where, once again, the acquiescence or consent of the political nation, in this case, no doubt, Theuderic, the Frankish aristocracy and the Gallo-Roman bishops, was necessary.

The events of 511 can never be known. Nevertheless an examination of the factors which may influenced these events is not without value for the study of early medieval kingship. In general, notions of Germanic tradition have not been impervious to scrutiny. Royal inheritance patterns, even for a dynasty as firmly established as the Merovingians could never be relied upon; kingdoms, if they were to be divided, did not have to be divided territorially. Above all kingship was an office which responded to political change.

Additional Note 1
The Kingdom as allod
 Most of the Germanic law codes imply that inheritance by all male heirs was the norm. This can be deduced from Pactus Legis Salicae LIX, Lex Salica XCI, Lex Burgundionum XIV 2, Leges Visigothorum IV 2 (1), (11) and the Edict of Rothari CLIII. But the majority of these kingdoms did not apply the laws of inheritance to the royal succession. For the Visigoths it is extremely clear that the kingdom was not treated as an allod; see the distinction drawn between the official and the personal property of the king in the Councils of Toledo VIII 10, 12 and XVII 7. On the other hand seventh century Visigothic kingship was not hereditary, whilst the Frankish

kingship was. The attitude of the Franks towards their kingdom was certainly less clear-cut than this by the mid-sixth century. This is illustrated by the fact that queens were given cities as *morgengaben*; see Gregory Hist IX 20. That is, the Merovingians seem to have come to regard their kingdom as personal property. This does not, however, explain how the practice arose. Seeing that the Germans did not automatically apply laws of inheritance to the succession, it is not enough to assert that the Franks did just that without some explanation. A study of Roman inheritance patterns, as opposed to a study of the imperial succession, is unlikely to provide a solution for the same reason; if the Franks adopted Roman laws of inheritance as a model for royal succession, why was this not done by all the tribes? Clearly a more specific context is required if we are going to assert that the Merovingians regarded their territory as allodial, whilst other kings did not.

Additional Note 2
Sacral kingship and the aristocracy

The link between the megistanes and the tribal cults, Thompson 1966 pp. 66–7, seems to require some emphasis. Without it, it is difficult to understand the facility with which a leader, elected for a time of crisis, could assume sacrality, only to discard it when his function as warleader ceased. This connection of aristocrat and cult is not confined to Gothic Society. Peter Sawyer has kindly pointed out to me the close relationship of aristocratic farm and cult centre in the Viking world. For this see Olsen 1966, English summary pp. 277–88. He also drew my attention to the interesting fact that the word used for the oligarchs of Iceland, Goði, is cognate with Gothic Gudja, a priest.

The classic interpretation of sacral kingship, Höfler 1954, has been much criticised. For the present context it is important that although Höfler stresses the importance of the *Thing* as an elective and sacral body, his discussion does seem to ignore the fluidity of political power. The source which most clearly supports Höfler's rather static view is Ammianus Marcellinus. But the famous description of sacral kingship among the Burgundians in Ammianus XXXVIII 5, 14 demands cautious treatment. Ammianus compares the Burgundian system with that in use in Egypt. But Egypt did not have a sacral kingship in the late fourth century A.D. This suggests that Ammianus is quoting a much earlier source. Whatever the source was, the evidence cannot be used at face value for a study of Burgundian kingship just before the migrations. Other evidence used by Höfler also needs handling with care. The very striking discussion of the fire-breathing Amals (Höfler 1954 p. 87) does not prove this is related to kingly rather than heroic activity. The line between the two may well be a narrow one, but it is as well to remember that there may be a difference. Not all kings were heroes and vice-versa. Naturally Höfler's arguments have not been the last word. Wolfram 1968 is an important attempt to reconsider the methodology used in the study of sacral kingship. Wallace Hadrill 1971 pp. 8–15 provides a magisterial survey of the evidence in a wider context.

Additional Note 3

Clovis' last years

The chronology of Clovis' reign has been much debated, but there is one point which suggests that Gregory's placing of Clovis' assault on the other Frankish kings belongs after the battle of Vouillé. Gregory Hist. II 37 records that Chloderic, son of Sigibert the Lame, fought with Clovis at that battle. This same prince was one of the latter's victims. Thus the unification of the Ripuarian and Salian Franks must belong to the years after 507. However Sigibert's Kingdom of Cologne differed from the other Frankish kingdoms mentioned by Gregory; first it was Ripuarian and not Salian, second it lay outside the centre of Clovis' early influence, the province of Belgica Secunda. This was not true of the Kingdoms of Cambrai and Thérouanne. Gregory may be mistaken in placing Clovis' attack on Chararic after the attack on Cologne and he may not have any reason other than thematic clarity when he describes the overthrow of Ragnachar as the final part of the sequence. Nevertheless some good evidence is required if we are to challenge the chronology of the assault on Chararic, given Gregory's precise dating of the event. Since such evidence is lacking, it is preferable to try and understand how Clovis could be but one king among many and at the same time governor of Belgica Secunda, rather than to resort to the argument that because Clovis' Roman power was so great we must assume that he had already overthrown the other Frankish kings. It may be that the 508 consulship at Tours was one of the spurs to Clovis' Frankish ambition.

Additional Note 4

Dates relating to royal dynasties and to the division of kingdoms.
511   Franks; division of kingdom after death of Clovis.
524   Franks; re-division of kingdom after death of Chlodomer.
531   Visigoths; fall of Balt dynasty.
532–4 Burgundians; destruction of kingdom; fall of Gibichung dynasty.
533–4 Vandals; destruction of kingdom; fall of dynasty of the Hasdings.
536   Ostrogoths; fall of Amal dynasty.
552   Ostrogoths; destruction of kingdom.
561   Franks; division of kingdom after death of Chlothar I.
567   Franks; re-division of kingdom after death of Charibert I.
568   Lombards; entry into Italy.
       Visigoths; division of kingdom, Liuva-Leovigild.
57 –8 Lombards; interregnum.
578?   Visigoths; Leovigild founds Reccopolis.
579?   Visigoths; division of kingdom, Leovigild-Hermenegild.
589   Lombards; Authari marries Bavarian (Lething) Theudelinda.
622   Franks; division of kingdom, Chlothar II — Dagobert I.
628   Franks; division of kingdom, Dagobert I — Charibert II.
632   Franks; division of kingdom, Dagobert I — Sigibert III.

700 Visigoths; division of kingdom, Egica — Witiza.
711 Visigoths; destruction of kingdom.
712 Lombards; end of Bavarian-Lething dynasty.
751 Franks; fall of Merovingian dynasty.

2

Julian of Toledo and the Royal Succession in Late Seventh-Century Spain[1]

ROGER COLLINS

On the first of September in the year 672 the Visigothic king Recceswinth died at the royal villa of Gerticos, at a distance of some one hundred and twenty Roman miles to the north-west of the royal capital, the *urbs regia* of Toledo. By Visigothic standards at least, his reign of nearly twenty four years was a long one, and, in terms of its legislative activity, amongst the most important of any of the seventh-century kings in western Europe. But apart from the legal legacy of the first version, as far at least as is currently extant, of the *Liber Iudiciorum*,[2] and those few sparse details about the date and place of his death, we know virtually nothing about the life and reign of this, one of the most significant of the Visigothic kings of Spain. Nor is this ignorance exceptional. Far less is known about the majority of the other Visigothic kings, and even the chronology of their reigns has had to be worked out by inference and cannot be accepted with absolute certainty.[3]

For Recceswinth we are, if anything, unusually fortunate in the quantity of information available to us, slight as this is. The place of his death, Gerticos, was identified in the thirteenth century with the small town of Bamba, now Wamba, in the province of Valladolid.[4] It is thus not far from the church of S. Juan de Baños, in the village of Baños de Cerrato, the only church to which an origin in the Visigothic period can be attributed with absolute certainty, and which we know, thanks to an extant inscription, to have been founded by this same king Recceswinth, in the year 661, and dedicated to St. John the Baptist. It may well have been erected as a votive offering for a cure effected by the medicinal properties of a nearby spring.[5] The relative proximity of S. Juan de Baños to the probable site of Gerticos may lead us to the reasonably plausible hypothesis that much of the land in this region, between Salamanca and Palencia, may well have belonged to Recceswinth, either as his family lands or as the royal lands he held during his reign, by virtue of his office.[6]

---

[1] I am most grateful to the members of the seminar for a very helpful discussion of this paper; to Ian Wood, for many valuable comments both then and afterwards; and above all to Judith McClure, for help and advice throughout.

[2] *MGH Legum*, Section I, Vol. 1, ed. K. Zeumer.

[3] Zeumer 1902.

[4] *Chronicon Adefonsi Imperatoris* c. 2, ed. L. Sánchez Belda, Madrid (1950).

[5] Garcia Górriz 1966. de Navascués, 1961.

[6] An important distinction in Visigothic Spain: for a discussion, see King, 1972, chapter 2.

Anyway, it may be seen from this how speedily information runs out and conjecture has to take its place. For other reigns, it might be noticed, that we have not so much as a hint about the siting of royal villas and residences outside of Toledo, nor any specific information about lands and estates, royal or otherwise, at all.

Now, this is not to say that there is a general lack of evidence available for the study of Spain in the sixth and seventh centuries. Quite the contrary, there is a surprisingly large amount of it. The problem lies more in the nature of the evidence, rather than in the quantity of it. There is a great corpus of law, from the late sixth and seventh centuries, both secular and ecclesiastical. The former is contained in the *Liber Iudiciorum* issued by Recceswinth circa 654 and revised and enlarged by Ervig in 681,[7] and which was intended to provide a comprehensive code of law for the kingdom.[8] For ecclesiastical legislation there survive the acts of all but one of many Councils of Toledo that were convened periodically throughout the seventh century. These acts together with those of a number of provincial councils were collected together into the famous canonical collection, the *Hispana*, in the early seventh century, possibly by Isidore of Seville, and then again in an expanded version in the last quarter of the century.[9] Then there is a remarkably large body of liturgical texts, far greater in number and providing a far fuller picture of the liturgical life of the Church in Spain than that available from any other comparable Church in this period, either eastern or western.[10] As well as these great legal and liturgical collections there are, of course, saints' lives, though far fewer of these than were written in Merovingian Gaul at this time, also monastic rules, a large, and as of yet little studied, body of poetry, much of it anonymous, and there are the literary products of a number of authors.[11] Amongst the latter, the works of Isidore of Seville are the best known, both to the generations that followed him and to modern scholars. But the literary pre-eminence of Isidore and the quantity of his output should not blind us to the varied and original contributions, both in style and content, made by other authors of the Visigothic period, in particular the three mid-seventh century bishops of Toledo, Eugenius II, Ildefonsus and Julian.

Obviously it would be possible to expand to far greater length this brief account of the kind of source material available to the historian of seventh-century Spain. But certain features must now be clear. For one thing, for Spain we are rich in certain kinds of evidence, especially legal and liturgical, and to a far greater degree than for any other part of Europe in this particular period, but, at the same time, we are extremely poorly off for the kind of source material that provides almost the staple diet for fellow historians working on Gaul, say, or Italy, or Anglo-Saxon England, or the Byzantine Empire for that matter. There are remarkably few saints' lives, and

---

[7] *MGH Legum*, Sectio I, Vol. 1, *Liber Iudiciòrum, praefatio*, pp. XVIII–XIX.

[8] See the paper in this volume by Patrick Wormald.

[9] Vives 1963, pp. XII–XV. Martínez Diez, 1966, and *idem*, 1971, 119–38.

[10] Pinnell 1965, pp. 109–64.

[11] E.g. *MGH AA* XIV, ed. F. Vollmer, pp. 271–82. For the *regulae*, see Campos and Ismael Roco 1971, II.

those that there are bristle with problems, both textual and interpretative,[12] and, what is perhaps even worse, there is virtually no history, in the literary sense at least. In the writing of chronicles there is a gap between the early seventh century and the middle of the eighth. Isidore, when he continues the chronicle of John of Biclar, takes his brief account only as far as the tenth year of the reign of Swinthila, that is to say 630.[13] For the rest of the seventh century no attempt was made to continue Isidore's work. Not until after the Arab invasion was there to be a resumption of the writing of chronicles in Spain, with the appearance of the two 'Mozarabic' Chronicles of 742 and 751.[14] What is striking about those two works is that their authors seem to have known little more about the history of the kingdom in the late seventh century than we do today. There are then no lost historical writings dating from the last decades of the Visigothic kingdom.

In terms of the writing of literary history, there is, needless to say, no Spanish Bede or Gregory of Tours. We have no large-scale narrative histories from the Visigothic kingdom at all. There is Isidore's *Historia Gothorum*, which, like his chronicle, terminates with the reign of Swinthila (621–31).[15] Braulio of Saragossa praised this work especially for the *brevitas* of its style, a quality much appreciated at the time.[16] It has occasionally been fashionable amongst historians to castigate Isidore for not writing a *History of the Goths* that would rival in size and doubtless outweigh in style and content the work of Gregory of Tours, or for not writing a Spanish *Historia Ecclesiastica*. They would be better advised to be thankful for what they have got and to ponder over why Isidore wrote the work he did and in the way that he did. At any rate this work of Isidore's, sparse as it is, was to have no successor.

This curious imbalance in the nature of the evidence for the history of seventh-century Spain is thus the most immediate problem that strikes the prospective historian of the Visigothic kingdom. It is also the most fundamental. Of course, there are a number of technical problems associated with all of the extant sources. For example, the liturgical manuscripts from Toledo had long been regarded as dating from the ninth century, but they have recently been redated as belonging by and large to the twelfth.[17] Also there has been a general lack of good editions of the major texts, with a few notable exceptions; something that has only recently begun to be rectified. Serious as some of these problems are, they are all ultimately soluble. The lack of certain kinds of evidence, to which I have been referring, is, of course, something to which there is no solution, barring the discovery, which must be unlikely, of hitherto unknown and unsuspected texts.

---

[12] E.g. the *Vita Fructuosi*, 1974.
[13] *MGH AA, XI*, ed. T. Mommsen, pp. 267–95.
[14] *Corpus Scriptorum Muzarabicorum*, I, pp. 7–54, 1973.
[15] *MGH AA* XI, ed. T. Mommsen, pp. 424–81.
[16] Lynch and Galindo 1950, p. 358, *Renotatio Isidori*.
[17] cf. the reassessment made of some Toledan liturgical mss. by Mundó 1964. More remains to be done.

Obviously every early medieval historian, whatever the period or the region of his enquiry, must be circumscribed by the nature and quantity of the evidence available to him. But for Visigothic Spain the problem, as I hope I have shown, is more extreme. This has exposed its historians to two dangerous temptations: the temptation of theory and the temptation of fantasy. The bulk of our evidence for Visigothic Spain is of a theoretical rather than a practical nature. We have these great codes of law and the enactments of an impressive series of Councils, which tell us what the legislators thought ought to be, but we lack the kind of evidence about the society that could tell us, firstly, how serious and prevalent were the ills that the civil and ecclesiastical legislators sought to reform, and secondly, how successful or otherwise they were in imposing their laws. The question of the treatment of the Jews provides a good case. The whole of the twelfth book of the *Liber Iudiciorum* is devoted to the enactments of various kings, from the time of Reccared (586—601) onwards, against those Jews who had not converted to Christianity, ending with their wholesale enslaving in the reign of Egica (687—702).[18] But we know practically nothing about the practical realities of Jewish life in Visigothic Spain; how they organised their communities, their position within the towns and their degree of integration into local society, the way in which they were patronised by the bishops, their learning and their contacts outside the Visigothic kingdom. In the absence of even a modicum of this kind of information, how can we possibly judge the effects of the legislation, or consider whether it could ever have been applied at all? Undeterred by such obvious limitations, some historians have assumed that the laws relating to the Jews provide not normative regulations but an actual description of social reality. They in effect ask us to believe that a Visigothic king or Council of bishops had but to legislate for their enactments to be applied absolutely and universally throughout the realm, a supposition for which there is not the slightest shred of evidence. Indeed the repetitive nature of the laws concerning the Jews would suggest the difficulty lay rather in getting them enforced at all.[19]

There is, then, in the study of Visigothic Spain, a very real danger of assuming that evidence that describes what ought to be is evidence that describes what is. The Romano-Gothic legislators have suffered for their own sophistication. They attempted to produce a comprehensive law book and have ended by being accused by some modern historians of having committed on an immense scale every crime and offence in the code. The existence of laws relating to run-away slaves has led some to depict late seventh-century Spanish society as being overrun by fugitive slaves, one hiding behind virtually every bush. By the time you have added up the oppressed Jews, fugitive slaves, black-magic practising bishops, and abortionists, all culled by credulous historians from the law code, a grotesque and totally fictitious picture of Romano-Visigothic society has emerged. This whimsical concatenation of fantasy has been spawned in support of a general thesis of the spiritual decadence and moral

---

[18] *MGH Legum*, Section I, Vol. 1, *Liber Iudiciorum*, Book XII, pp. 406—56, and in general, Katz 1937.
[19] Perez Pujol 1896, III, pp. 449—55.

decline of Visigothic society and its Church in the late seventh century, a conclusion of such staggering absurdity and banality that those unacquainted with the historiography of Visigothic Spain will surely believe that I am inventing all of this, as some sort of *jeu d'ésprit*. Could one believe that there are serious historians in this day and age who seek to interpret the end of Visigothic Spain in terms of a moral decline? Unfortunately there are.[20]

Now whilst it would be possible to expatiate at greater length about some of the ills besetting modern studies of Visigothic Spain, it is hardly necessary to do so now. I have raised the problems of the evidence for this period and the problems of its interpretation for two reasons. Firstly, to provide insight into an area of study that must be unfamiliar to most, and the peculiar difficulties of it. Secondly, it is by way of an apologia for not being able to talk about what I am supposed to.[21] In the context of seventh-century Spain it is virtually impossible to talk about kings, kingship and the Church, at least in practical terms. This is purely a matter of the evidence available. What I can and shall talk about is what an individual Churchman wrote about what he thought was happening or what ought to happen.

I stress the notion of the individual author. We have for too long been in the grip of what one might call a 'behaviouralist' school of interpretation of the early medieval Church.[22] We are told, and accept, a number of things about the behaviour of early medieval Churchmen and about their ideas, the validity of the underlying assumptions of which we never challenge. Thus we believe that in any specific situation there will be a clerical interest, independent of and often in contradistinction to an aristocratic and/or a royal interest.[23] Occasionally we are told there are alliances of self-interest formed between these parties. Thus to take, for example, the practice of royal anointing or unction in the early middle ages, how often are we given an interpretation of the introduction of this act in terms of the bishops, or the Church interest, wanting it for one reason and the king wanting it for another? Both parties agree on the action, but for different motives. It is assumed that bishops, or the clergy in general, will by and large always act together *en bloc* and will so act because of motives peculiar to themselves. What are these motives? So often these boil down to strange pieces of revealed clerical psychology. 'Clerics tend to ritualize', we are told, or, to take a precise example, there is that dictum of Bouman's, referred to by Dr. Nelson: 'Whenever bishops were present at an official function, it was in the nature of things that they accentuated the religious aspects of a long-standing usage by giving it a ritual turn.'[24] Now, when you think about it,

---

[20] Garcia Moreno 1974a.

[21] In the series of lectures in which this paper was first delivered, the general area assigned to me was that of the relationship between kingship and Church.

[22] This is largely German in inspiration; its influence has been detrimental to the pragmatic tradition of English historiography. All too often in its products abstract theorising takes the place of common sense and reason.

[23] E.g., the general thesis of Ullmann, 1969.

[24] See the paper in this volume by Janet Nelson. Bouman 1957, in its more concrete aspects, is a very fine book.

what on earth does this mean? '. . . it was in the nature of things. . . .' They could not help themselves, being bishops they just ritualized? This really will not do. There may well have been elements of common interest and common education amongst bishops, but we need it to be shown in every case. Interpretations based upon *a priori* assumptions as to how clerics think and behave must be regarded with some scepticism. Arguments about the development of early medieval kingship that seem to suggest virtually a clerical conspiracy to seize control of, ritualize, christianize, whatever you like, institutions and practices that 'simple lay folk' would have been happy to leave in their old, immemorial, unreformed way are particularly prevalent. They should not go unchallenged.

To turn to Spain, a favourite bone of contention has been whether in the seventh century the king controlled the Church, or the Church the king.[25] Of course neither is true and neither matters. If any sense is to emerge from an enquiry into Romano-Visigothic society, then everything will have to be examined piece-meal, one piece of evidence at a time. Only then will any general picture of the nature of the Visigothic Church, its various components and its relations with successive Visigothic kings emerge, and even then such a picture will be limited by the deficiencies in the evidence, mentioned before. So all that I can hope to do is to talk not about the Church in Visigothic Spain and its dealings with the kings, not even about the Church of Toledo in particular, but only about one of its bishops and only about some aspects of his thought.

I referred a while ago to the lack of historical writing from the last decades of the Visigothic period. There is, however, one exception to this general dearth. This is the work known by the abbreviated form of its ponderous title as the *Historia Wambae*, and written by the bishop, called after his see, Julian of Toledo.[26] This short work (which only takes up thirty-five pages of a *Monumenta* volume), at its simplest, provides an account of the main events that occurred between the death of King Recceswinth and the elevation of the new king, Wamba, on the same day, the first of September 672, and the suppression by that King Wamba of a major revolt that broke out against him in the province of Gallia Narbonensis, by the end of September 673; so, a year's events in all. As well as the narrative of the text of the *Historia* proper, there are a number of short subsidiary works appended to it in some of the manuscripts.[27] Firstly, there is a letter, purporting to have been written to Wamba by the rebel king Paul, during the course of their war. Then, secondly, there is the brief *Insultatio vilis storici in tyrranidem Galliae (Invective of the humble historian against the Gallic usurpation)*, and, finally, the *Iudicium in tyrranorum perfidia promulgatum (The Judgement promulgated against the Treason of the Usurpers)*.

As a whole this work has received remarkably little attention, and there are many problems connected with it that we cannot hope to deal with, or even refer to, now.

---

[25] E.g., Ziegler 1930, which cites the earlier bibliography.
[26] *MGH SSRM* V, ed. W. Levison, pp. 486–535, reprinted in *Corpus Christianorum* Vol. 115, pp. 218–44.
[27] *Corpus Christianorum*, Vol. 115, pp. 214–17, 245–55.

What is going to concern us primarily is that early section of the work, that provides, and in some detail, the only available account of a Visigothic royal election and consecration, from the seventh century.[28] Before considering particular portions of the text it may be sensible to provide some brief account of what is known of the work's author, and what initially can be deduced about its nature and purpose.

For biographical information concerning Julian, such as it is, we are virtually dependent on the short account given of his life and writings by his archdeacon and later successor as bishop of Toledo, Felix (bishop 693—c.700), in his *Elogium Sancti Juliani*, a continuation of Ildefonsus's *De Viris Illustribus*.[29] We may conjecture that Julian was born about 640.[30] Of his origins Felix says nothing, but in the Chronicle of 751 Julian is described as being of Jewish descent *(ex traduce Iudaeorum)*,[31] to which the Chronicler adds 'ut flores rosarum de inter vepres spinarum'! Although this unequivocal statement of Julian's Jewish origin has aroused some controversy, there seem to be no good grounds for doubting it. Julian thus belongs to a long line of distinguished Spanish clerics of Jewish stock. Of his education we know something more. He is described by Felix as being the *discipulus* of bishop Eugenius II of Toledo (646—657), himself the pupil and friend of Braulio of Saragossa, and thus, in the chain of master-disciple relationships that are so strongly emphasised in the seventh-century Spanish Church, in direct line of descent from Isidore himself.[32] Julian confirms this by referring on several occasions to Eugenius as *praeceptor noster*.[33] The nature and extent of Julian's debt to Eugenius, and also to Isidore, is something that still remains to be explored.

Another major influence on the early life of Julian was that exercised by a certain deacon, Gudila, with whom he seems to have led a common ascetic life in Toledo, until the death of the latter, on the eighth of September 679.[34] Unlike a number of the seventh-century bishops of Toledo, notably Helladius, Justus, Eugenius I, Ildefonsus and possibly Sisbert, Julian was not a monk. All of the bishops just mentioned came to the see from being abbots of the royal foundation of Agali, in the suburbs of Toledo.[35] Julian, like Eugenius II and Felix, was promoted from the ranks of the secular clergy, holding the offices of deacon and priest in Toledo before

---

[28] *Corpus Christianorum*, Vol. 115, pp. 218—20. Bouman 1957, p. XI.

[29] *PL* 96, cols. 445—52. Ildefonsus, *De Viris Illustribus*, (1972).

[30] *Contra* J. N. Hillgarth, *Corpus Christianorum*, Vol. 115, p. VIII, note 2, and Garcia Moreno 1974b no. 251. Their suggested date of 644, whilst feasible, would seem to be too conservative.

[31] *Corpus Scriptorum Muzarabicorum*, I, p. 28.

[32] See the accounts of Isidore by Braulio in Lynch and Galindo 1950, pp. 357—61, and of Isidore, Braulio, and Eugenius II by Ildefonsus, in his *De Viris Illustribus*, (1972), and of Julian by Felix, *PL* 96, col. 445ff.

[33] *MGH AA* XIV, ed. K. Zeumer, p. 291.

[34] *PL* 96, cols. 445—6.

[35] For the first three, see Ildefonsus, *De Viris Illustribus*, 132—4, and for Ildefonsus, see the *elogium* by Julian, *PL* 96, cols. 43—4. An abbot, Sisbert, signed the acts of XIV Toledo (684) and XV Toledo (688); Vives 1963, pp. 448 and 474.

his consecration on the twenty ninth of January 680.[36] The significance of the alternating appointment of monks and clerics to the see is by no means clear, and should not be pressed too far. Julian is certainly responsible for writing the *Elogium* on his predecessor but one, Ildefonsus.[37]

Of his other, more substantial, works Felix gives us some account. It is from this list of Julian's writings that we have confirmation that the *Historia Wambae* is unquestionably a work of his.[38] Unfortunately the list is clearly not put in any kind of chronological order, so there is no indication from this at what stage of Julian's career the *Historia* was written. Julian's literary output was considerable. Many of his treatises and compilations, notably the *Prognosticum* and the *Antikeimenon* have survived, but others have not. He is said to have written books of masses, sermons, hymns and poems, but very few of these have been identified from amongst the considerable quantity of anonymous Spanish material of these various types that has survived.[39] Julian's book of letters is totally lost, save for one letter to Idalius of Barcelona, prefacing the *Prognosticum*.[40]

Some of these works can be dated, the *Prognosticum* probably to 688 and *Apologeticum de tribus capitulis* to 686.[41] Likewise the dedicatees of some are known, though in a number of cases this adds little, as nothing else is known of these lucky recipients. One dedicatee is of particular interest. This is the Visigothic king Ervig (680—7), who commissioned the *De Comprobatione Sextae Aetatis* (of c. 686), a polemic directed against Jewish arguments opposing Christ's messiahship. Interestingly, this same Ervig was the dedicatee of an earlier work of Julian's, now lost, written before his accession, whilst still a count. Unfortunately it is impossible to tell whether Julian wrote this book, the *Libellus de divinis iudiciis*, between his own consecration and the election of Ervig, that is between January and October of 680, or at some earlier unspecifiable time.[42] In fact, it is impossible to know whether or not Julian wrote all of his books during his episcopate, or whether some of them date from the time of his sojourn in Toledo with Gudila. Some authorities have confidently asserted early dates for some of the works, but there is no proof.

Julian's relations with the Visigothic kings during the course of his episcopate are, when we can glimpse them, peculiarly fascinating. He presided over four Councils of Toledo, the XII in 681, the XIII in 683, the XIV in 684 and XV in 688.[43] His episcopate, lasting from January 680 until his death on the sixth of March 690,

---

[36] Felix: *PL* 96, col. 446.

[37] *PL* 96, cols. 43—4.

[38] Felix: *PL* 96, col. 450.

[39] *MGH AA* XI, ed. T. Mommsen, p. 349.

[40] *Corpus Christianorum*, Vol. 115, pp. 11—14. This is a letter by way of preface to the book, and probably not part of the original 'librum plurimarum epistularum' referred to by Felix, *PL* 96, col. 449.

[41] *Corpus Christianorum*, Vol. 15, pp. XV and XIX.

[42] *PL* 96, col. 450, and *Corpus Christianorum*, Vol. 115, p. XVIII.

[43] Vives 1963, pp. 380—474.

coincided with the end of the reign of Wamba, the whole of the reign of Ervig (680–7), and the beginning of that of Egica (687–702). With the mysterious events that terminated the reign of Wamba in October 680, Julian must have been closely involved. These are all too briefly hinted at in the acts of the XII Council in 681. Wamba, apparently in his last extremity, received, as was customary, canonical penance, having named Ervig, for no reason that is clear, as his successor. Unfortunately for all concerned he recovered, but, his penitential state being irrevocable, he was unable to resume the throne and seems to have retired to a monastery, willingly or not we do not know. This embarrassing state of affairs was regularised by the Council the succeeding year, when the nobility and clergy were absolved from their oath of allegiance to Wamba, still valid in that he was not dead, and Wamba's voluntary choice of Ervig as his successor was attested to.[44]

These murky events have allowed fantasists, ancient and modern, give free rein to their imagination, and to erect the whole affair into a plot on Julian's part to be rid of the apparently unacceptable Wamba.[45] This, of course, involved giving the king a potion that made his death seem imminent, and thus led to the taking by him of penitential status. One is tempted to ask why he did not use a good straight-forward poison instead of going through all the rigmarole of penance. But enough of such nonsense. The events of the ending of Wamba's reign, deeply embarrassing as they must have been, were the result of accident, not design.

Julian's relations with Ervig, both before and during his reign, were obviously close, and it is hardly fortuitous that the first Council of the reign, that of 681, saw substantial increase in the powers and prerogatives of the see of Toledo, particularly giving its bishops power to consecrate new bishops for the other ecclesiastical provinces of the kingdom. Effectively this Council recognised a primacy, both in honour and authority, of Toledo over the other sees of the peninsula.[46] Of Julian's dealings with Egica we know nothing. Certainly Julian's successor Sisbert did not get on with him, and became involved in an unsuccessful conspiracy to overthrow him in 692 or 693.[47]

But to turn from this all too brief account of Julian's life and some of his writings to the *Historia Wambae*, or, to give it its full title, the *Historia Excellentissimi Wambae Regis de Expeditione et Victoria, Qua Revellantem Contra Se Provinciam Galliae Celebri Triumpho Perdomuit*. What are we faced with? For a work of this period it is certainly odd. Nothing of its kind seems to have been attempted during the previous three centuries.[48] For its literary form is that of the short historical monograph, concerning itself exclusively with one particular theme or event. Its size and

---

[44] XI: Toledo of 681: Vives, 1963, pp. 386–7.

[45] *Corpus Christianorum*, Vol. 115, pp. XI–XIII. Murphy, 1952, pp. 1–21, for bibliography and reasoned assessments of these events.

[46] XII Toledo, canon VI.

[47] XVI Toledo (693), canon IX.

[48] At least since the fourth century. For some short military memoirs of that period, now lost, see Thompson 1966b, pp. 151–54.

selectivity thus distinguishes it clearly from the large-scale history, that seeks to deal with the whole of a chronological period. The most famous, and virtually the only extant, examples of this genre are the two works by Sallust, the *Bellum Catilinae* and the *Bellum Jugurthae*. For these books, both by reason of their style and their historical content, Sallust was much praised by his contemporaries and by succeeding generations, but from the end of the second century, at least, he was to have few emulators.[49]

Julian's debt to Sallust, in terms both of the literary form and in matters of literary style and content, is very clear, and has been fully expounded by the work's most distinguished editor, Wilhelm Levison.[50] It can be added that Julian's military theme will have made the model of Sallust's works most apposite, and it is not impossible that he will have been inspired to add the rhetorical *Insultatio* by the existence of the pseudo-Sallustian invectives, which at the time were accepted as genuine works of Sallust, and which may even have circulated in the same manuscripts as the historical monographs.[51]

That Julian should have had the writings of Sallust available to him is hardly surprising. They were extremely popular with the grammarians, especially Donatus and Priscian.[52] Julian himself was the author or inspirer of a grammar,[53] and the extremely rhetorical nature of the set-piece speeches in the *Historia*, of the supposed letter of Paul to Wamba and of the *Insultatio* and *Iudicum* are more redolent of works composed for the schoolroom than of pieces of official historiography, as some have seen them.[54]

Like Sallust, Julian expresses a clear didactic purpose behind his writing, and, like Sallust, he expounds this purpose in his prefatory remarks. In which, he says, if you will pardon a rather free translation: 'Any account that is given of glorious deeds in the past generally tends to defend the triumphs of virtue and to carry the minds of the young in the direction of virtue. For in the present the human character shows a certain disposition towards sloth in its inner nature and hence it seems to be more inclined towards the vices than attracted by the virtues. Thus unless it perseveres continually in being instructed by the challenge of valuable examples, it remains cold, and becomes torpid. Because of this, in order than an account of past events can serve as a remedy for sensitive minds, we have told this tale of our own times, that through it we may be able to provoke subsequent ages to virtue.'[55]

Such a prelude must inevitably seem sententious or merely formal, and statements about the didactic value of history are conventional parts of the prefaces of the

---

[49] Syme 1964, chap. XV, pp. 274–301.

[50] *MGH SSRM* V, ed. W. Levison, p. 492, notes 5 and 6.

[51] Though not in any of the manuscripts now extant; see preface to the Teubner edition by A. Kurfess, Leipzig (1957).

[52] *C. Sallustius Crispus*, ed. A. Kurfess, Leipzig (1957), *praefatio*, pp. III–XXXI.

[53] *Ars Iuliani Toletani Episcopi* (1973). See also Beeson 1924.

[54] Hillgarth 1970, pp. 299–300.

[55] *Corpus Christianorum*, Vol. 115, p. 218.

classical historians. Julian, who, as well as modelling the form of his work on Sallust, knew and quoted from Livy, can hardly be expected to omit such sentiments. But they may be more than clichés. The ideas expressed accord closely with some of the recommendations to be found in the pseudo-Isidoran *Institutionum Disciplinae*.[56] This short text is a product of Toledo of the later seventh century, and contains a series of practical suggestions for the education of the secular aristocracy, including one that the young be encouraged to listen to the poems of their elders, as a means of exciting them with a desire for glory.[57] These *carmina* have usually been taken for oral Gothic epics, never written down and hence long since lost, but which provided the foundations for the later Spanish medieval epic tradition.[58] Such a view rests on remarkably little evidence, historical or linguistic, and depends rather on romantic notions of venerable Goths passing on their hoary old epics from generation to generation in a society which did not speak Gothic and in which the social values enshrined in those epics will have seemed increasingly alien. The truth may be more prosaic, and the *carmina* Latin, Vergil rather than Ingeld.[59]

The *Historia Wambae*, the *Institutionum Disciplinae*, shorn of their Gothic overtones, Julian's *Ars Grammatica*, together with a number of other texts, combine to provide us with an impression of the educational ideals and instruction current in Toledo in the second half of the seventh century, an education that was not, it is important to note, the exclusive preserve of the clergy. A full exposition of this requires a study in its own right, but for our purposes now it seems reasonable to suggest that it is with the grammatical and literary concerns of the Toledan teachers that the origins of the *Historia Wambae* are going to be found to lie. Its stated didactic purpose, its peculiarly archaic literary form, its style and various aspects of its contents, especially a number of descriptions and set-piece speeches, and its strange rhetorical appendices are all indicative of such a genesis.

What it clearly is not is what it has been claimed to be, and that is a piece of officially-sponsored historiography, intended to glorify the king, Wamba.[60] If that was its intention, it has a most peculiar way of going about it. It patently has nothing of the panegyric in its literary form. Wamba is never apostrophised, as might have been expected, though the rebels are. Where specific moral deductions are to be made, as we shall see, they are concerned with abstract notions of legitimacy and illegitimacy of rule. Also, in contradiction to what has been suggested in the past, there are no clear indications that this work was written in Wamba's reign or lifetime at all.[61] In that, despite the somewhat unfortunate events of his enforced deposition, the

---

[56] Riché 1971, pp. 171—80.

[57] *Institutionum Disciplinae*, ed. P. Pascal, *Traditio*, XIII, pp. 426—7.

[58] In general: Menedez Pidal, 1956.

[59] Not least as there is no evidence for the continued use of Gothic in Spain after the sixth century. At the same time, the strength of the classical literary tradition in the Visigothic Kingdom has not been fully appreciated.

[60] Hillgarth 1970, p. 300. Also *Corpus Christianorum*, vol. 115, p. XVIII.

[61] Hillgarth 1970, p. 299.

kings who followed Wamba regarded themselves as his legitimate successors, receiving a measure of their legitimacy from his selection of Ervig to succeed him in 680, there is no good reason why it should not have been written after the end of his reign. The probabilities are hard to assess. At any rate there are no grounds for even the relatively limited assurance that the work was written in the 670s. It could have been composed at any time between 673 and 690.

But now to look at the important description, given immediately after the prefatory remarks of the work, of the election and consecration of Wamba as king. Firstly, then, to give the account in full in an uncouth translation of my own:

> There lived in our time the most illustrious prince, Wamba, whom God willed to be worthy to rule, whom priestly unction revealed, whom the community of the whole race and fatherland elected, whom the innate goodness of the people sought for and who was proclaimed worthy of ruling by the abundant revelations of many people before he achieved the honour of the kingdom. As for this most illustrious man; when the funeral rites and laments for the dead king, Recceswinth, had been completed, suddenly, all those present, acting in concord, as if they were one in spirit and in unison of voice, shouted out that it pleased them to have him as their ruler. He and no other should rule the Goths. This they shouted out loudly with their voices united and in droves they threw themselves at his feet, in case he should refuse their pleas. But he, trying to flee from them in every direction, overwhelmed with tears, refused to be overcome by their requests and would not be moved by any desire of the populace. He exclaimed that he would not put himself up for such imminent ruin and proclaimed himself to be too old. Faced with his reluctance one of them holding the office of *dux*, acting as if on behalf of them all, approached him fiercely and with a furious expression on his face, saying, 'Unless you promise us your consent you will be killed by the sword. We shall not leave here until either our army is to receive you as its king or, if you continue to refuse, we put you to death today.'
>
> Overcome not so much by their prayers as by their threats he finally consented and accepted the kingdom. He received all present into his peace, but he put off the time of his unction until nineteen days later, rather than be consecrated into the kingship anywhere other than at its ancient seat. For all of this was taking place at the villa, which had anciently been called Gerticos, situated nearly one hundred and twenty miles away from the royal city, in the territory of Salamanca. For there on that same day, that is to say the first of September, both the life of the old king had come to an end and the aforementioned man had come to succeed him, more as a result of divine pre-election than because of any popular acclamation.
>
> Now although he had already taken up his duties, as a result of divine pre-ordaining, the roaring acclamation of the populace and the receiving of the regalia, he did not allow himself to be anointed at the hands of the bishop before he reached the royal city and had sought out the seat of paternal antiquity, in which it was suitable for him both to receive the *vexilla* of holy unction and to receive the clearest assent of the men of standing *(positores)* to his election. This was naturally in case it should be imputed against him that, moved by ambition to rule, he had usurped or stolen, rather than occupied as a sign from God, so great a position of glory. Having then deferred this out of prudence, on the nineteenth day after he had received the kingdom, he entered the city of Toledo.
>
> And when he had arrived there, where he was to receive the *vexilla* of the holy unction, in the praetorian church, that is to say the church of Saints Peter and Paul, he stood resplendent in his regalia in front of the holy altar and, as the

custom is, recited the creed to the people. Next, on his bended knees the oil of blessing was poured onto his head by the hand of the blessed bishop Quiricus, and the strength of the benediction was made clear, for at once this sign of salvation appeared. For suddenly from his head, where the oil had first been poured on, a kind of vapour, similar to smoke, rose up in the form of a column, and from the very top of this a bee was seen to spring forth, which sign was undoubtedly a portent of his future good fortune.[62]

This translation, I fear, has done little justice to the style of the original, and has inevitably glossed over a number of difficult features in the text, particularly terms which may have a more precise and formal meaning than this might suggest.[63] However, it should have served to provide you with some idea of the stages of Wamba's elevation, as described by Julian. Let us look at some of the more peculiar features to be found in this account.

Firstly, there are a number of highy stylised descriptions, notably the much-stressed unanimity with which all present at the villa of Gerticos declared that they would have Wamba and none other to be the new king. Needless to say, we do not know, and never shall, why Wamba in particular was chosen to succeed Recceswinth. It is worth noting, in view of subsequent practice, that Julian makes no suggestion that Recceswinth had in any way chosen or selected Wamba to be his successor. It seems then, to have been a matter of his being chosen by those present at the time. What is more, if we are to accept Julian's chronology, and it is so deliberately precise that there seems to be no good reason for not doing so, their decision, and the surely inevitable political bargaining that must have accompanied it, must have been taken prior to Recceswinth's death, as Wamba was proclaimed on the same day as the old king died. In which case it is particularly notable that Recceswinth is not said to have had any part in it, or have confirmed the choice by his own notional appointing of Wamba as his successor. This was to be the practice when Wamba later chose Ervig, and Ervig subsequently chose Egica.[64] The large assemblage at Gerticos would suggest too that the death of Recceswinth was not unexpected. Who were those present at the king's death and who had a hand in the choice of Wamba? This again is not clear. We have a reference to the army, the *exercitum*, and to at least one man holding the office of *dux*. It is likely enough that the great officers of state were there, especially those with military responsibilities, the *duces*.[65] No bishops are mentioned by Julian as being present at all. What Julian does emphasise is the unanimity of all present. This is clearly, in his mind, an important feature in favour of the unquestionable legitimacy of Wamba's rule.

Wamba's reluctance and the charade with the *dux* threatening him with death, as described by Julian, is very interesting. This immediately brings to mind the late

---

[62] *Corpus Christianorum*, Vol. 115, pp. 218—20.

[63] E.g., the term *positor*, in the phrase 'et longe positorum consensus ob praeelectionem sui patientissime sustinere', *ibid.* p. 220.

[64] Vives 1963, pp. 464—71. Thompson, 1969, pp. 231—42.

[65] Thompson 1969, pp. 252—7. Perez Pujol, 1896, IV, pp. 191—204.

antique tradition of reluctance to accept power when offered.[66] One good literary parallel would be Ammianus Marcellinus's description of the supposedly forcible elevation of the Emperor Julian.[67] Now, is our author giving us here nothing more than a standardised literary cliché, a *topos*? Certainly the speech put in the *dux's* mouth is highly rhetorical and mannered. It really runs something like this: 'Unless you promise your consent to us, you must know yourself worthy to be killed by the sharp point of the sword. Nor shall we go hence until such time as either our army receives you as king or the bloody overthrow of death this day will swallow up the refuser.'[68] Equally stereotyped too is the description of Wamba's tearful refusal. It is unfortunate that we cannot tell whether this reluctance is no more than a literary convention or whether something of the kind was expected in practice, though not necessarily the little drama that Julian describes. Certainly many of the formal practices of the Visigothic monarchy were archaic and were continuations of late Roman customs. Thus the unsuccessful rebel Paul was exhibited publically on a camel after being mutilated, a similar fate to that meeted out to the usurper Johannes in 425.[69] Whatever the truth of the matter in Julian's account, reluctance, feigned or otherwise, was an important part of Wamba's claim to legitimacy.

Now the question might pertinently be raised as to whether there is not another influence to be detected here: that of contemporary ideas concerning reluctance to hold ecclesiastical office, that 'fleeing from the burden of pastoral care', described by Gregory the Great in the preface to his *Regula Pastoralis*.[70] This debate and the work of Gregory in particular were hardly unknown to Julian.[71] However, the *Historia* is, as has been said, unequivocably written in the secular tradition of classical historiography, and the imperial refusal of power is so clearly entrenched in late Roman practice that we are not forced to point any additional sources of inspiration for Julian's description.[72]

There is a wider implication to be drawn from this rejection of any overt influence of ideas on ecclesiastical office holding. This concerns the role of the Old Testament as a formative influence on the theory and practice of Visigothic kingship.[73] My contention would be that this should be minimised rather than emphasised. Of course, the accounts of the anointing of Saul and David may have served as the direct inspiration for the introduction of unction into the Visigothic consecration ceremonial, but there is no evidence for it.[74] As has been said, of the origins and date of

[66] Beranger 1948.
[67] Ammianus Marcellinus, Book XX, iv, 13–18, and for a sixth-century parallel, Corippus, *In Laudem Justini*, lines 175–88 (ed. A. Cameron, 1976). It is perhaps worth noting that this latter work survives in an exclusively Spanish manuscript transmission.
[68] *Corpus Christianorum*, Vol. 115, p. 219.
[69] Procopius, *History of the Wars*, Book III, iii, 9. See also Stein 1959, I, p. 284 and note 162.
[70] Gregory the Great, *Regula Pastoralis*, PL 77, col. 13.
[71] Hillgarth, 1971 pp. 97–118.
[72] See in general Congar 1966, pp. 169–97.
[73] Wallace-Hadrill 1971, chapter III, especially, pp. 53–5.
[74] Compare with Frankish anointing: *ibid.*, pp. 100, 133–5.

introduction of the royal unction, nothing is known. In the fragments of the liturgy of the royal consecration, dating from the late seventh century, there are no correspondences drawn between the new rite and the anointings of Saul and David; nor, for that matter, are there apparent links between the consecrating of kings and that of bishops, priests and the minor orders of the Church.[75] The Old Testament may have provided a useful vocabulary for the description of this and other features of royal activity when being used in an ecclesiastical context, and in an ecclesiastical literary tradition. But the existence of Julian's account in the *Historia Wambae* shows that it was equally possible to describe them in a purely secular fashion, and this in a work written by a bishop. It is a question of the right literary form. Thus it is not unreasonable, in Visigothic Spain at least, to see late Roman secular traditions having as much, if not more, influence on the shaping of Visigothic kingship and the expression of ideas about it, as the Old Testament.

Various points of procedure are quite clear from Julian's text. The funeral, accompanied by lamentations — would that we knew more about those — of Recceswinth took place on the day of his death, in other words at Gerticos. It is particularly interesting that the bodies of dead kings attracted no especial interest, and that the Church of Toledo made no attempt to secure them for burial in, say, the praetorian church of Sts Peter and Paul, or the church of St. Leocadia, where most of the seventh-century bishops of the see were buried.[76] There is a medieval legend that Wamba, too, was to be buried at Gerticos, and hence its modern name of Wamba. In the thirteenth century Alfonso X, *el Sabio*, secured the bodies of what were thought to be the two kings and had them brought to Toledo for re-burial.[77]

Other formal points are that, after his acceptance of the kingdom, Wamba admitted all those present into his peace. In other words, all old scores which Wamba the count may have had to settle with his aristocratic peers would be wiped out when he became Wamba the king. In seventh-century Visigothic society in which the throne passed not by dynastic succession but to elected or selected men, taken from the ranks of the aristocracy, this could otherwise have caused serious problems.[78] Wamba was also immediately invested with the regalia. Again it is not precisely clear what this will have consisted of. Doubtless it will have been the same as the regalia first adopted by Leovigild in the late sixth century. There was almost certainly a crown, and robes and a sceptre, doubtless of late Roman inspiration, there must have been.[79]

---

[75] *Antiphonario Visigotico Mozarabe*, ed. L. Brou and J. Vives, Madrid (1959), pp. 450—3.

[76] Ildefonsus, *De Viris Illustribus* (1972).

[77] The lack of concern over royal burial in the seventh century is not surprising, in view of the absence of established dynastic succession to the kingship.

[78] Thompson 1969, pp. 170—89.

[79] *MGH AA* XI, ed. T. Mommsen, p. 288: Isidore's account of Leovigild's use of regalia. See also the satirical description Julian gives of the coronation of Paul, who is forced to use a votive crown taken from a statue of St. Felix (given by Reccared) for the ceremony. *Corpus Christianorum*, Vol. 115, p. 240.

Now what is clear from Julian is that all of this could take place anywhere, and, in view of the generally peripatetic nature of the Visigothic court, it probably did. A king could die and be buried virtually anywhere, and his successor chosen at the same place, providing that those powerful enough to have a part in the selection process were present. The election and the subsequent investiture with the regalia do not seem, as far as we can tell, to have necessitated any clerical participation whatsoever. These procedures were certainly formal, long-established and, unless this be a distortion due to the literary nature of our evidence, Roman rather than Germanic in character. As mentioned before, Julian's account of the elevation of Wamba could just as well serve for a description of the creation of a fourth century Roman Emperor. Although there is a danger of deliberate archaising on Julian's part and dependence on literary models, the strength of Roman traditions in and the essential conservatism, in many respects, of Visigothic Spain, make such a comparison not improbable.

Where we do find a new element is in the ceremony of the royal anointing, of the unction. This is the first reference to the practice of royal unction in Visigothic Spain. If we take Julian's account at face value, then clearly the practice must have existed before the time of Wamba, but there is absolutely no indication anywhere as to when it may have been introduced. What is important to notice is that the anointing in itself is not a guarantee of anything, certainly not of legitimacy. The usurper Paul was also anointed. In his letter to Wamba he refers to himself as *rex unctus*.[80] Even if this letter be no more than a literary fabrication of Julian's, the point stands that Julian will not have considered it unsuitable thus to describe a usurping king. The action of anointing by itself is for Julian no more than a part of the process of constituting a new king. It is a part that is essential and not to be omitted, but it takes its place along with those other features of the process Julian describes: divine pre-election, which can to some extent be guaranteed by prior supernatural revelations, election by the *gens* and the *patria*, at least the leading figures of the aristocracy are referred to here; acclamation by the populace; and investiture with the regalia.

Whilst the ritual of anointing has to be seen in this context, as only part of the constitutive process, what is clearly of the greatest importance to Julian is the place where the unction is performed. Twice he points out, with great emphasis, that Wamba deliberately delayed his anointing until he had returned to Toledo, whereupon it finally took place, nineteen days after the other parts of the process had been carried out, in the praetorian church of Ss Peter and Paul.[81] For Julian, as for his predecessors, however much the king may in practice have been absent from it, Toledo was always the *urbs regia*, the *solium paternae antiquitatis*. In Julian's account the fact that the unction took place in Toledo was in itself a constitutive feature of the legitimacy of Wamba's rule, independent of the act of the anointing itself. The

---

[80] *Epistola Pauli, Corpus Christianorum*, Vol. 115, p. 217, line 1.
[81] *Ibid.*, pp. 219–20.

contrast with the account of the elevation of the usurper Paul is clear. Would-be kings could be anointed anywhere, but only kings who received the unction in Toledo could be legitimate.

This development of Toledo into the ceremonial centre of the Visigothic kingdom during the last part of the seventh century can clearly be seen from other sources too. Many of the actions of the king were coming increasingly to be put into a liturgical context. Some of the parts of what we may call this late seventh-century royal liturgy have fortunately survived. The most complete of these are the liturgical ceremonies created to mark the departure of the king on a military expedition: the *Ordo Quando Rex Cum Exercitu Ad Proelium Egreditur*.[82] These ceremonies are specifically stated in the text to take place in the church of Ss Peter and Paul, wherein which, of course, Wamba was anointed, as too will the liturgy to mark the return of the king and of his army. In the course of the service the king receives the golden cross, containing a fragment of the true Cross, that will be borne before him throughout the expedition.

Julian's attempt to link the royal unction specifically to Toledo and perhaps in particular to the church of Ss Peter and Paul is thus not exceptional. Many other standard features of royal activity, such as the waging of war, were likewise being annexed to Toledo and being given a specific ceremonial context. In this way, whilst the royal court could remain peripatetic, the status of Toledo as the unquestioned royal capital and the ceremonial centre of the realm would be assured, and indeed, enhanced. This city and no other was thus linked indissolubly with the kingship. A full account of this process, peculiar to the second half of the seventh century, would require a full length study in itself.[83] But in Julian's *Historia Wambae* we have the evidence for at least part of it. It is, however, worth noticing that there is a very good chance that Julian himself is the author of much, if not all, of that royal liturgy, which I have just been referring to.[84] His role in the process, although at the moment I can only hint at it, was obviously of the greatest importance.

There is one other element in Julian's description of the consecration of Wamba that is worth considering. That is the bee. The appearance of this sign, of the column of vapour and the bee emerging from the top of it, should not be taken as a reflection of some kind of sacral quality conferred upon the king by the action of unction. It was, if you like, a confirmation that the benediction, conveyed through the act of anointing, had been given to the right man, to the divinely pre-ordained king. What of the symbol of the bee, which must smack a little of bathos to the modern reader?

The classic account of the bee is to be found in Vergil's fourth *Georgic*. It is the war-like and bellicose qualities of the bees, as described by Vergil, which are what are likely to be at issue here. So, too, the existence amongst them of kings.

---

[82] *Liber Ordinum*, ed. M. Férotin (1904), pp. 149–55.
[83] This diverges from the interpretation of Ewig 1963, pp. 25–72, especially pp. 31–6.
[84] Madoz 1952, pp. 39–69. Also, Felix, *Elogium Juliani*, PL 96, cols. 449–50.

Whatever the merits of Roman entomology, it made a mistake there, in classifying what we would call queen bees as king bees. As Isidore, referring to the bees, put it: 'reges et exercitum habent.'[85] Although I have not yet been able to find earlier uses of the bee as a symbol it seems probable that it is its military and regal associations that must lie behind Julian's use of it.

Now for a slightly frivolous aside: Julian seems, from the evidence of his *Ars Grammatica* at least, to have been well versed in Vergil and if, as is likely, his idea of the bee had its origins in the fourth *Georgic*, what may he have made of a passage in that poem referring to a war between two king bees in which it is recommended that after the combat 'the one that appears worsted you must kill, lest he prove a waste and a nuisance, and let the winner be absolute in the kingdom'?[86] It sounds almost like the kind of political philosophy, if you care to call it that, employed in Visigothic Spain in the first half of the seventh century! For in that period principles by which legitimacy of any king could be judged, other than sheer success in holding onto his throne against all comers, seem to be conspicuously lacking. Thus Witteric had deposed and killed Liuva II in 603, Witteric had been murdered in 610, Sisebut's son Reccared II was probably deposed by Swinthila in 621, Swinthila was certainly deposed by Sisenand in 631, Tulga by Chindaswinth in 642. Ephemeral kings, such as Iudila, who managed to strike a few coins in Baetica and Lusitania in the early 630s, also made their bids for power.[87] Various Councils of Toledo in the 630s and 640s made attempts, at the behest of insecure kings, to regularise aspects of this situation. The V and VI Councils of 636 and 638, held under the short-lived King Chintila, were particularly active in this respect. The third canon of V Toledo, for example, forbade anyone from aspiring to the throne other than by popular election or by being the choice of the Gothic nobility, on penalty of excommunication and anathema.[88] The problem was, of course, that this was all very well in theory, but in practice if this regulation was breached nothing would be done about it. This had been the case in 631 when Sisenand seized the throne, with the support of a Frankish army.[89] Doubtless this canon was directed precisely against what he had done, and he himself by implication. But when in 642 Chindaswinth similarly deposed Tulga, no attempt was made to enforce this canon. For all the canonical pronouncements of V and VI Toledo, usurpation was only usurpation so long as it was unsuccessful. Isidore had recognised this long before.[90]

It is in contrast to this state of affairs and the somewhat *laissez-faire* attitude in Isidore's thinking, which effectively left it to God to make his will manifest through the success or otherwise of rival royal protagonists, that I would put the ideas of

---

[85] Isidore, *Etymologiae*, Book XII, viii, 1. (ed. Lindsay, 1911).
[86] Vergil, *Georgics*, IV, lines 88–90.
[87] For an account of these events, see Thompson 1969, pp. 155–89.
[88] V Toledo, canon III.
[89] *The Fourth Book of the Chronicle of Fredegar*, ed. J. M. Wallace-Hadrill, (1960), pp. 61–2.
[90] Wallace-Hadrill 1971, p. 53.

Julian in the *Historia Wambae*. His main concern is with legitimacy, how the legitimacy of a new king could be established and made manifest. Hence the heightened importance he gives to unction as a vital part of the constitutive process and above all the insistence that it was only in Toledo that that act of anointing could be carried out. This is a major development in the thinking about and the ceremonial of kingship in Visigothic Spain. It is certainly not a case of a bishop ritualising, just because that is what bishops do. The act of unction obviously existed as part of the procedures surrounding the elevation of a king before 672, otherwise Julian's words would make no sense. When it was first introduced we cannot tell. What Julian did was to enhance its significance by integrating it firmly with the city of Toledo, as part of the elaborate liturgical life in which the Church of Toledo was trying to enfold the kingship.

Now it may be objected that I have fallen into the very error, which I castigated so severely at the beginning of this paper, that of arguing from descriptions of what was felt ought to be to descriptions of what actually is or was. Perhaps so, but it should be conceded that I have underplayed my hand in throwing doubts on the description of the *Historia Wambae* as a piece of official historiography. As such it might be expected to reflect a more general level of approval of the ideas expressed. However, I do not think that it is anything of the kind, but I do feel that it is a valuable source for the ideas that led to the changes in the practices of Visigothic kingship that I have just been discussing, albeit too briefly. This view is tenable for a number of reasons. Firstly the *Historia Wambae* is not the only, nor even necessarily the best, source of evidence we have for those changes. As has been mentioned, its ideas and aspirations can be matched with those underlying the development of the royal liturgy in the late seventh century. Nor, as will be clear from this, is unction and the consecration of the king the only area of royal ceremonial to be affected. Royal warfare is clearly taken in hand by the Church of Toledo and, even more importantly, so too, from 680, is the royal death-bed and the procedures for the choosing of a new king.[91] After 672 Visigothic kingship is never again open to seizure by naked force. Whatever may happen behind the scenes, certain formal proprieties have to be observed publically. In this sense the problem of the succession has been solved, at least until 710.[92] To have given a full and proper account of this development would have involved a detailed investigation of each of the aspects of royal ceremonial and activity that were to be transformed in this period. Time, needless to say, prevents this for now. I can only hope to have made a start on the way by these few remarks about Julian and the royal unction.

Finally, to show that the ideas of Julian on this issue, as I have outlined them, were to have practical significance, I would draw your attention to the short regnal list, generally known, though somewhat deceptively, as the *Chronica Regum*

---

[91] I hope to produce some account of this in the near future. The evidence for this transformation has never been conveniently collected.

[92] The accession of Roderic has been interpreted as a usurpation, a seizure of the throne by force, against the interests of the heir of Wittiza: Thompson 1969, p. 249.

Wisigothorum, compiled in its final form probably between 700 and 702, and quite likely a work of Toledan provenance.[93] For the kings from Alaric I to Chindaswinth the author or authors knew no more than the length of their reigns, though that they knew to the day in most cases; but they mention no dates, until that of the death of Chindaswinth. But from the reign of Wamba onwards the precise dates of accession and of unction, which, as in the case of Wamba, are usually separated, are given. The place of the unction need hardly surprise us; in the entry for Egica we read: 'Unctus est autem dominus noster Egica in regno in ecclesia sanctorum Petri et Pauli Praetoriensis . . .' Notice too, '. . . unctus . . . in regno . . .'.[94]

There for now I must leave this quest. I hope that I may have been able to suggest to you, however tentatively, that Visigothic society in the late seventh century was in the process of undergoing various fundamental changes, particularly, for our purposes, in relation to its kingship. And that, *pace* Professor Fontaine, this was not a period of decline from the golden age of Isidore of Seville or from a so-called 'Isidoran constitution.'[95] It was rather a time of new ideas and new developments, the responsibility for many of which must rest with Julian of Toledo. However, if I have not succeeded in convincing you that the history of Visigothic Spain is interesting, at least I hope that I have suggested that, like most of us, Visigothic bishops were sensible men and that it was not just 'in the nature of things' for them to be interested in ritual.

[93] *PL* 96, col. 809–12.
[94] *Ibid.*, col. 812.
[95] Fontaine 1973, pp. 109–24. See my review in *Journal of Roman Studies*, Vol. 65 (1975).

3

Inauguration rituals
JANET L. NELSON

If I'd been addressing an audience of anthropologists, I'd have felt no need to begin by justifying my contribution to this series of lectures. Anthropologists have long been convinced of the importance of inauguration rituals. One of them who has contributed much on this subject, Meyer Fortes, said ten years ago: 'The mysterious quality of continuity through time in its organisation and values, which is basic to the self-image of every society, modern, archaic, or primitive, is in some way congealed in these installation ceremonies. . . . Politics and law, rank and kinship, religious and philosophical concepts and values, the economics of display and hospitality, the aesthetics and symbolism of institutional representation, and last but not least the social psychology of popular participation, all are concentrated in them'.[1] With such a lively appreciation of what they can convey, the anthropologist will expect to be able to 'read' from inauguration rituals a good deal about the nature of power, the structure, beliefs and values in this or that society at a given time.[2]

But are inauguration rituals equally useful to historians of early medieval kingship? For us the answer is not so simple. The time-dimension we work in raises two problems. First that of fossilisation: the congealing of ritual forms over time makes them suspect as historical documents. Some of the forms used at the coronation of Elizabeth II in 1953,[3] for instance, go back at least a thousand years; but who would claim that the 'politics and law' or 'religious or philosophical concepts and values' of post-war Britain were in any very real sense represented in that inauguration ritual. Already in the sixteenth century, Thomas Cranmer, himself ex officio a king's consecrator, said of royal anointing that it was 'but a ceremony', having 'its ends and utility yet neither direct force nor necessity'.[4] What did such rituals mean in the early Middle Ages?

Here we broach the second problem: that of origins. Another eminent anthropologist, Edmund Leach, recognised the existence of 'the philogenetic question "how come?"' as distinct from 'the functional question "what for?"'. But, he claimed, 'the enormous complexity of the ritual sequences which anthropologists

---

[1] Fortes 1968, pp. 5–20.
[2] See, for example Balandier, 1972, esp. ch. 5.
[3] Ratcliff 1953.
[4] Strype 1848, vol. 1, bk. 2, p. 206.

have to study makes any guesses of the "how come" type more or less absurd'.[5] And what about the ritual sequences which historians have to study? Well, as a mere historian, I claim the right to be absurd in my own philo-genetic way. Despite enormous difficulties, enough material survives if handled correctly to allow some kind of history of royal inauguration rituals to be reconstructed, including answers to some 'how come' questions. The liturgical rites of royal consecration, the *Ordines*, present special problems,[6] and we need the expert help of liturgists in their interpretation; but for the early Middle Ages, they do constitute contemporary evidence, becoming more or less stereotyped only from the eleventh century onwards. But *Ordinesforschung* should be only a part of our repertoire: we need to bear in mind the diversity of other available evidence and thus of the varieties of treatment required. Perhaps because of a certain tendency towards an 'abstract-legal' or *ideengeschichtlich* approach on the part of such scholars as E. Eichmann and P. E. Schramm who pioneered our subject,[7] many more sociologically-minded medievalists have as yet hardly cast more than side-glances at royal inauguration rituals or appreciated the potential contribution which they offer, so the anthropologists assure us, for our general understanding of early medieval society and not just of the political theory of some of its clerical elite. Yet it is half a century since Marc Bloch in his early masterpiece *Les Rois Thaumaturges*[8] blazed the broadest of trails for us to follow.

There is one point to stress at the outset: the significance, political and symbolic, of inauguration rituals arose largely from the fact that no early medieval king ever simply succeeded to his kingdom as a matter of course. A man might be born king-worthy, but he had to be made a king. In no kingdom of the early medieval West was there quickly established a very restrictive norm of royal succession. Sometimes a king was succeeded by a son or brother, sometimes by a distant kinsman, and sometimes by one who was no kin at all. Interregna happened: the Anglo-Saxon evidence is predictably clear, but clear also is that from Merovingian Gaul although, as Ian Wood reminds us,[9] dynastic continuity has tended to obscure historians' sense of the contingent in Frankish royal accessions. Kenneth Harrison, has recently written, tongue in cheek: 'much is known about the legal and "sacral" aspects of Germanic kingship. Far less is known of the events which could and sometimes did follow when personal power was extinguished by the death of a king, and the hungry athelings began to prowl'.[10] The inauguration of a new king, when it ended such a time of prowling, publicly indicated the victor of a political struggle: by no means

---

[5] Leach 1966, pp. 403 sqq., at 404.
[6] I indicated some of these in Nelson 1965, pp. 41–51.
[7] See Bak 1973 with full references to the work of Eichmann and Schramm.
[8] Originally published 1924, now translated into English as *The Royal Touch. Sacred Monarchy and Scrofula in England and France* (London, 1973).
[9] See above.
[10] Harrison 1976, p. 92.

'but a ceremony', it must have reminded all who participated in it of the powers and functions of kingship.

Having convinced you, I hope, that an interest in early medieval inauguration rituals is legitimate, I don't propose now to embark on a potted history of them. It would be all too easy to get bogged down at the beginning. For during the period before churchmen got closely involved in king-makings, the evidence all over the barbarian West is very sketchy indeed; and any case for which it's more than sketchy is more likely to be odd than typical. Of early Anglo-Saxon accessions, for instance, the Anglo-Saxon Chronicle will simply say that so-and-so 'took the realm';[11] and neither Eddius nor even Bede is much more helpful. Then suddenly the Chronicle for the year 787 reports that Ecgferth, son of Offa of Mercia, was 'hallowed to king'.[12] Caution has impelled some scholars to write in terms only of some kind of consecration;[13] but most interpret this as the first case of royal anointing in England.[14] Certainly this is the Chronicle's earliest use of the word 'hallowed' for a royal, as distinct from an episcopal, inauguration. But it is also its last, for almost a century and a half during which we know that royal anointings were practised in England. It seems possible that the Chronicle uses 'hallowed' for Ecgferth, simply because in his case the normal 'took the realm' was inapposite;[15] and that what was thought special was the pre-mortem character of Ecgferth's succession, not any novelty in its ritual form. It could be that kings had been anointed in England — perhaps were regularly anointed — before 787. In any case, the Chronicle is not the place we should expect to find such an innovation registered at the date it was introduced. For Scotland there is a similar general lack of evidence with information on a single case which could be the exception that proves the rule: St. Columba, according to Adamnan writing over a century later, 'ordained' a king in Scottish Dalriada as early as 574 by laying hands on him and blessing him.[16] But this obviously special case, cited by the hagiographer to show Columba's prophetic vision, need not imply that any sixth-century Celtic 'ritual' or 'ceremony' for ordaining kings existed, let alone that this was its normal form.[17] Historians seem sometimes to have forgotten that a saint's life demands different treatment from a chronicle. When Adamnan recounts Columba's vision of an angel bearing a glass book 'of the ordinations of kings' and then

---

[11] 'Feng to rice': on this, and on Bede's terminology, see Chadwick 1905, p. 355 sqq., esp. 360.

[12] Anglo-Saxon Chronicle s.a. 785 (recte 787), ed. B. Thorpe (Rolls Series, 1861), pp. 96—7.

[13] E.g. D. Whitelock in her translation of the *Anglo-Saxon Chronicle* (Cambridge, 1961), p. 35, n. 2.

[14] See e.g., Levison 1946, p. 119; Stenton 1971, pp. 218—9; Wallace-Hadrill 1971, pp. 113—5. On the possibility of earlier insular anointings see Kottje 1964, pp. 94—106. Bloch 1924, Appendix III: 'les débuts de l'onction royale', remains well worth reading.

[15] Compare the similarly exceptional case of the one-year reign of Cenwalh's widow, queen Seaxburh in Wessex, *Anglo-Saxon Chronicle* Preface to MS 'A', p. 1: 'þa heold Seaxburg . . . þaet rice æfter him'.

[16] *Adomnan's Life of Columba*, edd. A. O. and M. O. Anderson (Edinburgh, 1961), pp. 473—5.

[17] As inferred by Martène 1736, II, 10 col. 212; Ellard 1933, p. 13; Ratcliff 1953, p. 2. But see now Kottje 1964, p. 97.

describes the saint prophesying 'between the words of the ordination', we get a blend of scriptural reminiscence, liturgical phraseology and legendary motif.

For the historian, one saint's life may have very different evidential value from another: there is one remarkable passage in the late seventh-century Passion of St. Leudegarius which to my mind strongly suggests that a fixed inauguration ritual existed in at any rate later Merovingian times. This text is all the more credible here because the hagiographer, who is a contemporary of the events he describes, mentions king-making procedures en passant, in an unforced, unselfconscious way. He is out to blacken Ebroin, the enemy of Leudegarius, but he gives an essentially historical account of the background to Ebroin's fall. The date is 673:

> King Clothar (III) died . . . But while Ebroin should have summoned the optimates together and should have raised Clothar's full brother, Theuderic by name, to the kingdom with due solemnity as is the custom, puffed up with the spirit of pride he refused to summon them. So they began to be very fearful, because Ebroin would be able to do harm to whomever he wished with impunity, so long as he could keep under his control, and exploit the name of, the king whom he should have elevated for the glory of the public fatherland.[18]

Here we have the technical phrase *sublimare in regnum* (we shall meet it again presently) with a clear reference to a traditional ritual procedure: *solemniter, ut mos est*, which should be performed in the presence of the *optimates*, subsequently termed a *multitudo nobilium*. There is also a very significant indication that these same *optimates*, whose views the hagiographer is expressing at this point, saw the *gloria patriae publicae* as at stake in king-making: because they had not been rightfully summoned to play their part, they rejected Ebroin and his puppet-king and invited in instead another Merovingian from Austrasia. Clearly a power-struggle was fought out in 673, and the inauguration ritual became the focus of the political conflict. If only the hagiographer had stopped to say in detail what the customary procedures — the *mos* — consisted of. But that was no part of his concern.

That *mos*, from the sixth century onwards, seems to have centred on an enthronement.[19] I think it very unlikely that, as Levison claimed, 'the accession to the throne of the Merovingians was a secular act devoid of any ecclesiastical ingredient'[20] — unlikely, I mean, either that it was ever not religious (there is a difference between religious and christian) or that it did not also come under clerical influence before the mid-eighth century. The regal benedictions that survive in late eighth- and ninth-century manuscripts for use 'when the king is elevated into the kingdom'[21] seem to me to be of Merovingian origin; and the *pontifices et proceres* who appear together so often in late Merovingian sources would surely all have attended the inauguration of

---

[18] *Passio Leudegarii* I, c. 5, ed. B. Krusch, MGH SS rer. merov. V, p. 287.
[19] For a full discussion and references, see Schneider 1972, p. 213.
[20] Levison 1946, p. 116.
[21] See Bouman, 1957, pp. 163, 175 and pp. 91 and 189—90, for the texts of the regal benedictions 'Prospice' and 'Deus inenarrabilis'.

a king. The liturgist C. A. Bouman's remark about Carolingian inaugurations seems equally apposite in a Merovingian context: 'Whenever bishops were present at an official function, it was in the nature of things that they accentuated the religious aspects of a long-standing usage by giving it a ritual turn'[22] — though in the case of king-making what was new was not the ritual turn but the ecclesiastical twist.

As long as ecclesiastical blessings remained relatively subordinate adjuncts to such inauguration rituals as enthronement, investiture with weapons or regalia, symbolic marriage with an earth-goddess, or the mounting of an ancestral burial-mound, clerical writers would naturally tend to say little about procedures of king-making. They began to say more when their colleagues in the ecclesiastical hierarchies of the barbarian kingdoms took over, clericalised, 'liturgified' the conduct of a major part of the ritual. This happened at different times in the various kingdoms, but it had happened in the main ones by the mid-tenth century. This take-over centred on the introduction of royal anointing and came to involve the elaboration of a full ecclesiastical rite for the king's consecration, an *Ordo*, analogous to the other personal status-changing rites already provided for in liturgical books. Thus where an eighth-century Sacramentary might contain some regal blessings, a tenth-century Pontifical might well include — after ordination-forms for the seven ecclesiastical grades and for abbot and abbess, and consecrations for monk, nun and widow — *Ordines* also for the king and queen. The royal rite was thus regularised and recorded. But such a record by no means included the total process of a king's inauguration. Clerics rarely cared to document non-clerical procedures; yet when we happen to have evidence of these, we can see how partial a picture the *Ordines* give. Widukind, for instance, gives an account of Otto I's inauguration which begins with an enthronement ritual outside the church performed by the *duces et milites* making Otto king *more suo* — 'in their own traditional way'[23] — and ends with a description of the clearly very important feast that followed after the ecclesiastical rite was over.[24] The early Anglo-Saxon *Ordines* open with tantalising references to the immediately preceding election and a *conventus seniorum*, presumably the Witan, but we know nothing of what ritual procedures were enacted. One of these *Ordines* ends with a mention of the feast to follow, but it is an anecdote in the earliest life of St. Dunstan which happens to reveal how important this feast was felt to be by tenth-century participants.[25] The *Ordines*, then, though often our only evidence for the inauguration rituals of the ninth and tenth centuries, have to be married up with other types of evidence if we are to begin to appreciate their context, function and meaning for contemporaries.

If we have to think in terms of a whole process, consisting of extra- and intra-ecclesiastical ritual, constitutive only in its totality,[26] we also have to distinguish

---

[22] Op. cit., p. 127.
[23] *Rerum Gestarum Saxonicarum Libri Tres*, ed. H. E. Lohmann, rev. P. Hirsch (Hanover 1935), pp. 64–5.
[24] Hauck 1950, pp. 620–1. For other kinds of *mos*, see Schmidt 1961, pp. 97–233.
[25] Further details in Nelson 1965, pp. 42–3.
[26] See Mitteis 1944, pp. 47–60.

different observers and different periods in the rituals' evolution. Let's consider the rite of anointing — which historians seem to agree is very important but which has been too rarely considered in the context of a particular place and time, or studied comparatively in different kingdoms. There may be no point in asking who borrowed the rite from whom, if in fact it was not, or not always, diffused but 'invented' autonomously in various places: but if so, the question must become, under what conditions? It is probably equally pointless to ask what was the purpose of royal anointing, or to whose advantage did it operate, or was it indispensable:[27] I doubt if there is a single, generally-applicable answer to any of these questions. As to the constitutive character of anointing, for instance, the cleric who composed the 'Frühdeutsch' *Ordo* seems to distinguish between the *princeps*, or *electus*, before the anointing, and the *rex* after it.[28] But Widukind's terminology suggests nothing of the kind: he doesn't even distinguish consistently between *rex* and *dux*, Otto being termed now one, now the other. Hincmar of Rheims, when it suited him, stressed the constitutive character of Charles the Bald's anointing in 848;[29] but he certainly never questioned the fulness of Charles' kingly powers before that date (Rheims, after all, had benefited a good deal from their exercise)[30] nor did he cast doubt on the title of unanointed kings as such. The historical situation of the ninth century was too varied and too fluid for even a political theorist of Hincmar's stature to attempt to produce a clearcut or consistently-presented theory of royal anointing. What does seem to have happened is that once anointings had come to be regularly performed by the local hierarchy of a given realm, within a couple of generations or so anointing would tend to be regarded as indispensable. It joined, or rather was added to, the series of ritual acts which together made a king. For some kind of formal election, possibly culminating in procedures of elevation or enthronement, had invariably preceded it. The time-lag between these two main phases of the inauguration might be minimised, as in Otto I's case. But they remained distinct. In tenth-century England, for example, there is some evidence for the reckoning of reign years from the formal election rather than from the consecration. When practical difficulties enforced a longish delay between the two events, as in Athelstan's case (with Edgar's I deal in some detail below) we might hope to find some evidence, notably in charters, which might enable to test whether the royal powers of a *rex electus* before his consecration were less than complete in fact. But the results of such an enquiry are disappointing: whereas two of Athelstan's charters do clearly show reckoning of reign years in Wessex from a date before Christmas 924,[31] his earliest genuine one that is securely datable was issued on the day of his

---

[27] For these and other questions, see the discussion in *Settimane di studio del centro italiano di studi sull' alto medioevo*, VII, i (Spoleto, 1960), pp. 385–403.
[28] Ed. Erdmann 1951, pp. 83–7.
[29] Details in Nelson 1977a, pp. 245–50.
[30] See Tessier 1943, I, pp. 210ff., and 262ff.
[31] Birch, nos. 691, 692.

consecration 4 September, 925,[32] but the charter evidence as a whole is too scarce to warrant any suggestion that Athelstan was reluctant (or unable) to issue charters before he was consecrated. Edgar, as we shall see, certainly did just that. It is a commonplace that medieval men saw no incompatibility between the principles of election and heredity which to modern eyes tend to appear mutually exclusive:[33] we must also accept that a ninth- or tenth-century king exercised his royal powers from the time of his formal acceptance — *electio* or *acclamatio* — by some or all of his leading subjects, but still needed to be anointed as soon as possible thereafter for the king-making to be thought complete. Neither of the general statements in the preceding sentence will be found explicit in an early medieval text, but both are to be inferred from the evidence of what kings and others actually did.

In the light of all this, and especially of the need for more detailed preliminary work to be done before that general history of medieval inauguration rituals can be written (as, begging Leach's patience, one day it surely will be), I shall now examine three particular cases of inauguration rituals, including anointing, in practice in Francia and England in the eighth, ninth and tenth centuries. All three are problem cases, but they're perhaps more interesting, and certainly more instructive than so-called 'normal' ones. Together they reveal the dimensions of our subject. Firstly then, and inevitably: the case of Pippin. For only here do we have fairly good evidence as to the date and circumstances of the introduction of royal anointing in one realm. The background is well-known: Pippin's patronage of the Bonifacian reforms in the 740s, his sending of envoys to Rome, 'with the advice and consent of the Franks',[34] to ask Pope Zacharias 'about kings in Francia',[35] the receiving of the papal response that the name of king should be brought back into line with the reality of who held royal power, and that Pippin should therefore replace the last Merovingian. You did not make this *non*-Merovingian king of the Franks by letting his hair grow long and then enthroning him, but by anointing and enthroning him. Now medievalists have been all too eager to stress the revolutionary effect of 751: I say 'too eager' because the effect of this anointing on the nature of medieval kingship seems to me to have been sometimes exaggerated. Pirenne,[36] for instance, following Fustel de Coulanges,[37] drew rather too heavy a line between the allegedly quite 'secular' Merovingian *rex crinitus* and the Carolingian *rex dei gratia*. I would see a more continuous evolution of Frankish kingship starting with Clovis himself who, long-haired warrior-king though he remained, had a 'salvation-giving helmet of holy anointing'[38] put on his head when he received christian baptism. The royal

---

[32] Birch, no. 641 (strictly speaking, a memorandum based on a charter).

[33] A point best made by Kern 1954, pp. 13ff., 248ff.

[34] Continuator Fredegarii, ed. Wallace-Hadrill 1960, p. 102.

[35] *Annales regni Francorum*, ed. F. Kurze (Hanover 1895), SS rer. Germ. in usum schol., p. 8.

[36] Pirenne, trans. Miall 1939, pp. 136, 268ff.

[37] de Coulanges, 1888–92, vol. VI, 'Les transformations de la royauté pendant l'époque carolingienne', pp. 206–8, 226ff.

[38] Avitus of Vienne, Ep. 46, ed. R. Peiper (Berlin 1883), MGH AA VI(2), p. 75.

anointings of the Carolingians represent a quantitative rather than a qualitative change in the degree of integration between political power and ecclesiastical authority in Francia, and, underlying both, the development of the Franks' own self-image as a chosen people with a mission. Between Dagobert and Pippin — or even Charlemagne — is a difference more of style than substance.

But to return to 751: how do we explain the fact of Pippin's anointing? Fritz Kern in *Kingship and Law* had a crisp answer: 'Secular politics were the effective reason for the introduction of anointing into the constitutional law of the Frankish state'.[39] Underlying such an implicit assumption of royal initiative lies a rationalist view of politics as calculation operating in an autonomous secular sphere. This view, though apparently surviving in some of our contemporary practitioners of *Realpolitik*, is really an eighteenth-century one. Voltaire in his article, 'Roi' in the *Dictionnaire Philosophique*[40] imagined the following early medieval conversation: 'Le prince disait au pretre: Tiens, voici de l'or, mais il faut que tu affermisses mon pouvoir . . . Je serais oint, tu seras oint' ('I'll be greased — and so will you!') In similar vein Gibbon wrote of Pippin's royal unction as 'dexterously applied . . . and' (Gibbon could not refrain from adding) 'this Jewish rite has been diffused and maintained by the superstition and vanity of modern Europe'.[41] We should beware of projecting the cynicism of the Enlightenment back into the eighth century.

Now Pippin had been brought up in the monastery of St. Denis and may well have been literate. But how should a layman have understood how to operate in the clerical preserve of oil-rituals? Just what his own anointing may have meant to him we cannot know: one of his diplomas may mention it,[42] but that was of course drawn up by a cleric. We have some evidence, however, that the Frankish aristocracy, in the short run anyway, was little impressed by the new rite. The Continuation of Fredegar's Chronicle, written at this point by Pippin's uncle, does allude to the anointing of 751, but without enthusiasm:

> Pippin, by the election of all the Franks to the throne of the kingdom, by the consecration of bishops and by the subjection of the lay magnates, together with the queen Bertrada, as the rules of ancient tradition require was elevated into the kingdom.[43]

The use of the 'consecration' *(consecratio)* may be deliberately vague, for this could refer in the eighth century to any status-changing rite — the profession of a nun, for instance — without at all implying an anointing. But the chronicler's emphasis is not on the consecration anyway, but on the election and elevation of the Frankish king

---

[39] Kern 1954, pp. 77. I quote here from the English translation by S. B. Chrimes (Oxford, 1939), p. 41.
[40] Quoted by de Pange 1951, p. 557.
[41] *Decline and Fall of the Roman Empire*, abridged D. Low (Harmondsworth 1960), p. 636.
[42] MGH Diplomata Karolinorum, ed. E. Mühlbacher (Hanover 1906), no. 16, p. 22.
[43] Wallace-Hadrill 1960, p. 102. Rather than using Professor Wallace-Hadrill's elegant translation, I have translated this passage myself to reproduce the clumsiness and ambiguity of the original. The Continuator here is Count Childebrand, son of Charles Martel.

by the Franks — *ut antiquitus ordo deposcit*. Whatever the term *ordo* may mean in other documents or contexts of this period (and Pope Zacharias' desire 'that *ordo* be not disturbed', as reported in the *Annales regni Francorum* under the year 749, may well have Augustinian undertones[44]) here in the Continuation of Fredegar the *ordo antiquitus* is surely to be identified with the *mos* of Leudegarius' hagiographer.[45] The inauguration ritual of 751 accorded with that of Frankish tradition — which also happened to be Merovingian. In the eyes of contemporary Frankish laymen, and probably therefore of Pippin himself, this was what mattered most.

But the ritual of 751 also included the novelty of anointing. Its instigators should be sought, as von Ranke long ago surmised, in Pippin's clerical entourage, among such men as Fulrad of St. Denis and the enthusiastic reformer Chrodegang of Metz. Such men were on their home ground in the royal monastery of St. Médard at Soissons where the anointing took place. No doubt they acted under the influence of an Old Testament model, but why should a literal imitation now have been thought appropriate? Thanks to the lucky survival of the Missale Francorum, written somewhere in the Paris-Corbie-Soissons triangle in the first half of the eighth century,[46] we can be fairly sure that ordination anointings of priests were already being practised in precisely this region. If a literal interpretation of Scripture dictated the anointing of the priest's hands (the Vulgate rendering of Leviticus 16: 32 gave the erroneous translation: '*sacerdos . . . cuius manus initiatae sunt ut sacerdotio fungatur . . .*') it becomes understandable why priests thus anointed might then have found in Old Testament history their warrant for anointing the head of a king. I doubt if a special parallel was seen between Saul and David on the one hand, Childeric and Pippin on the other: David, after all, unlike Pippin, had observed the precept: 'Touch not the Lord's anointed', and had waited for Saul to be killed in battle. It was not a precise situational model, but a more general one that the Frankish clergy found in the Old Testament. The typological link existed not only between Carolingian and Davidic kingship and between reformed Frankish and Levite priesthood, but between the whole Frankish *gens* and the people of Israel. The 'inventors' of Frankish royal anointing belong in the same milieux that produced the Second Prologue to Lex Salica and the also contemporary Frankish *Laudes* with their invocations of divine blessings on the *iudices* and the *exercitus* as well as the king and princes of the Franks.[47]

A glance at Frankish inaugurations in the century after 751 shows no case in which royal anointing can be ascribed to a ruler's initiative. If anointings were performed in 768 or 771 (and the evidence is not clear-cut[48]) then Frankish clergy must again have

---

[44] As suggested by Büttner 1952, pp. 77–90.

[45] Compare the sense of *antiquitus* in *Passio Leudegarii* I, c. 7, SS rer. merov. V., p. 289.

[46] Ed. L. C. Mohlberg, Rerum Ecclesiasticarum Documenta, Series Maior, Fontes I (Rome, 1957), p. 10, with comments, pp. 64–7, and B. Bischoff's views on place and date, p. xvi.

[47] Kantorowicz 1946, pp. 41ff. See also Ewig 1956, pp. 16f., 47ff.

[48] See Brühl 1962, pp. 314ff.

been responsible. The Carolingians' own practice when they made their sons sub-kings reveals a remarkable lack of interest in the new rite: Charlemagne's second son Charles was made sub-king of Neustria in 790 without receiving any anointing,[49] and when Louis the Pious made his son Charles a sub-king in 838, he invested him with the weapons of manhood and with a crown, and, keeping abreast of the times, had all the magnates commend themselves with oaths of fidelity to the young man, but in neither of the two quite full accounts of this occasion is there any hint of an ecclesiastical rite.[50] I can't now go into the complicating factor of eighth-century papal involvement in Frankish royal anointings. But it may be worth noting that the anointings of Pippin and his two sons performed by Stephen II in 754 don't seem to have cut much ice with contemporary Franks: the Continuation of Fredegar (now being kept up to date by Pippin's cousin) simply does not mention these anointings, and the Frankish bishops implicitly ignored them if they indeed reconsecrated Pippin's sons in 768 and 771. Only at St. Denis was the memory of these anointings kept green,[51] and that was because they'd taken place at St. Denis and redounded therefore to *its* glory. It's surely a significant (and rather neglected) fact that not a single one of Charlemagne's court poets, panegyrists or correspondents, especially the prolific Alcuin, ever mentions that Charlemagne or his sons had been anointed. Don't courtiers write what kings want to hear?

One or two general points emerge from the obscure history of early Carolingian inaugurations. First, while anointing might operate at one level as a rival christian brand of sacral magic, a substitute for long hair, functionally it was bound to have some different implications, if only because it required artifice, clerical artifice, in addition to nature. It did not just grow; it had to be conferred at a point in time, specifically through an inauguration ritual, and this meant that churchmen became involved in the procedure of king-making in a new and prominent way. If relatively many reigning Merovingians and no Carolingians were assassinated, this can hardly be explained simply in terms of the protective effect of anointing for the latter dynasty, at least in its earlier period. More relevant here are such factors as the maintenance of a fairly restrictive form of royal succession[52] (and the Carolingians' abandonment of polygamy must soon have narrowed the circle of royals) and the growth of a clerically-fostered ideology of christian kingship.[53] Anointing in fact caught on slowly with the Carolingians — not because of its hierocratic undertones (can you imagine Pippin or Charlemagne afraid of being 'captured' by the Church?) but because Pippin, Charlemagne and, in this respect,

---

[49] See Eiten 1907, pp. 46ff.
[50] Astronomus, *Vita Hludovici Pii,* ed. W. Pertz, MGH SS II, p. 643; Nithard, *Historiarum libri quattuor,* ed. E. Mueller, MGH SS rer. Germ. in usum schol., p. 10.
[51] This is well brought out, in reference both to the Chronicle of Moissac and to the *Clausula de unctione Pippini,* by Levillain 1933, pp. 225—95.
[52] Compare the comments of Ian Wood, above p. 10.
[53] For some consequences in terms of juristic means of dealing with bad rulers, see Ullmann 1969, pp. 66f.

even Louis the Pious were traditionalists, making their sons sub-kings simply according to the pattern of the Frankish past, not deliberately by-passing clerical consecrators. And in practice the appointment of sub-kings, given a series of long-lived fathers, became a kind of pre-mortem succession, which meant in the end that no Carolingian between Pippin and Lothar II in 855 had to wait for a predecessor's death in order to become king. This effectively limited the extent of possible clerical intervention in, and ritual elaboration of, king-making procedures, and helps explain the absence of a developed liturgical tradition of Frankish *Ordines* before the mid-ninth century. It also accounts for the problem at the outset of my second case-study.

The consecration of Charles the Bald at Orleans is problematical because of when it occurred: how, if anointing had become — as it's often alleged — well-established in Frankish practice from the mid-eighth century, could Charles the Bald reign *un*anointed as king of the West Franks from 840, when his father died, until 848? Ganshof has concluded that for a Frankish king in the 840s, anointing, 'though something important, was not something indispensable'.[54] Well, it was dispensable, evidently. But what evidence is there that anointing was thought 'something important' by Franks, lay or clerical, before 848? It's likely that no Frankish king had been anointed since 800, and none anointed except by the pope since 771[55] (or possibly, even, since Pippin himself in 751). There *was* no real indigenous Frankish tradition of royal anointing. Not only Charles the Bald but his elder half-brother Louis in Bavaria and his nephew Pippin II in Aquitaine ruled unanointed after 840.

The problem therefore is to explain not how Charles reigned for eight years without receiving anointing, but why he ever was anointed at all. We must look at the situation in Aquitaine, which though it had been assigned to Charles in 843 had been held on to by Pippin II at first illegally, then from 845 under Charles' nominal overlordship. Early in 848 the Vikings burned Bordeaux. Pippin had offered no resistance: Charles had at least tried. So the Aquitainians, 'constrained by Pippin's inertia', deserted him and 'sought Charles'. But why was the decision then made to 'anoint him with sacred chrism and solemnly consecrate him with episcopal benediction'?[56] Why anointing? Alternative explanations have been offered: one is that Charles' position in 848 was so weak that he 'had himself anointed' as a last resort to protect himself with a 'sacred character' against his unruly subjects;[57] the other is that since Charles' position was looking healthier in 848 than at any time since his accession he could now assert his authority by 'having himself anointed'.[58] Well, oil may be versatile stuff, but both these explanations can't be right — and I doubt if

[54] *Settimane Spoleto,* VII, i (1960), p. 397.
[55] Brühl 1962, pp. 321f.
[56] *Annales Bertiniani*, edd. F. Grat, J. Viellard and S. Clemencet (Paris, 1964), p. 55.
[57] Levillain 1903, pp. 31ff. at 51.
[58] Lot and Halphen (part 1: 840–53; no other parts appeared) 1909, pp. 193f. Lot's suggestion, p. 194, n. 2, that the Aquitainian clergy had waited until Charles reached the Roman age of majority at 25, is not borne out by the consecration of Charles' son as king of Aquitaine at Limoges in 855 when the boy cannot have been more than 8.

either is. I see no reason to assume Charles' initiative. The idea, as in 751, was surely a clerical one, and the developing situation of the 840s with the increasing pretensions of the episcopate in general to a governmental role and the influence of Hincmar of Rheims in particular, supplies a credible context.[59]

If the object of Charles' anointing was to protect him from the infidelity of his *fideles*, it was not a success: the Aquitainians were not deterred from revolting in 853, and that was just the first in a series of stabs in Charles' back. But we ought not to apply such a crude yardstick to the question of whether anointing 'worked', for a ritual does not create a political situation. We need to ask, rather, what in 848 anointing signified, and to whom? Here, again as in 751, the broader ritual context is relevant: just around the 840s, the anointing of bishops, with chrism on the head, was coming into practice in north-western Frankish ordinations. This fact, and the importance attached to it, we know from a letter written by Hincmar himself giving details of an episcopal consecration in 845.[60] Some of the prescriptions in the rite for Charles the Bald's next anointing in 869 as king of Lotharingia show deliberate parallels with the episcopal anointing described in Hincmar's letter.[61] Though details are lacking for 848, I suggest that the bishops who devised and performed the Orleans rite were following the same model, making the king, like themselves, in a special way consecrated to God,[62] emphasising the gap between the man and the office and thus the responsibilities the office involved. If anointing was, as Arquillière wrote, 'la traduction liturgique du *ministerium regis*',[63] it became so explicity only in the ninth century: before that, kings might have been seen, in Scriptural terms, as *ministri* of God's kingdom, but not until the reign of Louis the Pious was the concept of royal office worked out and publicised.[64] The churchmen who did this had their feet firmly on the ground of contemporary politics. In the *Annales Bertiniani*, written at this point by Prudentius, bishop of Troyes, the 848 consecration is represented as the act of all the Aquitainians, lay *nobiliores* as well as bishops;[65] and in a subsequent reference to what came to be seen in retrospect as an anointing to his whole West Frankish realm, Charles under Hincmar's guidance stressed the *consensus* and *voluntas* of all his *fideles*.[66] If an enthronement also took place

[59] See Lot and Halphen 1909, pp. 130ff., and Nelson 1977, p. 245, n. 4. Devisse 1976 I, pp. 291f., seems rather to underestimate Hincmar's influence on Charles in the 840s.

[60] Andrieu 1953, pp. 22–73.

[61] MGH Capit II, pp. 456–7. This text, strictly speaking a protocol, not an *Ordo*, describes the *modus* and *materia* of the anointing in some detail.

[62] As stated explicitly in Hincmar's *adnuntiatio* preceding the 869 rite, MGH Capit. II, p. 341: '... ut in obtentu regni ... sacerdotali ministreio ante altare hoc coronetur et sacra unctione Domino consecretur'. Compare I Paral. xxix: 22, describing the anointing of Solomon: 'Unxerunt autem eum Domino in principem'.

[63] Arquillière 1955, p. 43.

[64] Anton 1968, pp. 208ff.

[65] *Ann. Bertin.*, p. 55. Compare ibid., p. 71 on the elevation of the younger Charles in 855: 'Aquitani ... Karlum puerum ... regem generaliter constituunt, unctoque per pontifices coronam regni imponunt ...'

[66] *Libellus adversus Wenilonem*, MGH Capit. II, p. 451.

in 848, laymen no doubt participated. Certainly West Frankish bishops were staking a claim to an indispensable role in the king-making ritual; and it then became possible for Hincmar, at any rate, to construct a theory of the king's accountability to his episcopal consecrators. But the bishops in their new role acted, in turn, as guarantors of the law and justice of all the king's subjects, as guardians of the christian people and thus as representatives, in some sense, of the realm as a whole. This became clear when something like a 'coronation-oath' was demanded of the king by the bishops as part of the ritual proceedings inside the church.[67]

I have stressed that anointing was by its very nature a clerical monopoly. This was not true of coronation, attested for the first time as part of a royal inauguration in Francia only in 838.[68] Before that popes had crowned Frankish sub-kings and Frankish emperors, and Carolingian kings themselves had experimented with the wearing of crowns and various other insignia on important liturgical occasions. But crown-wearing and *Festkrönungen* need to be kept distinct from coronation as part of the royal inauguration ritual.[69] 848 seems again to have marked an innovation in Francia, in that the archbishop crowned, as well as anointed, Charles.[70] This association of rituals was confirmed in the *Ordines* of Hincmar, who even used coronation as a metaphor for anointing itself in the anointing prayer, *'Coronet te dominus corona gloriae . . .',*[71] and when Charles was inaugurated to a new kingdom in 869, the scriptural model to which Hincmar appealed was not David, reanointed at successive inaugurations, but the Hellenistic king Ptolemy who when he acquired a second kingdom placed 'two diadems on his head, those of Egypt and Asia'.[72] Hincmar made coronation, alongside anointing, permanently part of the ecclesiastical procedures of king-making. In West Francia the 'liturgification' of enthronement had followed by about 900.[73]

Clearly the ninth century was a seminal period in the history of royal inaugurations in western christendom. Before leaving it, I'd like to make just one more general point about anointing rituals in the time of Charles the Bald. Personal anointing was conceived as one very special, peculiarly intense form of benediction whereby the recipient was exposed in a unique way to the outpouring of divine grace. The common factor was the fullness of the benediction, but the application varied with the context. The addition of anointing to episcopal ordination did not alter the character of the rite — the central blessing-prayer indeed remained unchanged — but it translated into visible, sensible terms what had hitherto been a metaphor: 'the flower of heavenly ointment'.[74] The sorts of grace requested for the

[67] See Nelson 1977, passim.
[68] Brühl 1962, p. 301.
[69] A point rightly stressed by Jäschke 1970, pp. 556–88, esp. 565ff., 584ff.
[70] MGH Capit. II, p. 451; for coronation in 855, see n. 65 above.
[71] MGH Capit. II, p. 457.
[72] MGH Capit. II, p. 340, with reference to I Macc. xi: 13.
[73] In the 'Seven Forms' *Ordo*, ed. Erdmann 1951, p. 89. See further Bouman 1957, pp. 136–40.
[74] Andrieu 1953, pp. 40–53.

bishop were specific to his office: 'constancy of faith, purity of love, sincerity of faith' and so on. The king's anointing, similarly, was intended to secure blessings needful for the carrying-out of royal functions — in particular the blessings of victory over visible as well as invisible enemies.[75] The point was that only God could provide the qualities a mere man needed to fulfil great public responsibilities. If an inauguration ritual as such presupposed a gulf separating the office from its incumbent, anointing focussed attention precisely here; for it was associated in the western liturgies with *rites de passage* covering the most drastic kinds of change in status, namely baptism and last unction, both involving a transition from 'death' to 'life'.[76] The anointings of bishops, priests and kings did not imply any functional likeness in the offices concerned, beyond their public governmental character and general importance (expressed in terms of divine foundation): anointing did not make the king into any sort of priest (any more than it made the priest a sort of king! Such a combination of functions was precisely a part of Christ's uniqueness.) If it had implied anything of the kind, what could we make of the anointing of queens, introduced in the time of Charles the Bald (another mid-ninth century innovation) and a feature thereafter of West Frankish ritual practice?[77] Priest, bishop and king each had his own specific function on whose performance the welfare of the christian people depended and for which special grace had to be acquired. The queen too had her function — one of the utmost public concern; and she too had specific needs: 'may she perceive through this anointing', prayed Hincmar over Charles' wife Ermentrude, 'cleanness of mind, safety of body. Crown her, Lord, with holy fruits . . . make her bear such offspring as may obtain the inheritance of your paradise'.[78] Though surely proving a lack of any necessary connection with priesthood, to use anointing as a fertility charm[79] was not to devalue it: rather to affirm the faith of Hincmar, Charles and their contemporaries in the sacramental outward and visible sign as guarantor of inward and spiritual grace.

And so to the tenth century: my third and last case-study is Edgar, king of the Mercians and, probably, Northumbrians from 957, and of the West Saxons from 959, to 975.[80] If there's one famous thing about Edgar, it's his 'delayed' or 'deferred' consecration at Bath in 973. 'One of the most puzzling things in our

---

[75] See Sprengler 1950/1, pp. 245—67, esp. 252ff.

[76] See Nelson 1976, pp. 108ff.

[77] The *Ordines* of Judith (856) and Ermentrude (866): MGH Capit. II, pp. 425—7, 453—5; the *Ordo ad ordinandam reginam* associated with the 'Erdmann' *Ordo* of *c*.900, ed. Schramm, 1968, II, pp. 220—1; the *Ordo ad reginam benedicendam* associated with the *Ordo* of 'Ratoldus' (=Schramm's 'Fulrad'), ed. Ward, 1942, pp. 358—9 (in use in France in the twelfth and thirteenth centuries). I do not think that Cont. Fred. as quoted above, p. 57, implies that Pippin's queen Bertrada was anointed, and the *Clausula* makes no such claim for her.

[78] MGH Capit. II, p. 455. Quoting the episcopal *adlocutio*, ibid. p. 454, Wintersig 1925, pp. 150—3, at p. 152 speaks of 'eine Weihe der Thronfolgermutter'.

[79] So, Kantorowicz 1955, p. 293.

[80] Stenton 1971, pp. 366—7.

history', E. A. Freeman called it,[81] just a century ago. Historians have been puzzling over it since the twelfth century. Osbern in his Life of Dunstan[82] told a story about Edgar's having run off with a nun whereupon Dunstan imposed a seven-year penance on him 'that he should not wear the crown of his realm during this whole period'. 973 thus became a spectacular crown-wearing when the seven years were up: *redeunte quasi jubileo termino*. William of Malmesbury[83] was clearly sceptical about this tale (which he nevertheless recounted with relish!) but still asserted that Edgar ruled 'from the sixteenth year of his age, when he was constituted king' until 973 'without any regal symbol' *(sine regio insigne)*. These twelfth-century writers seem to be invoking popular legend to explain the mystery of 973;[84] but a seven-year penance would take us back only to 966 and not to the beginning of Edgar's reign at all. In fact Osbern, in depicting 973 as a *Festkrönung*, a *coronatio* or festal coronation such as was familiar to him from the practice of his own day, thereby implied that Edgar *had* been normally consecrated already at his accession. Similar interpretations seem to be offered in the thirteenth century by Roger of Wendover[85] and Matthew Paris.[85a] On the other hand, William's contemporary Nicholas of Worcester[86] thought that Edgar himself had delayed his consecration out of 'piety . . . until he might be capable of controlling and overcoming the lustful urges of youth'. Well, if that took Edgar until he was nearly thirty, he must have been — for those days — a late developer! The two most recent attempts to solve the mystery are elaborations or revised versions of these medieval hypotheses: H. R. Richardson and G. O. Sayles[87] follow Osbern with their *Festkrönung* theory, while Eric John[88] thinks there's a kernel of truth in William's and Nicholas's belief that Edgar's consecration was delayed. Let's go back to the tenth-century evidence.

A first question: did Edgar really reign for over thirteen years without being consecrated as king? We have to start from the fact that no contemporary or near-contemporary witness actually states that Edgar received consecration when he became king either of the Mercians in 957 or of the West Saxons in 959.[89] But there is no valid argument from silence here, because literary or chronicle or charter evidence for *any* pre-Conquest royal inauguration is very rare. It's true that the Anglo-Saxon Chronicle's entry for 973 describing with uncharacteristic fullness the

---

[81] Freeman, 1887, p. 639.
[82] Ed. Stubbs, 1874, pp. 111–2.
[83] *Gesta Regum*, ed. W. Stubbs (Rolls Series, 1887–9), I, pp. 179–80.
[84] Note the comments of Stubbs, 1874, pp. xcix–ci.
[85] *Chronica sive Flores Historiarum*, ed. H. O. Coxe (London, 1841), I, p. 414.
[85a] *Chronica Majora*, ed. H. R. Luard (Rolls Series, 1872), I, p. 466.
[86] Stubbs, 1874, p. 423.
[87] Richardson & Sayles, 1963, Appen. 1, pp. 397–412.
[88] John, 1966, pp. 276–89.
[89] But no abnormality in the form of his accession is implied in the earliest Life of Dunstan, Stubbs, 1874, p. 36, or by Æthelweard, *Chronicon*, ed. A. Campbell (London, 1962), p. 55.

occasion at Bath gives no hint of any previous consecration,[90] though Æthelweard can be construed as doing so; but as I said earlier there was a tendency for only those inaugurations that were in some way odd to get written up. It is more remarkable, though even Eric John neglects this, that the regnal list '*β*' reckons Edgar's reign in Wessex from 11 May, 959, which since Edgar's brother Eadwig only died on 1 October, 959, is obviously a mistake:[91] in fact 11 May is the day and month of the Bath consecration in 973. Did the list's compiler get into difficulties because he simply assumed that the day and month supplied by his source must relate to the outset of Edgar's reign? He doesn't seem to have taken any multiple consecrations into account — and he was writing during the brief reign of Edgar's successor. Yet it would be hasty to infer that no consecration occurred before 973.

What historians medieval and modern alike have too rarely appreciated is the extraordinarily complex circumstances surrounding *both* Edgar's successive successions, in 957 and in 959. In both cases, it was actually impossible for Edgar to be consecrated king for some time after he had been chosen king. In 957, Canterbury was still in the hands of the elder brother against whom Edgar was in revolt, and the archbishop of Canterbury, Oda, until his death on 2 June, 958 remained loyal to Eadwig.[92] As for York, the new archbishop Oskytel, appointed in the 'unusual' situation following the less-than-complete reinstatement of the traitorous Wulfstan I, only attests charters as 'bishop' throughout 957 and 958 and therefore probably did not return from Rome with his pallium until 959.[93] His attestations before this date, as well as other evidence, suggest that English archbishops already at this period as later did not exercise full archiepisopal powers until after receiving the pallium, and again from just about this period, pressures seem to have been brought on these archbishops to go to Rome to fetch their pallia in person. In 957 then, since consecration by a mere bishop would hardly have done, Edgar had to wait. Some of his charters show reign-years being reckoned in the northern kingdoms from his election by the Mercians and Northumbrians.[94] His uncle Athelstan had experienced similar difficulties, and as we saw, seems sometimes, anyway, to have reckoned his reign-years from his election, not his belated consecration.

The situation in 959 was more 'unusual' still: the archbishop of Canterbury at the time of Eadwig's death on 1 October was Brihthelm, a recent appointee who had

---

[90] A point stressed by John, 1966, p. 278. The 'D' version of the *Anglo-Saxon Chronicle*, p. 225, after terming Edgar 'king' in annals for the earlier part of his reign, calls him 'Ætheling' in 973. But I cannot follow Mr. John in assigning great significance to this word, especially as it does not appear in versions 'A', 'B' or 'C': since, as I hope to show below, 973 was indeed an inauguration-rite, 'ætheling' could well represent a pendantic reflex on the part of the 'D' chronicler.

[91] *The Anglo-Saxon Chronicle*, trans. D. Whitelock (Cambridge, 1961), p. 5, with Professor Whitelock's comments, pp. 3 and 5, n. 2.

[92] As indicated by his attestation of Birch, no. 1032.

[93] For details, see Whitelock, 1973, pp. 232–47, at 240f. I am much indebted also to earlier correspondence with Professor Whitelock on this topic.

[94] Birch, nos. 1112, 1119, 1270.

not yet received his pallium. Edgar lost little time in, as the first biographer of Dunstan so frankly puts it, 'sending [Brihthelm] back where he came from'[95] — to make way for Dunstan at Canterbury. Then Dunstan had to go to Rome to square all this with the venial pope John XII (no doubt a good deal of grease was needed) and also to receive his pallium, on 21 September, 960. Dunstan therefore couldn't have been available to perform Edgar's consecration until the very end of 960, or more probably, allowing time for invitations to be issued, early 961 — which gives a delay of at least 13 or 14 months between Edgar's accession in Wessex and any possible consecration. Now it just so happens that all versions of the Anglo-Saxon Chronicle fail completely for the years 960 and 961; and the irregularity of Dunstan's appointment could account for a discrete silence of the part of other sources for these crucial years.

But arguments from silence are never entirely satisfactory. So I want now to offer two sorts of positive, if indirect, evidence that Edgar did indeed receive a royal consecration as soon as possible, at least, after his coming to power in Wessex. The first is composite, consisting of liturgical documents whose significance has only very recently been brought to light by liturgists.[96] Successive recensions of West Saxon *Ordines* contained in manuscripts of the tenth century and later can be shown to demonstrate the likelihood of a tradition of West Saxon royal consecration-rites, including anointing, continuous from the first half of the ninth century (and probably older still).[97] It is very likely that from 900 the same basic rite, the so-called Second Anglo-Saxon *Ordo*, remained in use until the Conquest, with relatively minor alterations being made sometimes, for specific consecrations, in the course of that period.[98] If then probably for more than a century before Edgar and certainly from 900 West Saxon kings had been consecrated according to a fixed rite as soon as possible after election,[99] I can't see Edgar suddenly breaking with that tradition for any of the reasons that have been alleged. Not only would such a breach have no known parallel either English or Continental (the difference between Edgar's case and that of Charles the Bald is clear), but Edgar, having been trained at Abingdon by

---

[95] Stubbs 1874, p. 38. Professor Whitelock, 1973, has shed light on this obscure episode.
[96] See Turner 1971, pp. xxx—xxxiii; Hohler, 1975, pp. 60—83; 217—27.
[97] I have argued this in 'The earliest surviving royal *Ordo*: some liturgical and historical aspects' (forthcoming).
[98] Turner 1971, p. xxxiii, associates this *Ordo* with Athelstan (925) but leaves open the possibility of an earlier date. I hope to show elsewhere that the earliest form of this Second *Ordo* was very probably used for the consecration of Edward the Elder at Pentecost, 900.
[99] Edward the Elder: Pentecost (8 June) 900: Æthelweard, *Chron.*, p. 51, with xxxf.; Athelstan: *Mercian Register* in *Anglo-Saxon Chronicle*, s.a. 924; Birch no. 641, with regnal list '*β*' (giving date, 4 Sept. 925); Edmund: '*β*' calculates from '*c*29 Nov. 939', according to Whitelock, *Anglo-Saxon Chronicle*, p. 4, no. 13, making an interregnum of just over a month from Athelstan's death on 27 Oct. (might Edmund's consecration have been on Advent Sunday, 1 Dec. 939?); Eadred: Birch nos. 815, 909, but the date, 16 Aug. 946, given by Florence of Worcester, *Chronicon*, ed. B. Thorpe (London, 1848), p. 134, does not fit with that implied by '*β*' (see Whitelock, *Anglo-Saxon Chronicle*, p. 4, no. 14); Eadwig: '*β*' suggests 27 Jan. 956, the third Sunday after Epiphany, Florence, p. 136, says archbishop Oda officiated, and the first Life of Dunstan, Stubbs 1874, p. 32, gives further details.

Æthelwold and come under the influence of Dunstan, was just the man to appreciate the divine gifts anointing was believed to convey. For their part Æthelwold and Dunstan needed Edgar to help realise their ambitions for reform: recent experience of royal mortality could hardly encourage confidence that Edgar would reach his thirtieth year,[100] and in my view it seems highly unlikely that they would have taken the dangerous risk of impairing Edgar's legitimacy as king by any such deliberate deferment of the consecration as Sir Frank Stenton postulated. And legitimacy was precisely what was involved — which is where my second bit of evidence comes in. On Edgar's death, supporters of his younger son Æthelred challenged the succession of his elder son Edward, Æthelred's half-brother: their main arguments were that Edgar had not himself been anointed at the time when he begot Edward, i.e. 959 or 960, and that Edward's mother had never been anointed at all.[101] Now obviously Æthelred's partisans would not have used these arguments against Edward if the same objections had applied to Æthelred too:[102] the two inferences must be, surely, that Æthelred's mother *was* anointed queen, something which we know from other evidence anyway, and that Edgar *had* been anointed at the time when he begot Æthelred, i.e. 966 or 967 — an anointing which can only be identified with the one which I have argued took place as early as possible after Edgar succeeded in Wessex. And there is the further point that if Edgar's anointing was credited with such retrospective significance, so to speak, for his heir, its significance for the reigning king himself surely follows *a fortiori*.

If Edgar was consecrated already at the end of 960 or early 961, whatever happened in 973 was not a 'delayed' or 'deferred' consecration. But what then was it? Clearly the rite at Bath was not just a *Festkrönung* but an inauguration, because Edgar was certainly anointed then (and no *Festkrönung* ever involved a repeated anointing). But an inauguration to what? On my argument, Edgar had already been ritually inaugurated to his Anglo-Saxon realm. Continental parallels show, however, that new inaugurations, including anointing, were perfectly in order — didn't the Old Testament offer the precedent of David? — when a king acquired new realms.[104] Charles the Bald in 869 is a case in point. What then was the new realm in 973? The

---

[100] Edmund was only about 25 when he was killed in 946, and Eadwig died aged about 15.

[101] Eadmer, *Vita Dunstani*, Stubbs 1874, p. 214: '. . . quia matrem eius (i.e. Edward's) Licet legaliter nuptam in regnum tamen *non magis quam patrem eius dum eum genuit* sacratam fuisse sciebant'. The accuracy of Eadmer's information about the two queens is confirmed by Nicholas of Worcester, who had made a special study of the subject: Stubbs 1874, pp. 422–4, and sent Eadmer his results. Though Eadmer is a late source, it is hard to see how the above intricate argument could be a later fabrication.

[102] Those historians who believe that Edgar was consecrated only once, in 973, have had difficulty explaining away this passage of Eadmer's: see, e.g., Freeman 1887, p. 639.

[103] Despite the objections of Richardson and Sayles 1963, pp. 397ff., I still regard the *Vita Oswaldi*, ed. J. Raine 1879, pp. 436–8, as a reliable witness to the use of the Second Anglo-Saxon *Ordo* in 973. A further and hitherto unrecognised pointer in this direction is the associated queen's *Ordo* prefaced by a very curious rubric which, in my view, can only relate to Edgar's wife Ælfthryth. I intend to argue this fully elsewhere.

[104] See Brühl 1962, p. 306 with no. 5.

key lies in the choice of ritual-site: whereas the royal vill of Kingston-upon-Thames was the place of all West Saxon royal consecrations whose site is known,[105] the 973 consecration took place in Bath — an ancient city whose Roman buildings and walls still stood impressively in the tenth century.[106] Then even more than now, this place must have conjured up the shades of Britannia, of the Roman and imperial past.[107] Here we enter a world of political ideas that have much to do with insular traditions but also with the tenth-century Continental present.[108] Henry, father of Otto I, like Charlemagne before him, was 'king and emperor of many peoples': Otto's great great diets were attended by 'a multitude of diverse peoples'.[109] The English kings of the tenth century, in touch fairly continuously with the Ottonian court through kindred, diplomatic and ecclesiastical links, could hardly have failed to be impressed by this contemporary imperial power. The West Frankish kings of the later tenth century, more alienated than impressed, were beginning to claim, or have claimed for them, an imperial status of their own, as 'lords of many sceptres'. If Abbo of Fleury, like Widukind in the East Frankish realm a generation earlier, used *regalis* and *imperialis* virtually as interchangeable concepts,[110] this was because the 'regal' now included a strong 'imperial' component, a real king, as distinct from a mere kinglet, being one who ruled over a plurality of realms or peoples. There are many signs that the Anglo-Saxon monarchy around the middle of the tenth century was coming to be regarded, anyway by those clerical authors whose work survives, in a similar light. Already in the 940s, Archbishop Oda hailed the *regalis imperium* of Edgar's father Edmund, to which 'all peoples *(gentes)* are subject'.[111] For Æthelwold, Edgar himself was a *rex egregius* to whom it was appropriate to apply the text of Jeremiah 1:10: 'Behold I have set you over the peoples and over the nations *(super gentes et super nationes)*'.[112] The biographer of St. Oswald, whose detailed information about 973 should in my view be taken very seriously, stresses the size and scale of the great assembly at Bath — suitable to 'the dignity of so far-flung a realm', adding, with an obvious reminiscence of Luke's Gospel (2:1): 'a decree went out from the emperor that all should flow together to him from east and west, north and

---

[105] Plummer 1899, II, pp. 133, 145, 149, 163.

[106] Biddle and Hill 1971, pp. 81–2.

[107] The Old English poem *The Ruin*, ed. Krapp and Dobbie 1936, pp. 227–9, with its reference (line 37) to 'the crowning city of a far-flung kingdom', is usually thought to relate to Bath. For the impact of Roman ruins on the Anglo-Saxons as reflected in their poetry, see Frankis 1973, pp. 253–69, esp. 257f.

[108] Stengel 1965, pp. 287ff. (England); 56ff. (tenth-century East Francia); Vollrath-Reichelt 1971, pp. 87ff. Despite the reservations of H. Hoffmann 1972, pp. 42–73, at 66ff., rightly noting that not every 'imperialis' means 'imperial', the existence of a non-Roman imperial idea of overlordship of other kings and peoples has been established beyond doubt: see esp. Erdmann 1951, and Löwe 1963, pp. 529–62.

[109] Widukind, *Rer. Gest. Saxon.* iii, pp. 38, 75. See Brackmann 1967, pp. 150ff.

[110] Werner 1965, pp. 1–60, esp. 16ff.

[111] PL CXXXIII, col. 952.

[112] Birch no. 1190.

south'.[113] These are, I think, the authentic voices of a hegemonial imperialism, an idea of empire smacking more of confederation than autocracy, and harking back, therefore, to an earlier Anglo-Saxon tradition of *ducatus* — leadership of allied peoples based on consent and common defence interests, as distinct from *regnum* based on conquest and military domination.[114] Edgar's revival (whether consciously or not) of this *ducatus* was in line with much previous West Saxon policy[115] but also showed his own sureness of touch. The need for collective defence was again being forced on the peoples of the British Isles from the later 960s onwards by the reappearance of the Vikings. That some of Edgar's closest advisers responded very quickly to the renewed threat just might be suggested by the appearance in charters from the late 960s of proems warning that the end of the world may be nigh.[116]

There is further evidence that imperial ideas of this kind were finding expression precisely in the early 970s. First, on the numismatic side, there is the special 973 'Circumscription' issue at Bath, which could have been produced partly for the purpose of an imperial *sparsio* following the consecration;[117] and the impact of the great coinage reform, later in the same year, must have been felt directly or indirectly throughout the British Isles.[118] Second, there is Edgar's fourth code of laws — that is, if we can accept the code's recently-proposed redating to this period of the reign.[119] One provision in this code is to be 'common to all the nations, whether Englishmen, Danes or Britons, in every province of my dominion'; another is to apply to 'all who inhabit these islands'.[120] Such phrases are unprecedented in earlier laws. Third, there is the submission to Edgar, very probably also in 973, of Kenneth king of the Scots, and the cession to him of Lothian under Edgar's overlordship.[121] Fourth, there is the ritual at Chester which followed the inauguration at Bath: eight 'sub-kings' rowed Edgar along the river Dee, including five Scots and Welsh and two sea-kings of the western and northern isles[122] — all members of a pan-Britannic

---

[113] *Vita Oswaldi*, pp. 436–7, compare ibid., p. 425–6.

[114] Vollrath-Reichelt 1971, pp. 182ff.

[115] See *Anglo-Saxon Chronicle*, s.a. 926, p. 199; s.a. 945, p. 212; compare the attestations of *reguli* in Birch nos. 815, 883, 909. For contemporary and later interpretations of Edgar's reign on hegemonial lines, see Æthelwold's account of Edgar's establishment of monasteries, in Whitelock 1955, I, pp. 846f., the 'D' version of the *Chronicle*, s.a. 959; Ælfric's *Life of St. Swithin* in Whitelock 1955, p. 853; Nicholas of Worcester, Stubbs 1874, p. 423; Florence of Worcester, *Chron.*, pp. 139, 143.

[116] See Whitelock 1955, I, p. 345.

[117] My suggestion is based on the evidence presented by Dolley 1973, pp. 156–9, that the Bath mint was uniquely productive in 973. Professor Dolley himself comments, p. 159: 'The need for largesse apart, the ceremony would have brought together a quite exceptional concourse of dignitaries . . .' whose board and lodging would have to be paid for from royal resources.

[118] Dolley and Metaclf 1961, pp. 136–68.

[119] Hart 1973, pp. 115–44, at p. 133, n. 6.

[120] Trans. Whitelock 1955, I, pp. 397–401: IV Edgar, 2,2; 14,2.

[121] Roger of Wendover, *Flores* I, p. 416. For the date, see Stenton 1971, p. 370; Freeman 1887, pp. 582–8.

[122] Ælfric, *Life of St. Swithin*, trans. Whitelock 1955, p. 853. Only six kings are mentioned in the *Anglo-Saxon Chronicle*, versions 'D' and 'E', p. 225. Florence, *Chron.*, pp. 142–3, using both these sources, gives the names of eight kings. For the substantial accuracy of his account, see Stenton 1971, p. 369.

alliance who presumably were also participants in Edgar's annual naval exercises around the coasts of Britain.[123] Fifth, there are the imperial styles in charters which, though not new, become now very prominent.[124] In one case Edgar is termed *'basileos anglorum et rex atque imperator . . . regum et nationum infra fines brittanniae commorantium'*.[125] Such political ideas did not grow in a vacuum. Sixth, there is the architectural innovation (for England) of westworks in several later tenth-century churches, notably Winchester, where the extension was begun in 971 but not completed until 994.[126] It has recently been suggested that the new church at Bath had a westwork already by 973.[127] Carolingian and Ottonian westworks, on which these English ones were modelled, were the settings for special kinds of imperial liturgical performance: were the English westworks designed, or could they have been used, for similar purposes? Seventh, there is the Benedictional of Æthelwold, now plausibly dated to 971–5, which displays a new and specifically imperial iconography of Christ, with a deliberate paralleling of Christ and the English monarch in the role of 'imperial king of kings', a model of tenth-century 'ruler theology' which may have gone from England to Germany, not vice versa.[128] Eighth and finally, there is a small piece of liturgical evidence from the royal *Ordo* which, despite some recent objections, I remain convinced was the one used in 973. Amongst the few changes made in the existing royal *Ordo* (and I should explain that in terms of the injection of imperial content into a pre-existing royal model) one makes perfect sense in the context of an imperial rite: in the prayer following the investiture with the sceptre, a prime symbol of Anglo-Saxon rulership, the word *Britannia* was substituted for the colourless *terra* of the scriptural model in the phrase, 'Honour him above *all kings of Britain*'.[129] None of these bits of evidence in isolation might mean much; but cumulatively they show that a case can be made (not a new case, certainly,[130] but stronger than previously realised) for seeing in 973 an imperial inauguration rite and Edgar in his later years as ruler of a British Empire, tenth-century style.

[123] Williams of Malmesbury, *Gesta Regum*, pp. 177–8.

[124] Stengel 1965, pp. 325ff; John 1966, p. 58f.

[125] Birch no. 1201 (original grant probably 967, assignment to St. Mary's Worcester, 973; dated 'anno . . . regno (sic) mei xiii'). Compare also Birch nos. 1266, 1268, 1270, 1307, 1316, and possibly 1302. In the light of Chaplais 1965, pp. 48–61, the specific connexions of these and earlier charters with 'imperial titles' are worth noting: Abingdon and Winchester, and, later, such houses as Ely influenced by Æthelwold and his circle, seem to be centres of imperial terminology.

[126] Cherry 1976, pp. 186–7; Biddle 1975, p. 138.

[127] C. A. Ralegh Radford, 'The architecture and sculpture of the tenth century with particular reference to the Bath area', unpublished lecture given at Bath in June, 1973. I am very grateful to Dr. Ralegh Radford for allowing me to use this citation.

[128] Deshman 1976, pp. 367–405, esp. 390ff. with 399–400, very pertinent comments on Edgar's imperial position.

[129] Turner 1971, p. 93, for the text in British Library, Cotton MS. Claudius A. iii, f. 14; for a list of the MSS. of this 973 recension of the Second English *Ordo*, see ibid. p. xxx, under (1), to which should be added the recently discovered BL Additional MS 57337.

[130] For an early fine exposition, see Robertson 1872, pp. 203–15. Compare Robinson 1918, p. 72.

I am not sure that my three case-studies will lend themselves to any summary generalisations. Instead, by way of conclusion I shall pose two very basic philogenetic questions. One: why anointing? Two: why kings? I recently suggested elsewhere that it was the existence of a permanent oil-crisis in the early medieval West which helped to make anointing with oil — a commodity potent and scarce — a 'natural symbol' to designate the power-holders in barbarian christian society. A first anointing made the christian; a second anointing identified the 'twice-born'.[131] But in glibly borrowing from India that notion of the twice-born as two specialist classes of men — priests and warriors — I evaded an important difference between India and the early medieval West. Within each barbarian kingdom while the priesthood did indeed constitute a class, only one individual was king. If the Indian analogy had been complete, there should have been anointing also of warrior lords, of dukes and counts for instance, in this age of 'guerriers et paysans'. The peculiar discrimination with which anointing was in fact applied mirrored, therefore, not simply an actual political situation but an ideal. Where aristocratic interests constantly threatened to tear apart society, kingship represented force contained, harnessed, institutionalised so as to unify each people in fact as well as in name. The very survival of kingship, under the later Merovingians for example, itself suggests that such an ideology was not just something ecclesiastically conceived and purveyed but represents lay sentiments too: how else could we explain those popular beliefs in the sacral powers of kings embodied in the royal touch? I will end where I began, with Fortes' comment about 'the mysterious quality of continuity through time . . . basic to the self-image of every society' and expressed in inauguration rituals. Since in the early medieval West 'society' was a kingdom or accumulation of kingdoms, to consecrate a king was to assert a society's identity. And its continuity through time? Here, finally, is where the queen's anointing came in; for it was through the provision of heirs to the royal house and the implied confining of those heirs to a single line, that the queen's divinely-blessed fertility helped assure integrity and the continuance of society itself.*

[131] Nelson 1976, pp. 117f.

*I should like to acknowledge a long-standing debt to Professor Walter Ullmann. Especially in relation to the last part of this paper, I must thank, for help on various points, Dr. Michael Lapidge, Professor Michael Dolley and most of all Professor Dorothy Whitelock. Harald Kleinschmidt generously allowed me to read his unpublished Göttingen dissertation on Edgar's consecration in 973: I benefited much from our discussions of many problems. The friendly advice and criticism of Ian Wood and John Gillingham have been, as usual, invaluable.

4

Kingship, Genealogies and Regnal Lists
DAVID N. DUMVILLE

Genealogies and regnal lists are two distinct, but related, types of evidence for the royal families of the early middle ages. To say this is to offer no controversial statement. Anthropologists, but perhaps as yet few medieval historians, would point out also that ideology is an essential aspect of the genealogist's trade; to discover the nature of his ideology is to acquire both useful historical evidence and a vital weapon in the historical criticism of pedigrees and king-lists. The implication of this last statement is rather less conventional, for it requires us to accept the possibility — even the likelihood — that surviving early medieval pedigrees and regnal lists are not the straightforward documents which they may at first sight seem to be; for example, they may seek to conceal, rather than merely to convey, information. In other words, the historian needs to ask many questions about the circumstances of the production and transmission of such documents before he can begin to apply the information which they contain. This paper will therefore be an essay in method, an examination of some methodological problems posed by a difficult class of source-material. Such a discussion is an essential part of any attempt to determine their relevance for the understanding of early medieval kingship.

In recent years, much historical work has been done in two related areas. Continental historians have made great use of genealogical evidence in demographic study which has been directed to the elucidation of kinship structures, patterns of succession to official positions, and so forth. With this we shall not here be concerned, since it rests not on genealogical documents but on genealogical information deduced from non-genealogical sources. On the other hand, historians of the Celtic-speaking peoples have begun to analyse the massive corpus of surviving Irish and Welsh pedigree-records,[1] and of Irish and Pictish regnal lists:[2] this is beginning to reveal the supreme importance of learning and ideology in the genealogical schemes of the medieval period. The recent publication of Professor Léopold Genicot's pamphlet on medieval genealogies[3] provides a convenient opportunity

---

[1] The Irish texts, still far from completely published, may be studied chiefly in O'Donovan 1844, Walsh 1918, Ó Raithbheartaigh 1932, Pender 1937, Pender 1951, and O'Brien 1976. There are also numerous items published in periodicals. There is a guide or index by Pender 1935. The earlier Welsh texts are edited by Bartrum 1966 and in various periodical publications listed by him; these and later texts are indexed, and published in diagrammatic form (which is not entirely satisfactory for textual study), in Bartrum 1975.

[2] The Pictish texts are best consulted in Anderson 1973.

[3] Genicot 1975.

both to review our ability to handle early medieval royal genealogies and regnal lists and to ask some questions concerning their contribution to our knowledge of early medieval kingship.

Most of the aspects of kingship studied in this volume are, in one way or another, linked to the types of document considered in the present paper. In the Celtic-speaking countries we find evidence which associates genealogy with inauguration ritual. Perhaps the best known example is the inauguration of King Alexander III of Scotland in 1249: as he sat at the ancestral place of crowning, surrounded by his French-speaking court, a Gaelic-speaking Scot knelt before him and read the king's genealogy back through the ninth-century Cinaed mac Alpine, and the fifth-century Fergus mac Erca, to Scota, daughter of Pharaoh, the invented eponym of the *Scotti*.[4] It was Alexander's legal title to rule which was being recited as part of the inauguration ceremony.[5] Other aspects of this same process can be seen at a much earlier date. In the Gaelic- (i.e., Irish-) speaking world it was the function of the *fili*, one of whose roles was that of court poet, to recite poems about the ancestors of the king and about their deeds of heroism. Some sixth-century Leinster court-poetry, surviving as part of the early Irish genealogical corpus, may be argued to have had precisely the same function as the Scottish royal pedigree read to Alexander III. It would have been sung before the new king at his inauguration as an announcement of his legal title and to remind him of the example set by his ancestors whom he should intend to emulate.[6] The same practice was still normal in Gaelic Scotland in the seventeenth century.[7]

Legal title, as we shall see, was naturally very important. It was one of those elements which enabled a man to be a candidate for the throne. It was one of the factors leading to the patterns of consent to a particular candidate which Ian Wood has studied, above. And in our period legal title was normally, though not invariably, established by descent. Royal genealogy may be expected to state that claim, often retrospectively, and it need have no necessary relationship with biological fact. For example, it may be shown that in the historic period of pre-viking England, succession to the throne usually depended on descent from the fifth- or sixth-century founder of the dynasty;[8] there is no guarantee that by the eighth or ninth century the relationships claimed were statements of biological fact; nor is it certain that early (i.e., prehistoric) kings in the regnal lists belonged to the dynasty in question or that anyone in, say, the seventh century had the means of demonstrating this. But given the nature of this usual qualification for kingship, it was inevitable

---

[4] Duncan 1975: 555; Hughes 1977: 4.

[5] As Williams 1971: 41 notes, this 'suggests why the *filid* wrote so many genealogical poems and why such poems were considered to be important'; for a late example of a versified pedigree see Knott 1922—6, Poem 32.

[6] The earliest examples of such poetry are printed by Meyer 1913—14 with German translations.

[7] Martin 1703; cf. Bergin 1970: 8.

[8] See Dumville 1978. Compare the use of *Uí*-names for Irish dynasties and population-groups who claim descent from eponyms of that date — Mac Neill 1911: 85.

that candidates for the throne would state their claims in these terms or that successful usurpers might subsequently manufacture a pedigree claiming the appropriate descent.

An ecclesiastic who decided to write a history, to keep annals, or to compile a chronicle might or might not be conversant with conventions of this sort. This is a question we should always put when such a source offers us genealogical information, particularly about a period for which the writer is not a contemporary witness. In short, we might accept without too many qualms a statement that Z was son of Y, or even that Z was son of Y son of X. But if we are offered more than that, we shall do well to ask a series of questions: does the writer show any signs of ideological, or genealogically learned, inclinations? What was the nature and origin of his source? Does *that* show any ideological proclivities? Over the years, we have heard much from students of early medieval European cultures about the ability of primitive peoples to preserve genealogies for many generations,[9] with the implication that they are therefore historically accurate or subject at worst to some degree of muddle in transmission. It is now clear, however, from both historical and anthropological study, that many more complicated historical factors must be taken into account:[10] for example, a pedigree may be accurately transmitted, but bear no relation to biologico-historical facts because it seeks to explain a phenomenon other than descent from father to son or because it seeks to assert a claim which is not historical in kind. We need to ask such questions about the sources of the pedigrees in the Anglo-Saxon Chronicle. Kenneth Sisam discerned three strata:[11] the short West Saxon pedigrees probably originating (as far as the written record is concerned) in the earlier eighth century, perhaps in a set of West Saxon annals; additions from the Anglian collection,[12] probably the penultimate stage in the compilation of the Alfredian chronicle (the last being the adoption of entries from Bede's summary chronicle in *Historia Ecclesiastica*, V. 24); and the extended West Saxon pedigree of Cerdic (or Cynric) seen *sub annis* 552, 597, and 855, which Sisam so devastatingly examined. This is a matter of source-criticism and form-criticism: these processes are just as relevant to genealogies as to other items in the text. We can therefore ascribe the conventions only of the last stratum to the Alfredian compiler; he cannot be held responsible for the nature of the other items, though we may wish to draw conclusions from his interest in and use of them.

Genealogies and king-lists are also associated with early medieval royal legislation, as Patrick Wormald notes below.[13] The ecclesiastical connexions of the early

---

[9] cf. Sisam 1953: 337 for an example related to Anglo-Saxon England.

[10] See below (pp. 85–89) for the discussion of factors involved in oral transmission, and for the necessity to assess the nature of the transmission (whether oral or written, etc.).

[11] Sisam 1953: 332–7.

[12] We may include here the use of regnal lists: see, for example, the Mercian information in Anglo-Saxon Chronicle *s.a.* 755 (*recte* 757). On the Anglian collection of royal genealogies and regnal lists, see below, pp. 89–93.

[13] Page 134.

Germanic law-codes suggest that churchmen felt king-lists and royal genealogies to be important mirrors of a king's right to rule. A king had a long line of royal predecessors: he belonged to a royal tradition. A king possessed an appropriately royal pedigree: therefore he was of royal blood. A king legislated: therefore he was a king. Of course, one might equally note that of the laity only a king could legislate anyway; and that without a royal genealogy he could not be a king. The circularity of the arguments is evident, but these points nonetheless seem to have been considered proofs of kingship. It is not clear that we can separate the appearance of these royal records from their clerical milieu; therefore we cannot say to what extent the early Germanic royal legislators themselves regarded a record of their predecessors in the kingship or of their own royal descent as a necessary complement to their kingship and their power to legislate. The most impressive such document,[14] containing a king-list *and* a genealogy, is part of the Edict (of A.D. 643) of the Lombard King Rothari.[15] A king-list is also found in association with the laws of the seventh-century Visigothic King Reccaswinth.[16] Manuscripts of Frankish laws reportedly also contain king-lists.[17] There may be a direct connexion, perhaps stemming from Visigothic practice,[18] between these three applications of this type of royal record. In England, the situation is rather different, for there appears to be no direct early connexion between royal legislation and royal pedigrees or regnal lists.[19] It is no more than a conjecture that Æthilberht's code began with his pedigree, short or long;[20] nor is there unambiguous evidence for a direct association of laws with either genealogies or regnal lists before the eleventh century.[21] Consideration of this aspect of kingship is therefore principally concerned with continental developments.

---

[14] The least impressive is in the *Lex Gundobada* where, in § III, King Gundobad names four Burgundian kings as his ancestors: Fischer 1949: 24 = Drew 1972: 24. But, against Wallace-Hadrill 1971: 35, it is far from clear that this is a regnal list. On the knowledge of these names in Anglo-Saxon England, see Malone 1962: 154–5, 156–7.

[15] Edited by Beyerle 1947; translated by Drew 1973.

[16] Wallace-Hadrill 1971: 34.

[17] Wormald, p. 134.

[18] Wallace-Hadrill 1971: 34. He also conjectures that an earlier form of the Visigothic king-list was found in the laws of the seventh-century King Liuvigild; he is followed by Wormald, *infra*.

[19] Against Wormald, *infra*.

[20] For this conjecture (based on two arguments, neither of which seems sound), see Wallace-Hadrill 1971: 34, 39 (and 44, 45), repeated by Wormald, *infra*.

[21] Corpus Christi College, Cambridge, MS. 383 (*ca* 1100, from St. Paul's, London) ends with an incomplete copy of the West Saxon 'genealogical regnal list' (printed by Dickins 1952), but it is an addition of *saec.* xii[1]. The compilation of laws in this manuscript is closely related to that in the early-twelfth-century *Textus Roffensis* which is supposed to derive from a Canterbury manuscript of the early eleventh (Sawyer 1957: 20). That copy ends (fos 101–16) with a collection of genealogies, regnal lists, papal and episcopal lists (and lists of the twenty-four old men of the apocalypse and the seven archangels) which have a distinct provenance in a probably Christ Church Canterbury manuscript of the year 990 and enjoy a long common history before that (see Dumville 1976). The West Saxon 'genealogical regnal list' occurs there on fos 7v–8v, at the head of the Laws of Alfred, but with the regnal list extending to Æthelred (978–1016); there is accordingly no evidence of an early connexion, especially as it is lacking from the early manuscript, CCCC 173, section II, a Winchester text of the

The Church had, of course, a large stake in kingship. In the Celtic countries, it also developed a big stake in genealogy, and for much the same reason. There are two main aspects of this. From at least the ninth century onwards[22] we find collections of genealogies of saints, establishing both the good blood of the saints and their descent from appropriate tribal groupings.[23] Many saints' Lives also begin with a genealogy,[24] similarly establishing the aristocratic status of this Christian hero in society. The essential connexion of saints with prophecy (and of the Celtic saint with cursing[25]) leads to the incorporation in saints' Lives of *ex post facto* prophecies by the saint that descendants of a particular king said to be hostile to the saint will never succeed to the kingship: we find this in the Lives of St. Patrick[26] and in the Life of the Welsh Saint Beuno.[27] These prophecies are partly intended to be a demonstration and a warning of the saint's power of intervention with God (or, at the very least, of the saint's prescience); they are sometimes partly an ideological statement which expresses traditional hostility between an ecclesiastical foundation and a particular royal line. But the main point is that they depend on a knowledge of genealogical sources, and the retrospective exploitation of a terminal line. We see ecclesiastical interest in genealogical sources in Anglo-Saxon England also. The Anglian collection of royal pedigrees and regnal lists[28] — our major source of Anglian genealogies — was put together, I think, in Northumbria between 765 and 774 by a cleric. Several of the Church's contemporary demands are mirrored there. In particular, all kings known to be illegitimate or to be descended from such a ruler are excluded from the collection.[29] Here we see an ideological motive determining excisions from a genealogical collection;[30] and it is not only the Church which may be seen in this role.

Genealogy is thus an important aspect of kingship: in eligibility, in inauguration, in the Church's view of a king. We need to pursue all these matters, but there are also many other points of method which must be considered.

A notable feature of the distribution of genealogies and regnal lists is that the farther west one goes, the more there are. A massive corpus of medieval Irish

---

Laws (accompanied by episcopal lists) of the mid-tenth century (which came, between 1001x1050 and 1070, to Christ Church Canterbury where a Kentish regnal list was added, after the episcopal lists, in the early twelfth century). The text of that inferred Æthelredian copy of the West Saxon 'Genealogical regnal list' may, on internal evidence, have had an exemplar of Edgar's reign (as did that in the exemplar of the related MS. BL Cotton Tiberius B. 5/1); but that is no evidence for an association of that text with the Laws in 959x975 (much less in Alfred's reign).

[22] The date is that given by Kelleher 1968: 143.
[23] cf. Kelleher 1963: 119.
[24] For example, most of the Lives in Stokes 1890 begin in this way.
[25] For a brief note on this practice see Dumville 1973b: 305.
[26] In connexion with King Lóeguire.
[27] For the Welsh text see Wade-Evans 1944: 18 (§ 10); for translation, Wade-Evans 1930: 317.
[28] Edited by Dumville 1976.
[29] Dumville 1978.
[30] For an example of ecclesiastical views influencing excisions from a regnal list, see below, p. 81.

genealogies,[31] a sizeable body of Welsh ones, a small but interesting quantity of Anglo-Saxon records,[32] and an exiguous group of single patrilines from the Continent constitute the surviving evidence. My remarks will therefore be largely, though not wholly, confined to the British Isles.

THE PEDIGREE

Consideration of the evidence may begin with the pedigree or genealogy. The point has been made above that a king's genealogy constituted his legal title to rule. In its capacity as a legal document, it might therefore be expected to embody legal fictions or conventions; these might relate merely to the individual (for example, reflecting modes of adoption) or — more broadly — to his tribe, kingdom, or nation. In the latter circumstances, the convention or fiction will have political implications. The pedigree or pedigree-collection has, in fact, a wide variety of political applications which will require our attention. It can be an expression of something wider than kingship: it can proclaim political alliances and overlordships; it can announce belief in the existence of a racial grouping; it can seek to express an harmonious political order. Let us take an example from each of England, Wales, and Ireland.

The Anglian collection of royal genealogies and regnal lists has only recently been published as a collection. Little or no work has yet been done to identify the various strata of which it is composed. But, as it stands, it is arguably a Northumbrian compilation of the later eighth century.[33] We may begin by examining one aspect of the collection as a whole. All the lines of descent go back to the Germanic god Woden. As written, the trunk-lines of the pedigrees (those which go back to Woden, rather than the short side-branches) are all of approximately equal length, having no regard to chronological discrepancies. The heptarchic kingdoms of Bernicia and Deira, Lindsey, Mercia, East Anglia, Kent, and Wessex are thus provided with rulers descending from a Germanic god. When we recall that the collection is probably the work of a cleric, a number of questions comes to mind. For example, did Woden no longer hold any terror for the Anglo-Saxon churchman? Or did he represent something other than Germanic heathenism? Already in 731, Bede had recorded the descent of the Kentish kings from Woden, adding that 'de cuius stirpe multarum prouinciarum regium genus originem duxit' (*Hist. Eccl.*, I. 15).[34] Even if Woden had been a human who was subsequently euhemerised — as Kenneth Harrison has recently argued[35] — it is clearly not possible that all the post-migration

---

[31] See n. 1 above for references. Volume One of O'Brien's *Corpus* runs to 750 pages.

[32] In addition to the Anglian collection, there are Wessex texts chiefly connected with the Anglo-Saxon Chronicle. For other scattered items, see Dumville 1976: 29 and notes.

[33] Dumville 1976: 23–4, 45–50; cf. above, p. 76.

[34] cf. Anglo-Saxon chronicle *s.a.* 449E and the Old English Bede for translations of this passage into English.

[35] Harrison 1976a. I am not at all disposed to accept his argument.

royal lines descended from him, even though Bede speaks as if of a family.³⁶ We are therefore in the presence of an ideological statement. But what does it mean, and how are we to interpret it?

There survives from the reign of King Alfred (871—99) a manuscript-fragment (British Library MS. Add. 23211) containing, *inter alia*, a group of East Saxon royal pedigrees³⁷ and a West Saxon regnal list. The East Saxon dynasty's origin is traced not to Woden but to Seaxnet. We know, too, that in the eighth and ninth centuries the pagan Saxons on the Continent worshipped a deity of this name (Saxnot), as well as Thor and Woden.³⁸ It has from time to time been unfashionable — following changes in archaeological thinking — to draw Bede's sharp division between Angles and Saxons. It seems to me, however, that we must allow this division at least in general terms. If the people comprising a kingdom comes to be known as East Angles or West Saxons, we may conclude both that this name appealed in some way to a dominant element of the population and that we may use it as a guide at least to the tribal affiliations of the ruling dynasty of that people when it emerges into history.³⁹ If the East Saxon royal dynasty did trace its descent from a tribal or national god of the Saxon people, we may suspect that, originally, similar descent may have been asserted by the royal dynasty of Sussex (for which we lack genealogies) and by that of Wessex. In this connexion we may recall that Kenneth Sisam drew attention to evidence which suggests that the higher reaches of the West Saxon royal pedigree (which, in its extant forms, goes back to Woden) was borrowed from the Bernician.⁴⁰

What, then, is the implication of the universal descent from Woden ascribed to the heptarchic kings by the Anglian collection? Molly Miller⁴¹ has argued — and I am sure she is correct — that for Bede, in *Hist. Eccl.* I. 15, Woden expresses no more

---

[36] Bede's use of *stirps* and *genus* requires further study for the elucidation of this passage.

[37] The texts are printed by Sweet 1885: 179; cf. Hackenberg 1918: 94—5.

[38] cf. Hodgkin 1952: I. 302, who gives a text of the Old Saxon *Abrenuntiatio diabolae*.

[39] We must bear in mind that we are unclear as to the exact nature of the Germanic groups which settled in England in the fifth and sixth century. There may in fact have been a general lack of tribal homogeneity, each main group comprising the leader and his immediate relatives with a motley ragbag of racially-mixed followers. This suggestion could also be taken with the possibility that the apparently racial groupings may rather have consisted of those who owed allegiance to a particular god. I owe these points to Ian Wood. Both in Ireland and on the Continent in the early middle ages, we see genealogical schemes used to express ideas of racial or national groupings. The early Irish genealogists held that the population of contemporary Ireland consisted of a number of distinct racial groupings, representing successive immigrant groups (in the scheme put forward in its most extended form by *Lebor Gabála Érenn*, edited and translated by Macalister 1938—56). It is not clear what points of contact, if any, this scheme has with (pre)historic reality, nor does there seem to be any reasonable hope of developing a method which will allow these to be discovered; the classic attempt is O'Rahilly 1946, a brilliant study but one whose unhistorical methods and main results are quite unacceptable. On the Continent, perhaps about 700, someone saw the peoples of Europe in a genealogical framework and expressed this in a document known as the *Genealogiae Gentium* or 'die (fränkische, richtiger) deutsche Völkertafel in Prosa', printed by Müllenhoff 1873: 163—4; see Kienast 1968: 20 and n. 16, and, for bibliography of older discussions, Levison 1952: 118 n. 269.

[40] Sisam 1953: 302—5.

[41] Miller 1975a: 254 n. 1.

'than a means of defining royalty'. For Bede, therefore, no questions arise in this context as to the historicity or paganness of Woden:[42] he is a convention, and *his* inclusion at least is not intended to be taken literally in any reading of the genealogy. While agreeing with Dr. Miller, I should like to go a stage further and conjecture that the inclusion of Kent and Wessex in the Anglian collection expresses their inclusion in the eighth century within the Anglian world. In other words, I suggest that descent from Woden expresses an Anglian origin, or perhaps — more cautiously — belief in an Anglian origin. When extended to non-Anglian peoples, it reflects a political link: in this case, subjection to Anglian (Northumbrian or Mercian) overlordship. Only in the early ninth century, when political circumstances changed, might there have been the opportunity to rewrite these records. But by Alfred's reign, from which our first *ninth-century* West Saxon pedigree records derive,[43] the political situation was so different that there can have been little motive to reconstruct the pedigree conventions. (In any case, we may wonder if, in ninth-century Wessex, the necessary knowledge was available.) The West Saxon pedigree above Cerdic, the founder of the dynasty, is in whole or in part — as Sisam showed[44] — a construction; whether it belongs to the eighth century or the seventh is another matter. If an earlier pedigree for Cerdic was ever known, it has disappeared entirely from our sources; but we should not *necessarily* insist that there ever was one.[45]

If such a general assertion of political unity may be made through the use of a genealogy (and we shall see from the Celtic sources that there is nothing unusual about this), we can see too that more specific links may also be expressed in these terms. Let us proceed one generation below Woden and examine his alleged sons. For the seven heptarchic lines there are five sons. This in itself is a potential source of information. The Mercian, Lindsey, and East Anglian lines are independent. But through Wægdæg son of Woden are descended the lines of Kent and Deira,[46] and through his 'brother' Bældæg come the lines of Bernicia and Wessex. If we enquire about historical links between the members of each pair, two seventh-century connexions come immediately to mind. Edwin of Deira married the sister of Eadbald of Kent; Cynigils of Wessex gave his daughter in marriage to Oswald of Bernicia. In

---

[42] A different approach is hinted at by Wallace-Hadrill 1971: 22–3, 44–6: 'Christian kings needed pagan ancestors of heroic standing'; 'Æthelberht's pagan ancestry mattered to his Christian advisers: why not to him?'; 'That Æthelberht liked to represent himself as descended from Woden is plausible enough, surely. . . . Æthelberht would surely have learned how to make the most of his blood. There were missionaries at hand to see that he did it.'

[43] As opposed to probably eighth-century records embodied in some Anglo-Saxon Chronicle entries: Sisam 1953: 336–7.

[44] Sisam 1953: 300–7.

[45] Sisam 1953: 305, and pp. 80–81, below.

[46] Bede gives the form *Uecta* where the Anglian collection has *Wægdæg*. It is all very well for Sisam (1953: 325) to say that the two forms are 'not philologically equivalent'; since we are ignorant of the principles on which shortened forms of Old English names were created, such assurance is unacceptable. One may suspect that Sisam's insistence derives from his view *(ibid.)* that 'it is against the practice of these genealogies that the kings of Kent and Deira should be content to share a fictitious link with Woden'. That is a prejudgement, which is hardly supported by the evidence.

each case one king was being associated by marriage with the line of the heptarchic overlord, the *Bretwalda* or whatever we may call him.[47] If in early Anglo-Saxon England the pedigree convention operated which expressed political or dynastic links in genealogical terms, then our pedigrees may display precisely that convention.

What evidence can be brought to bear on these points from the pedigree-texts themselves? The Deiran and Bernician pedigrees are chronologically consistent with one another, while the other two show wild variations from this standard.[48] In fact, by comparison with the Northumbrian lines, both of them are much too short for the time which they seek to span. On the other hand, the trunk-lines all contain, in the extant text of the collection, the same number of names. We shall explore the reasons for this symmetry later. The Kentish pedigree presents the greater problems. In two parts, it appears already in Bede's *History* (I. 15; II. 5), published in 731. It is one of the most unstable genealogies, each source having some point of disagreement with the next. This hardly suggests a fixed, generally agreed, ancient pedigree. It extends only three generations above Oisc (from whom the Kentish dynasty took its collective name of *Oiscingas*) and two above Hencgest (his alleged father, according to Bede and the Anglo-Saxon Chronicle, and the first of the line to arrive in Britain) before we come to a son of Woden; in the West Saxon pedigree there is but one generation above Cerdic before the eponymous Giwis and, just like the Kentish line, only three before we come to a son of Woden. If we seek an historical context for the joining of a short Kentish pedigree (to Wihtgils or Witta) to the Deiran stem, Edwin's marriage with Æthilberg of Kent seems the only possibility.[49] We know the West Saxon genealogy to have been modelled on the Bernician;[50] in particular, we may note the employment of an eponym *Giwis* (for the Gewisse, as the West Saxons were known in the seventh century[51]) just as the Bernicians (in Old English, *Beornice*) had an eponym *Beornic*. The form *Giwis*, which is transmitted mechanically, is archaic and arguably seventh-century;[52] Bede in 731 already has *Geuissae* (*Hist. Eccl.*, III. 7), and the Northumbrian dialects were the most conservative on this particular point.[53] If we were to associate the confection of this pedigree with the dynastic marriage of Oswald and Cynigils's daughter in 635, when Oswald stood as godfather at his father-in-law's baptism, it would be a most suitable documentary complement to the inauguration of a new alliance, Christian and Bernician. The

---

[47] But Edwin did not rule Kent (*Hist. Eccl.*, II. 5), though he was overlord of the rest of England.

[48] This, of course, makes the Northumbrian pedigrees the standard. But if we regard them as bogusly consistent, there is no standard at all, and all lines are chronologically discrepant. cf. Sisam 1953: 328.

[49] Note how Bede states the link between Kent and Deira (*Hist. Eccl.*, II. 9): 'Huic autem genti occasio fuit percipiendae fidei, quod praefatus rex eius cognatione iunctus est regibus Cantuariorum, accepta in coniugem Aedilbergae filia Aedilbercti regis, quae alio nomine Tatae uocabatur'.

[50] Sisam 1953: 302–5 demonstrated this, while leaving the mechanics of the link unclear.

[51] Bede refers to it as an outdated name, *Hist. Eccl.* III. 7; cf. Walker 1956.

[52] Sisam 1953: 303 n. 2 provides the information, but his conclusion (which requires a Welsh intermediary) is unacceptable.

[53] But cf. Campbell 1959: 153–4.

pedigree link would express the political relationship of the two dynasties. Another possible moment would be the marriage of King Aldfrith of Northumbria (685–704) to the sister of King Ine of Wessex; here the political ramifications are less clear, though one may wonder if an alliance in face of the power of Æthilred of Mercia is a possibility (the same, directed against Penda, was presumably the intention in 635). A likely *terminus ante quem* is provided by the addition of the names Wig and Freawine to the West Saxon pedigree, probably to reflect the political circumstances of Offa's reign, as Sisam argued.[54] Wig and his father Freawine were known in heroic legend as subordinates of the first, or Continental, Offa; their appearance in the West Saxon dynastic pedigree is a natural way of expressing the late-eighth-century relationship in terms of genealogical convention.

If I have taken the implications of these structural discrepancies correctly, we are faced with the proposition that in seventh-century Northumbria conjunction of royal pedigrees to express political situations was accepted practice. On the question of date, however, we cannot rule out the possibility that such genealogical links were created retrospectively with antiquarian and learned, as much as ideological, motives. If we should associate the Kentish link with Edwin's reign, it will predate the main period of Irish influence in Northumbria; we could not then so easily suspect a reflex of Irish practice.[55] A more promising context is perhaps offered by Bede's words in *Hist. Eccl.*, III. 1 ('cunctis placuit regum tempora computantibus, ut, ablata de medio regum perfidorum memoria, idem annus sequentis regis, id est Osualdi, uiri Deo dilecti, regno adsignaretur'), that those who count the length of kings' reigns have agreed to delete the reigns of Edwin's apostate successors in Bernicia and Deira and assign the year in question to Oswald's reign. This well-known passage points to a learned group keeping royal records. These would be just the sort of people who would record and similarly adjust pedigrees. Who they were will exercise us later.

In Wales, we can see the same processes at work, but we have more (if later) evidence. The trauma which brought the post-Roman Brittonic kingdoms into existence also posed a problem of legitimacy. For various reasons,[56] Welsh political thought came to associate the transition from Roman to native rule with the death of Magnus Maximus in 388. As the last Roman ruler in Britain, according to this scheme, Maximus was the fount of legitimacy. Accordingly, a number of major Welsh royal lines claimed descent from Maximus, either directly through the male line or indirectly by the alleged marriage of the head of their dynastic pedigree to an invented daughter of Maximus. In this way they stressed their legitimacy. We have early (that is, ninth- and tenth-century) examples of this for the kingdoms of Dyfed

---

[54] Sisam 1953: 306–7.

[55] As does John Morris, *The Age of Arthur* (London, 1973), p. 143. For a suggestion of a generally Celtic context, see Sisam 1953: 328–9 and Wrenn 1967: 29. We cannot, of course, rule out pre-616 cultural contacts between the Irish and the Northumbrian kingdoms.

[56] On which see Dumville 1977: 179–83.

and Powys. At the head of Dyfed's line, immediately below Maximus, as his son, stands an eponym *Dimet*.[57]

We see this feature repeated in the North Welsh kingdom of Gwynedd. Gwynedd comprised a number of distinct sub-kingdoms. In the case of most of these, we are uncertain if they were originally independent kingdoms; but where we have royal pedigrees they show that at the head of the line stood an eponym — Dunod in Dunoding; Ceredig in Ceredigion.[58] At some point, each of these was declared to be a son of the head of the main Gwynedd dynastic pedigree, one Cunedda. By about 800, the list of sons seems to have become fixed, so that when another kingdom, Meirionydd, is incorporated into Gwynedd, its eponym Meirion has to be made the son of one of the already created sons of the founder.[59] We may compare the cases in the Anglian collection which I have discussed already.

All the dynasties of the sub-kingdoms of greater Gwynedd therefore shared the same ancestor, Cunedda, who was said to have achieved power in Gwynedd in 388, the year of Maximus's death. Political unity was expressed genealogically in this way. The same is true of Powys: the sub-kingdoms shared an ultimate ancestor (Gwrtheyrn) with the dynasty of the main kingdom. Their recognition of its overlordship is expressed thus in genealogical terms.

A genealogical system can be employed in this way to express a political situation. We may recall here my suggestion to that effect about the Anglian collection: it can be argued that there individual pedigrees have been attached to a scheme (showing universal descent from Woden) for a specific political purpose. It is knowledge of the possible conventions, and exploitation of the discrepancies in any such scheme, which allows us to make some headway against what may otherwise seem impenetrable lists of names.

The polity of early medieval Ireland is believed to have been based on up to 150 tiny tribal kingdoms,[60] which were normally gathered in small groups (or mesne kingdoms) under an overlord who was also king of one of the petty kingdoms. These mesne kingdoms or overlordships were themselves gathered in groups under a provincial overlord who was also an intermediate overlord and, in his own right, a petty king as well. These groupings came to be expressed, at an early date, in genealogical terms.

Among the innumerable examples of manipulation of Irish pedigrees, to suit changing political conditions, perhaps the best known is that which sought to take account of the rise to power in the province of Munster (the so-called 'southern half' of Ireland), in the later tenth century, of the Dál Cais dynasty at the expense of the earlier Eoganacht dynasty.[61] Propagandist genealogists sought to give the Dál Cais

---

[57] Bartrum 1966: 10 (HG § 2).
[58] See, for example, Bartrum 1966: 11 (HG § 17), 12 (HG § 26).
[59] See Bartrum 1966: 13 (HG § 32) and, for comment, Miller 1976: 102 n. 1 and Miller 1977.
[60] Byrne 1973: 7, increasing on Mac Neill's number (endorsed by Binchy 1970: 5) of 80–100.
[61] Ó Corráin 1971: 38–9 and 1974: 9; Byrne 1973: 11.

kings genealogical legitimacy, in their usurped status as provincial overlords, by establishing (falsely) that the Dál Cais belonged to the *same* dynasty as their Eoganacht predecessors. This was done by inventing a founding Munster ancestor who divided the province between fictional progenitors of the Eoganacht and the Dál Cais.

It is examples of blatant manipulation such as this which help us to establish what were the conventions of the keepers of genealogies.[62] Criticism of genealogical texts whose systematics cannot be trapped in this way by external evidence must depend on an awareness of the possibilities of manipulation. What may seem hyperscepticism in a critical approach to texts where external checks are not possible must be viewed in the light of the genealogists' conventions, which have nothing to do with *our* requirements concerning historical veracity.

At least one Irish text has been identified which discusses possibilities of corruption of genealogies.[63] Gilla in Chomded Hua Cormaic, a poet of the earlier twelfth century, lists in verse 'six ways *of special note* that confound the tree of genealogy'. His poem is preserved in a manuscript of his own century. Four of the six reflect the results of social developments, such as the rise of the base-born and the decline of noble lines; but the possibility is not to be overlooked that some of these processes could be alleged, rather than real, in specific cases. We must not forget that one of the poet's prerogatives was satire; we do not lack instances of a poet threatening to satirise a ruler by attributing a servile descent to him, and the threat would be all the more effective in that the poet was the hereditary keeper of genealogical lore. Gilla in Chomded himself notes two causes of deliberate falsification: invincible ignorance (a category employed, then as now, to include the work of other scholars with whom there was fundamental disagreement); bribery and corruption of the learned (the *fili* as genealogist, not only the *fili* as court poet, evidently had his price). These were ways 'of special note'; we may be sure that Gilla in Chomded had more humdrum means of genealogical error in mind.

Genealogy, we have seen, could have a propagandist function. Propaganda is no modern invention. Encapsulated in verse (particularly in praise-poems), in heroic tales, and in the less literary genealogical records, royal or dynastic propaganda could be broadcast via the learned classes whose responsibility it was to maintain 'knowledge' of this type. Genealogy allowed the ruling dynasties to present the past (and, by implication, the future) in terms of their own history;[64] such total exclusion of other lines was a powerful propaganda weapon.

The ideologies propounded by genealogical texts do not merely relate to political propaganda. Learned elements, such as the toponymic, must also be noted: for

---

[62] Byrne 1971: 146–50 studies the difficulties of the tricks of the early Irish genealogists, and discusses their ability to alter genealogical relationships to suit changing politics.

[63] Byrne 1971: 146. The text was unearthed by Mac Neill 1911: 93. It is printed by Best & O'Brien 1957: 574–87 from LL 143a39–145a; this is the only copy of this verse sketch of universal history, *A Rí ríchid réidig dam*. For the relevant passage, see p. 579, lines 17903–14.

[64] I owe this formulation of the point to Eric John; cf. also Henige 1971: 380.

example, there survive groups of Irish pedigrees which seek to establish relationships between geographically proximate groups who have no political or biological connexion, or between peoples who live in widely separated locations but happen to enjoy the same names.[65]

The genealogy is therefore able to be a legal title, a political weapon, and an expression of learning. To what extent was it a necessary means of establishing a person's identity? In other words, to what depth was an accurate knowledge of ancestry essential? Any answer to this question must embrace two approaches. First, there is the direct evidence of the use of means of identification, and here the simple patronymic generally seems sufficient (though cases of 'Z son of Y son of X' or 'Z grandson of X' are sufficiently numerous in the early medieval British Isles to warrant special mention). Secondly, there is the question of legal liability arising from membership of a kindred-group within a certain number of generations. This still requires a great deal more investigation, but its principal relevance to our subject of kingship is in questions of succession, and these are tied up with the political considerations we have already noticed. In the Germanic, Brittonic, *and* Gaelic parts of the British Isles, membership of the relevant royal dynasty seems to have been the appropriate requirement for succession to the throne, at least up to the tenth century. While in theory that might involve knowledge of an inordinate number of generations of genealogy, in practice the immediate family surroundings would be sufficient to provide an awareness of such membership and the rest could be left to the skills of the professional genealogist.[66]

We have seen some of the manipulative and systematic techniques which may be employed in the written transmission of royal pedigrees, and we shall see more. In the consideration of any pedigree, however, we must ask whether we are dealing with a text which has at any stage enjoyed a period of oral transmission. The question is particularly acute for the Irish records. Large collections of Irish genealogies are extant in manuscripts of the twelfth century and later. They have undoubtedly had written ancestors, probably going back *at least* to the eighth century. There is evidence also of successive revisions of the corpus, with a view to updating.[67] Yet we know genealogy to have been an orally cultivated profession throughout the Gaelic middle ages. The problem which afflicts the whole study of early Irish literature — that of the varying relationships between the oral and the written — is relevant to our present concern, for the genealogies sit on the border between that which constitutes documentary record and that which is essentially part of the oral culture.

---

[65] Ó Corráin 1971: 27 n. 18; Mac Neill 1911: 62; Byrne 1971: 142—3 on Ireland. cf. Bohannan 1952: 310, 'In Tiv doctrine lineage ties and territorial distribution should be compatible', and Peters 1960: 30—1.

[66] One might note here the poem in which the sixteenth-century poet Tadhg Dall Ó Huiginn tells his patron that he will, *inter alia*, give him knowledge of the 'genealogical branches' of his ancestors — Williams 1971: 4.

[67] Kelleher 1968: 151, 152.

If we should accept, for Anglo-Saxon England, that the pre-Christian parts of the pedigrees back to the dynastic founder (*viz*, for Kent, from Æthilberht back to Oisc or Hencgest; for Wessex, from Cynigils and his generation back to Cynric or Cerdic; and so on) have any claim on our attention as records of those two protohistoric centuries, we must conclude that they were orally cultivated (though not necessarily, of course, as they stand at present) in the seventh century. Nor is it impossible that parts of the further reaches of some pedigrees originated (perhaps in the seventh or eighth century) in an oral rather than a written context, or even that — having been created in a written document — they gained subsequent oral currency, later re-entering or (more likely) influencing the written transmission.

All these possibilities must lead us to consider the role of pedigrees in pre-literate societies, and in non-literate contexts within societies in which writing is practised by one element of the population. In the last few decades, social anthropologists have made great advances in the study of the place of genealogy in such societies, especially in contemporary Africa and Polynesia. Understanding of the varying treatments and relevance of genealogy in different social structures has helped historians of these cultures, as well as anthropologists, to a juster assessment of the evidential value of orally cultivated pedigrees (and regnal lists). This had led, in turn, to new attempts to examine the role which other orally transmitted information might be able to play in writing the history of pre-literate societies.[68] It seems to me that students of early medieval European history and literature cannot afford to neglect these developments which have a direct bearing on some of their primary concerns. Plainly, it is impossible to review and adapt the whole subject in this paper, but some main points are of immediate relevance.

It is now common ground for social anthropologists that pre-literate peoples only preserve versions of their history which explain current social groupings and institutions, and that these versions may bear little relation to an historical sequence of events.[69] In other words, their oral tradition constitutes both a validation of existing social relationships and a mnemonic device for their transmission and explanation. This applies with particular force to genealogies. Anthropologists have come to speak of this scheme as a 'charter'.[70]

The essential corollary of such a system is that changes in the social and political structure will necessitate changes in the genealogical expression of that system.[71] Since genealogies do not merely express present relationships but also validate them, it is essential that they change.[72] Many tribal societies will have a social dynamic which ensures that certain changes are inherent in the social structure; in other

---

[68] On this see, for example, Vansina 1965. An excellent article, clear and wide-ranging, which is likely to become a classic, is Henige 1971.
[69] Richards 1960: 177.
[70] Bohannan 1952: 315; Lewis 1962: 35.
[71] Bohannan 1952: 311.
[72] Bohannan 1952: 312.

words, viewed from the present, there will be periods of the past, interrupted no doubt by historical accidents, in which typical social processes are merely repeated.[73] Lineages will grow and divide; rulers will succeed each other. These regular changes will necessitate equally regular restructuring of the pedigrees. But the basic identity of a series of such events can also allow a degree of foreshortening in the record,[74] a manipulative technique to which we shall return below.

The criteria of validity of genealogies in a pre-literate society are therefore almost certain to be far removed from what the modern historian is likely to require as a record of the past. The criteria will be social relationships between the groups or the persons referenced in the genealogies. As one anthropologist has put it: 'Genealogies validate present relationships; these relationships prove the genealogies; and the form of the genealogy is modelled on the form of present relationships'.[75]

The form of a genealogy is also important. Its main line(s) may run for a dozen generations or even extend to thirty or more. Part, at least, is likely to be rigid: that which expresses the ultimate unity of a tribe is likely to be fixed; and those immediate relationships in the present or very recent past which are well known are unlikely to be immediately manipulable. Given the need for continual alteration, however, there must be within a genealogy an area of ambiguity where adjustments are made.[76]

Various types of adjustment will require to be made. Strangers who come to be associated with the tribe will need to be grafted on to the genealogies; conversely, lineage segments which go their own way may require to be detached.[77] The rise of new lineages by the division of older ones will require a restructuring of the genealogy to provide a suitable place for a new ancestor and eponym. In some cultures the waxing and waning of the numerical strength of lineages is reflected in the length of the genealogical span allotted to them.[78]

At the remotest extremity of the genealogy, further additions — sometimes of very many names — may sometimes be made. In this way genealogical expression might be given, for example, to trading connexions of long standing or, more commonly, to the religious beliefs of the owners of the genealogy.[79] Nor, of course, must one omit — in societies where long patrilines are handed down (either orally or in writing) — the effects of a desire to appear superior through possession or knowledge of a notably lengthy pedigree.[80]

---

[73] Bohannan 1952: 311.
[74] Richards 1960: 178.
[75] Bohannan 1952: 312.
[76] Peters 1960: 41.
[77] Peters 1960: 41–2.
[78] Lewis 1962: 42.
[79] Lewis 1962: 44–6.
[80] Cf. the example quoted, from a written context, by Henige 1971: 376.

All this simply allows one to endorse the maxim that 'tribal genealogies are true only in the sense that a parable is true'.[81] However, in any pre-literate culture, one can expect there to be a period — however short — which anthropologists have come to call 'historical time', a span of years within which real events are remembered and for which historically accurate genealogical information is available.[82] The length of this period will nonetheless vary according to the structure, interests, and environment of the society in question; it can only hope to be determined with the aid of a study of the social structure. At least where royal or chiefly genealogies are concerned, one may expect to find for the historical period a fairly complex genealogy with collateral pedigrees; that part, however, which has been transmitted for a long time by oral tradition down to the point of record will have resolved itself into a long series of simple father-to-son successions. This pattern is stereotypical.[83] In other societies, only that extent (perhaps four or five generations) which is essential to the smooth running of the social structure will be remembered, while more distant ancestors (who may even be worshipped) are not recalled in the context of exact genealogical relationships.

Given a view of a timeless past in which known social processes produce an identical recurring pattern of historical events, the conditions of ideological history are met.[84] In these circumstances genealogies may well be telescoped, often very drastically: fifteen generations might be reduced to six, or a whole epoch into one generation or into the reign of a single ruler.[85] This last process may also occur with reference to the period of the foundation of a dynasty or a nation: the first, or the greatest, of the founding rulers comes to stand for the whole founding era. The point that greatness is a non-numerical quantity is seen not to be taken, especially in cases where the one representative king is assigned an abnormally long period of rule.

Other aspects of this genealogical elision may be related to the means of growth of tribal or dynastic lineages. Lineages will grow by the successful procreation, survival, and development of a number of new lines at each generation. Given the random nature of these developments, some lineages will suffer a decrease in size relative to the more successful groups on account of high mortality or infertility. The relative strengths may be genealogically represented by longer and shorter pedigrees. Where there is no significant point of branching in the pedigree, a name is likely to drop out of the record and be forgotten. This can lead to two or more lineages claiming descent from the same ancestor by widely differing numbers of generations.[86]

This 'structural amnesia'[87] is common in genealogies.[88] But in different societies

[81] Lewis 1962: 36.
[82] Richards 1960: 178.
[83] Henige 1971: 379.
[84] Richards 1960: 178.
[85] Henige 1971: 375; cf. Boston 1969.
[86] Lewis 1962: 42.
[87] Boston 1969: 41.
[88] Lewis 1962: 42 and the references cited there.

the foreshortening takes place in different parts of the genealogy. It may occur in the more recent portions, just beyond those who have recently lived;[89] it may take place in the central or upper portion of a genealogy from which segments branch, especially in cases of politically insignificant or numerically small lineages;[90] it is unlikely, on the whole, to take place in the highest reaches of the genealogy which often constitute its most rigid part.

In fine, there is a need for a method, or methods, of manipulation which will allow the genealogy to remain constant in length and of fixed form despite the dynamic content provided by the historical developments inherent in the social structure.[91] The mechanics of this process are intimately connected with that of the transmission of genealogical information from one generation to the next.[92] Direct teaching is rare in pre-literate societies, and professional learned classes are even less common. Much will therefore depend on whoever is the 'owner' of a genealogy. If transmission is not an official function, the most prosaic cause of error may well operate — faulty collective memory.[93] The context of the transmission of genealogies is also important: if, in a chiefly society, it travels with a regnal list, its history may be different from that of a genealogy whose primary context is a tribal origin-legend. We may expect these materials to interact.

All these considerations suggest two main conclusions. Different parts of any given genealogy, orally cultivated, will have a different social function and therefore, ultimately, a different historical worth. As I. M. Lewis has put it, 'even in the same society a particular type of oral tradition — in this case the genealogy — does not necessarily have a uniform social function or a uniform historical validity'.[94] Secondly, the methods by which a genealogy can be altered, and the (by no means frivolous)[95] reasons for which manipulation is necessary, will vary considerably according to the social conditions obtaining within different cultures. Certain manipulative patterns will recur, but we cannot fully understand the motivation behind the mechanics if we do not study the structure of the society with whose genealogies we are concerned.

The concentration of earlier generations of students of early medieval European history and literature on the question of the period, counted in generations, over which information could be accurately transmitted by word of mouth now seems somewhat misplaced. Universals of this sort are probably not to be found; and without the aid of modern social anthropology the complex of factors discussed in the last few pages would not have been available. What is apparent is that, without the minutest examination, acceptance of any genealogical record is extremely rash.

[89] Peters 1960: 36–8, 32–4.
[90] Lewis 1962: 42–3.
[91] Peters 1960: 32.
[92] Richards 1960: 180.
[93] Henige 1971: 375.
[94] Lewis 1962: 47.
[95] Richards 1960: 178–9.

Given the range of manipulative possibilities, whether in a literate or in an oral culture, it is unlikely that we can place much faith in such records as statements of biological fact even for a few generations above the first historically attested character (such as Æthilberht in Kent), much less above the first character presented by historical sources (Hencgest, in the case of Kent).

A surviving early medieval pedigree, like any other, is as good only as the contexts to which it belongs. In addition to the social context, we must look at its physical situation. If it is found in a manuscript, we need to know not only the age of its manuscript but also its reason for being there, and the antecedent history of both manuscript and pedigree. This will necessitate a close look at any collection of which it is a part. Otherwise we risk asking the wrong questions of the pedigree. A written pedigree in a book of a given date does not necessarily tell us anything of the pedigrees orally cultivated at that date, either at the place of record or elsewhere.[96] A genealogy may have a prehistory; it will almost certainly have an afterlife, either oral or written or both. All these stages need to be clearly distinguished.

In addition to context, the form of a genealogy is important.[97] It may be couched in ascending or descending form. The ascending, or retrograde, pedigree was the normal form among the peoples of the early medieval British Isles. Occasionally, however, in a Latin context, one finds the formula 'A genuit B, B genuit C' etc., which derives from the biblical 'begat' model: one can perhaps draw a conclusion from this reversal of the usual (vernacular) order. A genealogy may comprise the usual patriline or it may contain an element of matrilinear descent. It may or may not show collateral branches from the main, trunk, stem. It may well be part of a collection of pedigrees, or even a collection of collections.

An individual pedigree will by definition extend back to an ancestor. That ancestor may be near or remote; in trunk-lines in a collection he will almost invariably be remote. He may be a figure either of myth or of legend; he may, alternatively or additionally, be an eponym, real or fictitious. With a single line, little headway can be made with form-criticism. When faced with a group of pedigrees, however, one can expect to detect any formal systematics which may be involved.

Let us return to the Anglian collection. Sisam observed,[98] a quarter-century ago, that all the trunk-lines were of much the same length. He concluded that there was a recognised length for a pedigree of some fourteen names, including the ultimate ancestor. But this is not a notably useful conclusion, taken by itself. Although there is formal symmetry, the lines end (or begin, depending on one's vantage point) at varying points over a century and a half. In other words, Æthelberht II of Kent (725x762) appears in the same genealogical position as Edwin of Deira (616–32). If the lines are set out in a table, some discrepancies are also visible in the form. The Bernician line has one name too many, and this may result from scribal error (or, of

---

[96] I agree with Miller 1975b: 255.

[97] As stressed above, p. 86, where other aspects of form are considered.

[98] Sisam 1953: 326–8.

course, from some design) near the head of the genealogy. The Lindsey line presents special problems. It appears to be three generations shorter than the rest, but finishes more than half a century later than them. Only the latest of these kings, Aldfrith himself, has been identified.[99] There is no assurance that the line belonged to the collection earlier than 796.[100] Its length is more than made up in the extant text by having the 'ancestors' of Woden added to this line, when properly they belong with the whole collection. How this arose (whether by chance or design is another question) may be seen from the arrangement in the oldest surviving manuscript (British Library MS. Cotton Vespasian B. 6), where the lines are set out in parallel across a double page. The recent extension of the pedigree from Frealaf back to Geot would then have sat at the bottom of the page, beneath the whole collection, and belonging to all the lines. A subsequent copyist or reviser will then have incorporated the names either into the shortest line for the sake of symmetry or into the line beneath which this extension sat on the page. The short Lindsey pedigree (ten names from Aldfrith to Winta) may have been that cultivated by or for Aldfrith himself, in which case it may simply have been joined to the collection without extra padding; alternatively, some names may have dropped (or have been dropped) when those from Frealaf to Geot became connected exclusively with the Lindsey line. The appearance as a pair of the famous names Biscop and Beda in positions which would place them in the years surrounding 700 may or may not be a cause for suspicion; on the other hand, the Celtic *Cædbæd*, here allegedly of the first half of the seventh century, might be felt to carry some conviction. We may note the alliterative regularity: Winta, at the head, alliterates with Woden; then three names alliterate on C-, another three on B-, and the last group vowel-alliterates. Here is a very neat regularity, which invites further suspicion. We see the same in the pre- and proto-historic sections of other pedigrees. Without external checks, however, we can only harbour suspicions that this is not, in our sense, an historical record of a royal line.

For all the other lines, we can establish a point at which apparently historical sources first bring the dynasty to Britain: for Kent, this historical horizon occurs with Hencgest, according to Bede and the Anglo-Saxon Chronicle; for Deira, with Soemil of whom the *Historia Brittonum* says 'Ipse primus separauit Deur o Birneich'; for Bernicia, with Oesa of whom it is said by a chronicle-fragment (deriving from Bede and composed before *ca* 850) that 'Iste Oessa primus uenit in Brittanniam';[101] for Wessex, with Cerdic, according to the Anglo-Saxon Chronicle and the West Saxon 'genealogical regnal list'; for Mercia, with Icil, according to Felix's Life of Saint Guthlac;[102] and for East Anglia, with Wehha of whom the *Historia Brittonum* says 'ipse primus regnauit in Brittannia super gentem Estranglorum'.

In the lines of Bernicia, Wessex, and East Anglia, more detailed genealogical

---

[99] Stenton 1970: 129–31, reprinting a discussion of 1927.

[100] This is absent from the *Historia Brittonum*, though that may be due to a mechanical fault; there are no extant witnesses to an earlier form of the collection as a whole.

[101] Edited by Dumville 1973a.

[102] See Colgrave 1956: 75, 176–7.

information begins two generations below these names; in Deira and Mercia the fuller collateral information begins four generations below the historical horizon.[103]

Yet where we know the dynastic name — Oiscingas in Kent, Wuffingas in East Anglia (for both of which Bede is our source), and Iclingas in Mercia (according to the Old English Prose Life of Guthlac)[104] — it is by no means always derived from the alleged first ruler in Britain.[105] The Kentish dynasts are not *Hencgestingas, nor the East Anglian *Wehhingas. We do not know if the Northumbrian dynasties were called *Soemlingas and *Oesingas; in eighth-century Northumbria Ida, as the first recorded and dated king, seems to have been regarded as the crucial dynastic ancestor. In Wessex, however, at least in the ninth century, Cerdic was plainly seen as *the* ancestral dynast (though lines go back to him *via* Cynric, two generations later).

What are the implications of all this for the historicity of the pedigrees and therefore for our view of early Anglo-Saxon kingship? There are reasons for suspicion about the names above that of the dynastic founder in almost every line: it is here that borrowings from heroic legend (as in the Mercian pedigree) or from another genealogy (as in the West Saxon line) are apparent, and here that the text-tradition is most unstable. If, on the other hand, we approach the pedigrees from the historical end, we shall find few discrepancies or difficulties, even in comparison with early external sources. But inevitably there comes a superior limit of immediate credibility, and in each case this is somewhere in the second half of the sixth century. It is interesting that it should be here, for that tallies in respect of potentially reliable record with the situation as far as Welsh and Irish records are concerned. We may care to remember the devastating plague of the late 540s. We may also care to consider that this might represent the limit of normal human memory at the time of the English conversion to christianity in the first half of the seventh century. As in Ireland and the Brittonic world, fragments of information about the century 450 to 550 will remain, but they will be disjointed and perhaps contradictory. We must accordingly be the more suspicious of any assertions about the century preceding *ca* 550x575. Back to this point the genealogical history of the Anglo-Saxon heptarchic dynasties depends on Christian recording in the seventh century. What of the further stages?

If we accept the pedigrees as they stand, in the section between the point (generally in the seventh century) where external evidence can be brought to bear

---

[103] Kent presents special problems. If we count from Hencgest, there are three generations (owing to a chance reference by Bede, we know of a sister of Æthilberht); if from Oisc, one or two generations, depending on whether he is made son or grandson of Hencgest. If we ignore Ricula, Eormenric's daughter, and use evidence comparable to that available for other kingdoms, then there is a depth of five generations from Hencgest and three or four from Oisc.

[104] Edited by Gonser 1909; cf. Colgrave 1956: 176–7.

[105] The Ravenna Geographer (V.31) wrote that Britain was inhabited by 'the nation of the Saxons which came long ago from Old Saxony with their chief, Ansehis by name': Chadwick 1907: 47. This is taken to refer to the invasion of Kent, and, with an emendation of *Ansehis* to *Anschis*, an old form of Oisc is produced. A rival emendation produces the name of Hencgest. Against Sisam 1953: 325 n. 1, I feel that Chadwick's view does less violence to the text.

and the historical horizon, some striking points on dating emerge.[106] It has been common ground that the origins of the West Saxon dynasty of the early middle ages must be placed much later than the evidence provided by archaeology for the major English settlements in Wessex. Cynric, who stands at the head of the branching lines, should have enjoyed a floruit in the second quarter of the sixth century (the Anglo-Saxon Chronicle, we may note, places the creation of the kingdom *s.a.* 519), while Cerdic — if seen as his grandfather[107] — would have flourished in the last third of the fifth century. What is perhaps not so well recognised is that the conclusion applies with increasing force to Mercia and to East Anglia. If the Mercian pedigree back to Icil is correctly preserved, he should have died in the first quarter of the sixth century; the early location of his dynasty is of course problematic, but he can hardly represent the first generation of immigrants into midland England. In East Anglia, the tension is most acute: if we take Wehha as the first king, we have to do with a ruler whose death occurred in the last third of the sixth century; but if we calculate from the dynastic eponym, Wuffa, then the dynasty begins with a king whose most most likely floruit is the last quarter of the sixth century.[108] Yet this is an area of primary migration and settlement. If these genealogies represent sixth-century facts, we must accept at least one of two conclusions: that the dynasties of the early Christian period could not recall any names in their pedigree earlier than Wehha, Icil, etc., and therefore concluded (or allowed it to be concluded) that these were the first who reigned in the new land; secondly, that these dynasties came to power only at a comparatively late date, for example when immigration had completely ceased and relatively unchecked internal movement (such, perhaps, as give rise to those place-names — studied by Ekwall and Copley[109] — which indicate the settlement of East Saxons far from Essex, Angles deep in Saxon territory, and so on) had largely abated. This would mean that, in the fifth century and part of the sixth, many areas would have been controlled either by dynasties crushed by those which survive into the historic period or by intensely local rulers who came under the sway of the leading dynasties by the end of the sixth century or even (as a final possibility) by communities of classical 'Germanic free peasants'! Whichever of these options we adopt, a necessary corollary would seem to be that men such as Wuffa and Icil had made themselves kings, and had established their dynasties, not by virtue of ancient royal descent (as eighth-century writers — and, we may suspect, kings like Offa —

---

[106] Here, as elsewhere in this paper, I have used a generation-average, for the purposes of calculation back from externally attested dates, of 27.5 years. This is at once a convenient middle-point between the rival schemes of 25 and 30 years per generation, and is that argued for by the demographer J. A. Newth, in Miller 1970.

[107] With the Anglian collection, rather than with the Anglo-Saxon Chronicle which makes Cynric Cerdic's son.

[108] We may compare the dates given by the thirteenth-century St Albans chronicler Roger of Wendover for Wuffa (571—8) and his son Tyttla (from 578): Plummer 1896: II.106—7. Roger may, of course, have made the same calculations as I have done, but in some other contexts he uses earlier sources not available to us.

[109] Ekwall 1936; Ekwall 1953, esp. p.138; Copley 1951—3 and 1954/5.

would have us believe)[110] but by their own accumulation of power and influence in the closing years of the migration period.

The Mercian pedigree above Icil, which is a roll-call of legendary heroic names, is hardly to be taken seriously as a biological statement. We have seen how related names were imported into the upper reaches of the West Saxon pedigree in the eighth century.[111] Whether the names of Eamer, Offa, Wærmund, and Wihtlæg were in the Mercian pedigree before the time of the eighth-century Offa is a moot point: it has frequently been asserted that Offa's actions were inspired by those attributed to his ancestral namesake, a view which rests ultimately on acceptance of the pedigree (or, at least, on a belief in Offa's acceptance of it). Offa's powerful predecessors may have chosen to incorporate these names, which would have provided sufficient motivation for his parents to name him thus; on the other hand he may have been named after a legendary hero, and have subsequently arranged to have the legendary Offa and his relatives translated into his pedigree. At all events, we cannot afford to draw such conclusions about royal motives without an appreciation of the full range of possibilities provided by the pedigree-evidence.

Let us look very briefly at a continental pedigree which we know to have been manufactured, that produced by Cassiodorus for Theodoric, Ostrogothic king of Italy in the early sixth century, or for his grandson Athalaric.[112] We are ignorant as to Theodoric's real ancestry, but we can conjecture from the evidence of Cassiodorus's other writings and our knowledge of his milieu as to his motives and intentions. We may believe that he sought to convince the Romans of Italy of Theodoric's hereditary right to rule as a king. According to Professor Wallace-Hadrill it was 'the devouring interest of the great Roman houses in all that pertained to genealogy' which led to Cassiodorus's attempt to make Theodoric respectable to them;[113] Wallace-Hadrill summarises Cassiodorus's propaganda view of Theodoric as 'a ruler of Romans, devout in the service of *Romanitas*'.[114] The claims of Theodoric's own family to an hereditary right to the throne did not go back even a century, but Cassiodorus's genealogy asserts that for seventeen named generations, from Athalaric back to Gapt, the family had produced kings, and an attempt was made to associate them with the greatest name in Gothic history, that of Ermanaric.

---

[110] Cf. the remarks above, p. 83, on propaganda.

[111] Above, p. 81.

[112] It is preserved in the abridgment of Cassiodorus's Gothic History by Jordanes, *De origine actibusque Getarum*, §§ XIII—XIV: Theodor Mommsen (ed.), *MGH, Auctores Antiquissimi*, V/1 (Berlin, 1882); for a translation see Mierow 1915.

[113] Wallace-Hadrill 1967: 35. There are other romanising tendencies observable in genealogies from other contexts. For fabricated ninth-century Carolingian genealogy (from Metz) which made Arnulf the grandson of a Roman senator, see Kienast 1968: 55 (who suggests that the political motivation was to gain the indulgence of the contemporary Aquitanian magnates) and Oexle 1967: 252—79. Note also the appearance of *Caser* (apparently Latin *Caesar*), as a son of Woden, at the head of the East Anglian pedigree in the Anglian collection; there the motivation is not clear.

[114] Wallace-Hadrill 1971: 9; cf. the remarks of Patrick Wormald (pp. 125f below) about the function of the barbarian lawgiver in this same propagandist scheme.

I shall not go into all the details, for these have been well studied, but the upshot is that scholars have been unwilling to accept it either as a biological statement or as a king-list; we have, in part at least, the names of miscellaneous kings moulded into genealogical form. I wonder if this is not what we see, too, in the fifth-to-sixth-century section of the Kentish pedigree, where an extreme instability in the textual transmission accompanies a dark lacuna in the Anglo-Saxon Chronicle record and the shift in archaeological culture from a Scandinavian-oriented to a Frankish-leaning province.

For another example of an early continental Germanic genealogy, we may look at that incorporated into the prologue of the Edict of Rothari, the code of Lombard laws issued in A.D. 643.[115] At the very end of the prologue the genealogy (for twelve inclusive generations) of Rothari himself is given; it is a simple retrograde patriline, and appears to include no previous kings. The preceding king-list, which names seventeen kings including Rothari (of whom the eleventh led the Lombards into Italy in 568), can hardly extend back beyond the fourth century if taken as a consecutive record. It contains some scattered genealogical information as well, which seems to tell us that, over the three centuries which the king-list may span, some seven to nine families were represented among the kings. One family, represented by Leth (the third ruler) and his descendants, held the kingship for six consecutive generations, we are told. Otherwise, two generations was not exceeded. The genealogy of Rothari's non-royal ancestors, if well-founded, would place the birth of the earliest, Obthora, *ca* A.D. 300. There is thus an apparent agreement between two bodies of Lombard record, brought together in writing in 643 but probably separately transmitted to that point, as to the upper limit of Lombard history. Further investigation of Rothari's information must depend on the use of sources external to his Edict. His wording, however, does not suggest that a regnal list was actively cultivated at the Lombard court: repeated changes of dynasty were perhaps scarcely conducive to that. He writes,[116] 'In these matters our concern for the future assures us that what we do here is useful, and so we have ordered to be noted down here the names of the Lombard kings, our predecessors, and from what family they came, insofar as we have ascertained them from the older men of the nation'. Here, presumably in unofficial oral transmission, lie many possibilities of error.[117] Rothari's own pedigree, on the other hand, was family property, a status which gave it different conditions of transmission and different chances for error or manipulation.

Pedigrees may be manipulated: they may be manipulated into a particular form; they may be manipulated for political reasons. But manipulation is rarely perfectly achieved, and the contradictions or inconsistencies which result give us the opportunity to prise open the holes in the scheme. As Professor John Kelleher has

---

[115] For details of edition and translation, see n. 15 above.
[116] As translated by Drew 1973: 39–40, with one change of word-order.
[117] Cf. Henige 1971: 375.

put it,[118] 'we may take it as an axiom of historiography that in source-materials of this age and kind a good, glaring contradiction is worth a square yard of smooth, question-begging consistency'.[119]

Genealogies might be invented and manipulated; they might also be suppressed. Large collections, such as the Irish, which were a guide to the structure of the contemporary polity, would need to be updated; at that moment, some lines would for varying reasons be excised. In that corpus, Kelleher has noted that there are stratum lines mostly from three to five generations apart, which are indications of attempts at updating. As he says, 'all sorts of intriguing questions are raised by this, not the least being who the genealogists were and how they cooperated'.[120]

In Ireland, there was a decline in the fashion of genealogy-writing from the late eighth century.[121] The same is true of Anglo-Saxon England within the next century. Genealogical materials of the eleventh and twelfth centuries are in both countries very poor in quality, and are collected with antiquarian intentions.[122] Only in Wales — within the British Isles — did the practice continue unabated. But in England in the ninth century a great deal of energy was devoted to the backward extension of the royal genealogies, principally that of the West Saxons as their dynasty was now the most powerful among the English.[123] The incorporation of a wild profusion of legendary and mythical figures, back to Scyld Scefing, followed by a biblical pedigree back to Adam, was intended first to establish for the dynasty a commanding position within the world of Germanic heroic legend, and then to anchor it firmly in universal history and a Christian context.

To whom were genealogies proper? In early Anglo-Saxon England, the answer seems clear: only to segments of the ruling dynasties. At least, that is whose pedigrees were committed to writing. In Wales, matters started that way: only royal pedigrees were committed to writing at an early date; but we need not doubt that others were orally cultivated, and innumerable pedigrees in manuscripts of late medieval and early modern date trace the ancestry of high-born families back to the tenth century. In Ireland, however, pedigrees of thousands of family-lines were committed to writing already in the early eighth century,[124] and some earlier no doubt; many aristocratic families were discard segments of royal dynasties,[125] and with so many kingdoms there were very many segments and even more discards;

---

[118] Kelleher 1968: 142.

[119] We may note also a distinguished anthropologist's opinion that it is the existence of an inconsistency in the record which very often leads to an attempt to manipulate or harmonise; this is not done frivolously — Richards 1960: 178–9. Kelleher 1968: 142 also notes the existence, a millenium ago, of problems never solved by the compilers of the corpus of Irish genealogies.

[120] Kelleher 1968: 151; cf. 152.

[121] Ó Corráin 1974: 64–5.

[122] For Ireland, see Ó Corráin, *ibid.*; Byrne 1971: 155–6, 165; Kelleher 1968: 147.

[123] The classic study is Sisam 1953.

[124] Byrne 1971: 153–5.

[125] Headmen of vassal peoples were also often treated by the genealogists as remote discards of the ruling house: Ó Corráin 1971: 32.

many other lines are shown by the genealogies often to have no interlinking blood-ties whatever.[126] I have, of course, begged the question of what constitutes a king. That has been the subject of another paper, above. But in Ireland at least, in the Celtic world, there is a strong suspicion of a pagan religious background, with early lines claiming descent from a tribal deity, often a goddess.[127] The Germanic evidence on that point is ambiguous: the Woden and Seaxnet of the Anglo-Saxon genealogies, not to mention the Geat who is said also to be a god, may suggest some belief at some stage in a sacral monarchy. The Ostrogothic Amals are also possibly candidates for this role, as *semidei* (according to Jordanes)[128] and descendants of the racial eponym Gapt (or Gaut, the *Geat* of the English) whom Jordanes calls a 'hero'. There is no sign that whoever reduced genealogies to writing in the early medieval Germanic world saw fit to record non-royal pedigrees:[129] may we therefore safely deny their cultivation?

If the cultivation of genealogy was a feature of Germanic kingship in the early middle ages — and, given the available witnesses, this seems a reasonable statement — there is nonetheless a lack of evidence for the antiquity of this practice. For all that we may, *a priori*, believe to the contrary, we seem to lack convincing evidence that prehistoric Germanic society was pedigree-conscious. (Quite the reverse was the case in the Celtic world.) If the suspicion be just, then we must look to the Church as the cultivator of Germanic royal pedigrees. We may relate this to the intense concern shown by the established early medieval western Church for aristocratic descent and breeding. Within the English context, we may note as relevant the accumulating evidence for the dynastic affiliations of religious houses.[130] Behind the Church's view of genealogy, apart from biblical precedents[131] we may see Roman practice.

THE KING-LIST

The regnal list, or king-list, is related to the genealogy, but is nonetheless distinct. Those familiar only with one or the other might confuse them.[132] In Wales, for

---

[126] Binchy 1970: 7—8.

[127] Mac Neill 1911: 64, 83 (but cf. 80—1).

[128] *Loc. cit. supra*, n. 112.

[129] I exclude Scandinavia from consideration here. The genealogies recorded in the Icelandic *Landnámabók*, particularly of the *góðar*, are usually taken to be non-royal; however, as Peter Sawyer points out to me, there may be reason to dispute this and to view the *goði's* power and land *(goðorð)* as, in effect, a petty kingdom. As this is hardly the place to begin such a far-reaching discussion, I leave the matter there.

[130] The numerous works of B. Colgrave, N. K. Chadwick, D. P. Kirby, and P. Hunter Blair have all contributed to this understanding.

[131] See, for example, Genesis V and Luke III. 23—38. But note also the sentiments of I Timothy I.4, 'Neither give heed to fables and endless genealogies, which beget controversies'. Matthew XXIII. 9 — 'Call no man your father upon the earth: for one is your Father, which is in Heaven' — seems also to have had some effect on genealogy: in the Christian Roman world, unlike the Celtic, one did not record on a memorial inscription the filiation of the dead person; Nash-Williams 1950: 6.

[132] cf. Sisam 1953: 294—5 for another reason for confusion. Confusion persists into modern times: Wallace-Hadrill 1971: 33, 34, 45 is an example; Boston 1969: 40—1 also seems to make this mistake. cf. Henige 1971: 379 n. 39.

example, regnal lists were not cultivated; an early genealogist faced with a list of Roman emperors converted it into a patrilinear pedigree.[133] We shall examine below the interaction of the two forms.

The king-list will normally present a simple list of kings with an indication of the number of years each reigned; in some contexts, only the names are found. It too is of course perfectly open to manipulation,[134] though in a smaller variety of ways than a genealogy. It will also face technical problems: it will have difficulty in dealing with more than one king ruling at the same time and with interregna. Multiple kingship was not uncommon in a number of Anglo-Saxon heptarchic kingdoms but, unfortunately, no detailed regnal list for these kingdoms has survived, though East Saxon and Kentish lists were available to Bede.[135] Kenneth Harrison has discussed interregna with reference to the Northumbrian situation,[136] where it is apparent that the period of the interregnum was not counted in any king's reign; in a regnal list kept under those conditions, there will accordingly be cumulative error. In short, as Professor Kelleher has said, 'there is no such thing as a non-defective regnal list'.[137]

Its principal purpose, however, would seem to be purely chronological.[138] Although we find it in many manuscript contexts — historical, legal (here, as Patrick Wormald points out, clearly associating kings with legislation), and computistical —, the last is its natural and most common milieu.[139] We may be certain that it has its origin, in Anglo-Saxon England at least, in pagan times. Kenneth Harrison has recently examined the evidence for the primitive Anglo-Saxon calendar[140] and has concluded that 'it was able to have furnished a reliable sequence of years, running from midwinter to midwinter'. One may recall, too, the passage from Bede (*Hist. Eccl.*, III. 1)[141] about how those whose job it was to keep regnal lists decided to exclude the apostate successors of Edwin from their reckonings. There is no overt suggestion that these people were clerics, but they were clearly open to clerical persuasion. If we may envisage the existence of such people attached to royal courts in pagan England, we shall appreciate the *possibility* of the existence of an accurate record. However, we must balance against this not merely the obvious risk of faulty

---

[133] Bartrum 1966: 11 (HG § 16).

[134] cf. Richards 1960: 182 for a variety of regnal lists within one kingdom.

[135] cf. Henige 1971: 377–8 for examples of the results in other cultures. He notes (p. 380) the attractiveness, from a propaganda point of view, of the concept of a single ruler from each generation.

[136] cf. Harrison 1976b: 80–95. The point is developed by M. Miller, 'The dates of Deira' (forthcoming).

[137] Kelleher 1968: 149.

[138] Though aspects such as the ritual (in ancestor-worship) or ideological (as constituting a 'charter' of society) should not be overlooked. On these two aspects see, respectively, Richards 1960: 188 (cf. 182) and Boston 1969: 41.

[139] We may note that the first identifiable written examples in England and in Pictland belong to the period of the paschal controversy, which greatly stimulated computistical activity. On the Pictish texts, see three forthcoming articles by M. Miller: 'Matriliny by treaty: the Pictish foundation-legend'; 'The disputed historical horizon of the Pictish king-lists'; 'The later Pictish kings'.

[140] Harrison 1973.

[141] See above, p. 81.

transmission, but also the possibility of deliberate intervention for ideological reasons — as in the case reported by Bede — which will effectively deprive us of basic knowledge by offering a falsehood or half-truth.

If a society has developed, or is prepared to acknowledge, the concept of 'usurpation' of the throne, another reason for the distortion of a regnal list becomes apparent. We may illustrate this from eighth-century Mercia. After the killing of King Æthilbald by his household in 756 or 757, there was civil war in Mercia. A Latin marginale of the early ninth century in a Mercian manuscript[142] briefly records the course of events:[143] 'Anno dominicae incarnationis .dcclvi. Æðilbald rex occisus. Eodem anno Offa rex Beornredum *tyrannum* bello superauit et regnum tenuit Merciorum.' This view of Beornred as a usurper *(tyrannus)* is reflected in the extant copies of the Mercian regnal list which omit him, even though other brief reigns are included. Nothing is known of Beornred's pedigree, though there is room for a suspicion that ninth-century Mercian kings whose names alliterate on *B-* (Beornwulf, Berhtwulf, and perhaps Burgred) and who are genealogically unplaced may belong to the same lineage. He was presumably declared a usurper because he had actually held the kingship[144] to which Offa considered himself the rightful heir; had Beornred been wholly unsuccessful in his attempt, there would not have been the need to stigmatise him as *tyrannus*, for he would simply have been a disappointed contender of whom there were often many.[145]

Notwithstanding the risks of ideological intervention, the basic function of the regnal list is a much more matter-of-fact, day-to-day one than that of the pedigree. It will have served first as a crude means of providing some chronological or historical perspective. It may perhaps have been preserved in mnemonic verse, but (as far as I am aware) we have no evidence on the point. How far the knowledge of the professional keeper of regnal lists would extend is an interesting question, but the answer would probably be 'only as far as the head of the dynasty'. There was no reason, and probably no opportunity, to retain details of the kings of superseded dynasties. Within the Christian period, the dating of letters, charters, and official acta involving kings came to be most naturally expressed in terms of regnal years; whether this means of dating communications extended back, via the use of runes and wood, into the pagan period I could not say. It was left to a chronologist and historian of Bede's stature to attempt to reconcile the welter of often unrelated information of this sort into a coherent and cross-referenced system.[146]

---

[142] British Library MS. Cotton Vespasian B.6, fo 104r, col. 2.

[143] See Dumville 1976: 41 n. 1 for the whole marginale.

[144] Cf. Anglo-Saxon Chronicle *s. a.* 755 (and Whitelock 1961: 31); Plummer 1899: 47–8 discusses this episode and the career of Beornred.

[145] That he survived by a decade his defeat by Offa, and that he probably had descendants who would remember his rule, no doubt gave added point to the insistence on the illegality of his reign.

[146] We may note that Bede seems to have had access to Northumbrian, East Saxon, and Kentish regnal lists. He may also have used a Mercian king-list, but this is less certain for his figures may be the result of his own calculations.

The compilation, as opposed to the continuous recording, of a king-list was a difficult task, requiring, in effect, the use of archival material. Similar techniques would be necessary for the synchronising of regnal lists from different kingdoms. These points were, of course, well taken by Bede in his work for his *Ecclesiastical History*.[147] Successful achievement of this process in the context of numerous small kingdoms was a considerable achievement. Irish scholars were specialists in the techniques of synchronising reigns from different kingdoms, and of harmonising variants in regnal lists and genealogies. Among the corpus of Irish genealogies, for example, are various tracts on the interrelationships of the various major genealogies and how to synchronise them in time;[148] there are also collections of synchronisms,[149] modelled on the techniques of the Eusebius-Jerome world chronicle.

Another difficulty for the compiler (even more than for the contemporary recorder, who would very likely hold partisan views) of a regnal list would be a period of chaos or, above all, of foreign rule.[150] A limited perspective on this may be gained from the variants in the Mercian regnal list. In the copy which belongs to the Anglian collection, Penda's son Peada is assigned a reign of a single year. This seems to coincide with the information known to Bede,[151] who states that King Oswiu of Northumbria (who ruled Mercia from 655 to 658) made Peada king of South Mercia, retaining the rest under his own control. Bede gives no absolute date either for this act or for Peada's assassination (perhaps with Northumbrian connivance) a year later. On a strict reading of Bede's words (*Hist. Eccl.*, III. 25) all this could have occurred anywhere within 655x658.[152] The Worcester copy of the Mercian king-list, however, assigns Peada a reign of three years, which could derive partly from a less cautious reading of Bede. In 653 (*Hist. Eccl.* V. 24, *recap.*, and III. 21) Peada, as (under) king of the Middle Angles (to which position Penda had appointed him), approached Oswiu for a wife. If his appointment be taken to have dated from that year, a reign of three years would have put his death in 656, the earliest possible date by which he could have ruled one year under Oswiu.[153] On either view, the years during which Oswiu ruled Mercia directly are ignored in the regnal list; on the latter view, the correct total is preserved by chance for the later user, but at the expense of giving a false impression of consecutive rather than partly concurrent

---

[147] See Harrison 1976b for a sympathetic study.
[148] O'Brien 1976: 137–8, 358; cf. Kelleher 1968: 141, 142.
[149] Examples of this genre are edited by Meyer 1913 (commentary by MacNeill 1915), Thurneysen 1931, Boyle 1971.
[150] Cf. Henige 1971: 374.
[151] From whose work (*Hist. Eccl.*, III. 25) it could perhaps derive, but this seems unlikely.
[152] For a discussion of the issue see Plummer 1896: II. 175, 187 (and 1899: 24, 25).
[153] Or the three years might derive from a view that after Penda's death Peada was the legitimate king until his assassination, which would be placed in 658 and be immediately followed by Wulfhere's accession. Whether or not this was the view of the author of this version of the regnal list, it is the least probable of the interpretations of these difficult years.

reigns.[154] We see a wholly different view in the ninth-century section of the Worcester list, where Ecgberht of Wessex's one-year period of direct rule in Mercia (829–30) is recorded as if that of a Mercian king. His Mercian opponent, Wiglaf, is given two separate reigns, one on either side of Ecgberht's; this coincides with the dating formulae of Wiglaf's charters.[155]

The regnal list is, in itself, a straightforward enough form. In the Roman world, there were lists of consuls and emperors. Papal lists developed in great detail — years, months, *and* days[156] — but the episcopal lists which are extant rarely give even the number of years. But there is no compelling reason to link the keeping of Anglo-Saxon regnal tables with Roman models. Although the Church had a monopoly of Latin script and of parchment, we can perhaps believe in the oral cultivation of king-lists at royal courts.

The extant early Anglo-Saxon examples are, however, a singularly unsatisfactory group. The earliest, as they stand, belong to the early eighth century: this is also the period of the compilation of the Pictish regnal list.[157] That for Mercia, first found in a very late eighth-century context, begins only with Penda, assigning him a barely credible reign of twenty-one years, which seems much too short.[158] The whole question of the early history of the Mercian monarchy is thus left in the air, almost seeming to justify the statement of the Welsh-Latin *Historia Brittonum* that Penda was the first who redeemed the Mercians from the Northumbrians: 'Ipse primus reparauit regnum Merciorum a regno Nordorum'.[159] The fact that the Mercian list begins at this point, however, may be a reason for confidence in it: it commences at a point from which a continuous written record was possible.[160]

The Northumbrian list, which Bede plainly knew, and which makes its first appearance in 737 as an addendum to the Moore manuscript of his *History*, has rightly attracted criticism from David Kirby though his attempt to rewrite it is

---

[154] For a different version again, see the Anglo-Saxon Chronicle, *s. aa.* 653, 655, 657; on this see Plummer 1899: 24, 25, and Whitelock 1961: 20.

[155] cf. Sawyer 1968: 119, no.188 (an original charter) which is dated 'anno uero dominicae incarnationis, DCC° XXX° 1ª... anno primo secundi regni mei'.

[156] Cf. the regnal list studied by Roger Collins, above. The West Saxon 'genealogical regnal list' begins to give information in this sort of detail in its later sections.

[157] Cf. n. 139 above.

[158] A tenth-century copy, surviving in a Worcester manuscript (BL Cotton Tiberius A. 13, fo 114v) of *ca* A.D. 1000, gives him thirty-two years, however. This version is printed by Hearne 1723: I. 242.

[159] The only recorded earlier king is Cearl (Bede, *Hist. Eccl.*, II. 14) who is genealogically unplaced. (But we may note the *C*- alliteration of the immediate ancestors of Penda's father Pybba, and of one line of Pybba's descendants.) Of course, the words of the *Historia Brittonum* can be taken to have many different implications. I here take them to mean that Mercia was dependent on, or subject to, Northumbria until Penda's time.

[160] It also avoids a common error of orally transmitted king-lists, namely the attribution of an excessively long reign to the 'founder' of the dynasty (Henige 1971: 383; cf. p. 375, and Boston 1969). The West Saxon list may not have avoided this: the possible elision of Croida (though he may, of course, never actually have reigned) represents a typical development in the oral record of a foundation-epoch in a kingdom's history.

unacceptable.[161] It projects back into the sixth century the Bernician control of Northumbria in the seventh. It includes kings who are genealogically unplaced. And it begins with Ida, in a year which may be calculated as 547: Bede says that the Northumbrian royal family derives its origin from Ida (*Hist. Eccl.*, V. 24, *recap.*). As we have seen, however, another view was that Oesa had been the first of the line to come to Britain:[162] did he therefore not rule? Why else would the list omit him and Eoppa, Ida's father?[163] In the absence of controlling evidence, we cannot alter the scheme though we may view it with extreme suspicion. But we do not know, of course, what its intention was. Is it a semi-genealogical document, recording only Bernician rulers? The inclusion of Edwin of Deira would seem to deny that. Is it then a provincial king-list, on the Irish model, which lists those rulers who controlled the whole of Northumbria? If so, what do we make of the early rulers, who seem unlikely to have exercised control over Deira? Could it be the conflation of a Bernician and a Deiran king-list? Or is it, as I first suggested, a list of Bernician rulers to Æthilfrith, who may have been the first king of a united Northumbria, and then of his Northumbrian successors? However we look at it, it is certainly a document of the winning, Bernician side in the Northumbrian struggle, and this should warn us to approach it with caution. King-lists can all too easily conceal information.

The reliability of a king-list is guaranteed, therefore, only if it can be checked to some degree against other sources. These may be other, varying copies of the same list (the West Saxon regnal table is a possible case in point which needs a good deal of consideration), or genealogies, annals, and other historical sources. This sort of checking has allowed Dr. Ó Corráin to identify an example of manipulation of a Leinster king-list for the eleventh century by a twelfth-century compiler whose own dynastic sympathies left him with 'little taste for recording the reign of a king from a rival segment', which was accordingly deleted.[164] The Irish materials are often sufficiently full to allow such checks; the English records, especially for the sub-historical sixth century, are not. In theory, there is nothing easier than to delete a king from a list and assign his years to one or two other kings. In practice, especially with Roman numerals, things tend to go wrong, giving the modern historian his chance; the worst corruptions of transmission are always those of numerals, however, and it is here above all that Kelleher's dictum is most appropriate. The chronological aid can become a chronographic monster.

As a form, the regnal list can be expanded into, or (less easily) reduced from, a chronicle. In the early-ninth-century *Historia Brittonum*, we see a Welsh writer

---

[161] Kirby 1963. It is methodologically unsound in that it uses unreliable and very late sources which are hardly an adequate basis for a challenge to this list.

[162] Above, p. 90, and Dumville 1973a.

[163] Confusion of king-list data (the first, second, and third kings) with genealogical information (Ida as the point from which the genealogies branch) is implied here; but note also the remarks in n. 160, above, about elision of names in the record of a foundation-era.

[164] Ó Corráin 1971: 23–4.

attempting to develop a narrative history of sixth-to-seventh-century Northumbria by the synchronisation of the Northumbrian regnal list with a motley collection of other items of Welsh and English origin. The subject-matter common to regnal list and royal genealogy naturally leads to interaction of these two genres. In a culture unfamiliar with one form or the other, false deductions and misuse can occur.[165] A more common type of interaction is represented by the prologue to the Edict of Rothari or the West Saxon 'genealogical regnal list', where genealogical information is given in the context of a king-list in order to provide some links between the various rulers; this can be managed more coherently in a situation where a single dynasty monopolises power (as in Wessex) than where dynasties change frequently (as among the Lombards). Finally we may note the possibility of the use of a genealogy to provide a king-list where one was wanting but became necessary for a political or ideological purpose: an example is found in Ireland, where the pedigree of Niall Noígiallach (eponym of the Uí Néill dynasty) was used to provide a list of the prehistoric kings of Tara, his alleged predecessors.[166]

In the end, however, as with genealogies, much of our response to a regnal list must be determined by our appreciation of the means of its transmission and, in particular, the question of whether that transmission has been oral or written. There are well-tested procedures for dealing with the results of written transmission; but, as David Henige concludes, 'a major task of research is to determine why some orally transmitted king-lists are remarkably accurate while others are much less so'.[167]

THE PROFESSIONAL LEARNED CLASS

I must end, therefore, with some brief remarks about the keepers of genealogies and regnal lists — the professional learned class.[168] Alone in Western Europe in the early middle ages, the Celtic countries seem to have had professional secular learned men. Elsewhere, in the Christian period, the Church seems to have served this function. Before the coming of Christianity, the Germanic kings, in England at least, may have employed officials to reckon time, including the lengths of their own reigns. It is possible that this function had been performed by pagan priests; I know of no evidence on the point,[169] though we may doubt that Bede would have spoken so

---

[165] As when an early Welsh genealogist converted a list of Roman emperors into a patrilinear pedigree; see above, p. 97, and n. 133.

[166] Mac Neill 1927: 154.

[167] Henige 1971: 386. On this whole question, and the matter of how to assess the reliability of orally transmitted king-lists, see the important paper by Jones 1970.

[168] Note the remark quoted by Henige 1971: 376 that the genealogist (of the Rajput bardic caste) is 'both the preserver and creator of myths'.

[169] The employment of comparative Celtic-Germanic philology may help towards an answer, however. It has been suggested (by Williams 1971: 6–8) that the Anglo-Saxon *scop*, as also the Scandinavian skald, was a professional genealogist. Williams (1971: 8) goes so far as to describe the *scop* as 'court genealogist and historian'. Plainly, if this were so, the *scop* would be an important figure in the present discussion; but I wonder if this is not to say more than the Anglo-Saxon evidence allows.

matter-of-factly about them[170] if that had been the case. The task would eventually have devolved upon the king's chaplain-clerk, but by that stage the knowledge would have been widely diffused, especially in ecclesiastical centres.

Ireland presents the paradigm of the secular learned class. The divisions of functions among its various members are still a subject for dispute among celticists, but it seems clear that the *filidh* (generally translated 'poets', though they were much more) were responsible for the cultivation of genealogy and of other tribal and national records such as king-lists, origin legends, toponymic lore, and so forth.[171] The practice was hereditary in various families, who might be related to the ruling dynasty in their kingdoms. There was a national network of communication, based on a standard non-dialectal language and on freedom of movement for the *filidh* throughout the Gaelic world. Royal patronage was taken for granted. Their learning was orally cultivated, and it is not clear how the process of reducing this knowledge to writing, chiefly beginning in the eighth century, was accomplished.[172] Members of the profession becoming clerics, and the necessary interest of the widely spread monastic federations in this subject-matter, were doubtless important factors. This type of learned organisation appears to have been an inheritance from a Common Celtic antiquity,[173] so that it was shared by the British-speaking peoples as well. It is accordingly no surprise to find similar cultivation of genealogy and related subjects in medieval Wales.[174]

It is the techniques ultimately of these learned seculars which we have been observing in this paper. There is naturally a temptation to wonder[175] if the influence of the Irish learned class on Anglo-Saxon England was simply a matter of religion, writing, and art, or whether learned clerics did not also introduce some knowledge of pedigree-conventions to the kings whose countries they evangelised,[176] along with their distinctive script and those traces of Old Irish orthographic conventions which have been said to have left their mark on Old English.[177]

Be that as it may, the cultivation of the pedigree and of the regnal list was a professional task. Legal documentation and propaganda must, after all, both be handled

---

[170] *Hist. Eccl.*, III.1; see above, pp. 81, 97.

[171] Williams 1971: *passim* (esp. 4–5, 6–8, 15, 16, 41); Carney 1973: 238. See Bergin 1970: 4 (reprinting a paper of 1912) for a classic description of the functions of a *fili* in the late medieval period. For an example of genealogists using earlier praise-poetry as a source for a king-list, see Carney 1973: 242. And on the general relationship of genealogy and origin-legends, see Williams 1971: 41 n. 4.

[172] Mac Neill 1922 and Mac Cana 1970 discuss this issue.

[173] cf. Williams 1971: 15. Indeed there is evidence that this is a modified survival of Indo-European practice: compare the *suta* of ancient India (Williams 1971: 16). See also Dillon 1947: 15–20.

[174] But, in Wales, by the twelfth and thirteenth centuries, the practice was not hereditary — Williams 1971: 6.

[175] Though the possible chronological difficulties noted above (p. 81) must be remembered.

[176] cf. Sisam 1953: 328–9 and Wrenn 1967: 29.

[177] Details may be extracted from Campbell 1959, chapter 1.

with care. A mistake in the record of one's patron's ancestors could, if detected,[178] be more than just embarrassing in a violent age. To practise the technique of *damnatio memoriae*[179] required a good grasp of the political situation or a very steady nerve. We see this practice (called by its classical name which referred to the systematic creation of an unperson — usually a traitor or a previous emperor — by the erasure of his name from public monuments and records) employed by the Irish and the Welsh, as well as by those Anglo-Saxon professionals to whom Bede refers. In Ireland, pagan deities' names are erased from ogom inscriptions cast in genealogical terms.[180] In Wales, Gwrtheyrn of Powys — identified as the man (Vortigern) who let in the English — is subjected to such a campaign which appears to have begun, with ecclesiastical support, even before the demise of the dynasty which claimed descent from him. Here is a case of genealogical controversy, with rival schools of thought supporting rival ancestors.[181] All this activity centred on the king and his dynastic line: we see his affiliations, in societies where cultivation of genealogy is important, through the work of the learned men whom he or his relatives patronised; if we are to understand his beliefs, his aspirations and his fears, as well as his alliances, we must strive to understand the terminology and the conventions of his servants.

[178] One is bound to recall the suspicion (cf. above, n.66) that a king might not have been personally genealogically well-versed.

[179] Henige 1971: 373 n. 9 draws attention to the practice in three other cultures: Pharaonic Egypt, early Assyria, and Korea.

[180] Mac Neill 1909: 333—4; Macalister 1945: xi—xiii, xvii. For comparable inscriptions in ancient India, see Henige 1971: 379 n. 39 and Trautmann 1969: 574—7.

[181] The attempt was made to supplant Gwrtheyrn by one Cadell; it was left to later scholars (after the demise of the dynasty in question and the absorption of Powys into Gwynedd, both in the mid-ninth century) to make an antiquarian reconciliation of the two traditions — Dumville 1977: 185—7.

5

Lex Scripta and *Verbum Regis*: Legislation and Germanic Kingship, from Euric to Cnut

PATRICK WORMALD

I

I must confess at once that my objectives in this paper are more limited than its title may imply.[1] I am not here concerned with the relationship between Kingship and Law, to which Fritz Kern devoted a classic study, and which has recently been discussed with reference to the central figure of Hincmar of Rheims by Dr. Nelson.[2] Nor am I directly concerned with the extent to which a Germanic king of the early Middle Ages was considered responsible for making and promulgating law; this is an issue which cannot but come up in the course of my discussion, but, for the moment, I wish to take the fact of royal responsibility more or less for granted, and ask not what kings did for legislation, so much as what legislation did for kings. Why, in fact, did Germanic kings make laws in the period between the fall of the Roman Empire and the revival of Roman Law? And how far did this activity change the status and authority of kingship within Germanic society?

The answer to the first at least of these questions may seem obvious. Why does anyone ever make laws? The prologues to many barbarian codes and edicts give the legislator's ostensible motives, and in their emphasis on the promotion of peace and order, the redress of injustice and the resolution of difficult cases these are exactly what one would expect.[3] Why should one suppose that the purpose of Germanic law-making was other than the enforcement of law in the courts, as at least some of the texts imply, and as the giants of the nineteenth century German *Rechtsschule*, upon whose shoulders we all stand, never doubted?[4] But my impression, derived admittedly from only a few years consideration of material that demands a lifetime's study, is that it is not easy to account for the existence of much barbarian legislation in its extant form, simply in terms of the needs of justice and government. Some of

---

[1] I am very grateful to Mr. Ian Wood, Dr. Michael Clanchy and Dr. Jenny Brown for constructive criticism and helpful suggestions.
[2] Kern 1954; Nelson 1977.
[3] cf., e.g., *L. Vis.*, I ii, pp. 40–2; *Ed. Roth.*, Pr., pp. 1–2; *L. Gr.*, Pr., p. 91; *L. Liut. (717)*, Pr., pp. 109–10; *L. Liut. (724)*, Pr., p. 128; *L. Liut. (731)*, Pr., p. 155; *L. Ra. (746)*, Pr., pp. 185–6; *L. Ah. (755)*, Pr., pp. 197–8; *L. Sal.* (C), Pr., p. 2; *Capitularia*, no. 22, Pr., I, pp. 53–4; no. 33, c.1, I, p. 92; no. 77, Pr., I, p. 170; no. 98, Pr., I, pp. 204–5; no. 137, I, pp. 273–5; no. 185, II, pp. 4–6; *L. In.*, Pr., pp. 88–9; *L. Ew. II*, Pr., pp. 140–1; *L. As. V.*, Pr., pp. 166–7.
[4] cf. Brunner 1906, I, p. 425. Brunner's great book represented the consummation of the tradition and it is unnecessary to refer to his predecessors and successors; but a convenient modern summary is Buchner 1953.

the difficulties were implicitly acknowledged by Boretius, the editor of the Frankish capitularies for the *Monumenta*:

> I take it for granted that, even if the understanding of particular details in the outward expression of the public life of the time escapes us completely, we are better able to recognize and distinguish the essentials of the matter, the underlying forces, than contemporaries. In fact, I am convinced that today we are better able to understand the legal sources of the Frankish period, to appreciate their meaning and implications, than the scribes and compilers of the period.[5]

In other words, we know what the Frankish legislators were trying to do and why, even if the texts themselves do not entirely support our views. Boretius was far from the most distinguished member of the *Rechtsschule*[6]. but a convoy is exposed by the speed of its slowest member, and similar, if more subtly refined, assumptions underlay the work of all the great scholars who laid the foundations of the study of Germanic law. Quite apart from more detailed objections which will concern us shortly, Boretius' views are today unacceptable on principle, but the problems of interpretation to which they testify remain. We need to be able to postulate a *raison d'être* for barbarian legislation which takes account of *all* its features, including some which look very like warts.

My impression is also that the solution lies mainly in the ideological aspirations of Germanic kingship. To quote Professor Wallace-Hadrill:

> *Lex Salica* is new law; and it is royal law . . . What holds it together is the king's will . . . The mere fact of legislation makes him more of a king.

And:

> (The barbarian codes) . . . record just that fraction of custom that seemed enough to satisfy royal pride in legislation. This was their immediate practical use . . . The fact of their existence as books was what mattered most . . . The Kentish laws . . . reveal a little of contemporary practice . . . and they place it under the king's name . . . By causing them to be written down, the king makes them his own. Lawgiving is a royal function; it is something that the Emperors, through the Church, can give kings.[7]

These perceptions are basic. But there is, as we shall see, a problem about describing some legal texts (and especially *Lex Salica*) as royal law, and other problems are here hinted at rather than fully brought out. *Why* did kings make a fraction of contemporary custom, 'their own', and how was this of, 'practical use'?

---

[5] Quoted by Stein 1926, pp. 291–2. The judicious Plummer was less confident: 'The study of the Anglo-Saxon laws often reduces me to a state of mental chaos. I may know, as a rule, the meaning of individual words; I can construe, though not invariably, the separate sentences. But what it all comes to is often a total mystery'; Plummer 1902, p. 102.

[6] For criticism of his edition, cf. Ganshof 1957, pp. 40–1; and of similar assumptions by his colleagues, Goebel 1937, pp. 1–61.

[7] Wallace-Hadrill 1962, pp. 179–81; Wallace-Hadrill 1971, pp. 37, 43–44. This is the right place for me to acknowledge my profound debt to Professor Wallace-Hadrill for his inspired and inspiring teaching on this, and other problems of early medieval western history.

How did the fact of legislation make one, 'more of a king'? In what sense did the Emperors or the Church, 'give' kings the function of lawgiving? And are we to conclude that the royal role in lawmaking was something new in Germanic society?

My paper, then, will involve more on legislation than on kingship. First and foremost, we must investigate the nature and purposes of our Dark Age legal texts. But whatever the results of this investigation, they are at least bound to reflect on the peacetime duties of kings; and I hope it may also be found that the suggestions I have to offer have important implications for the evolving ideology of medieval European kingship.

II

I had better begin with a definition. By legislation, I mean 'written decrees by secular authority with ostensibly general application'. I thus exclude, first, the charter incorporating only a particular judgement for a particular beneficiary, and, second, such ecclesiastical legislation as was not taken up and given sanction by secular government. My definition remains very broad, but nothing more precise is possible. One of the points that I want to bring out in this paper is that it is much more difficult to generalize about early medieval legislation than many historians seem to have supposed. Partly, this is because of its variety, and partly because it yet obstinately refuses to fall neatly into clearly distinguishable categories.

The diversity of barbarian legislation will emerge from much of what follows. But one illustration of this point which is of central relevance to us may be given at once. By no means every legal text in our period was explicitly ascribed to a king. Royal initiative is clearest among the Lombards and Anglo-Saxons, at opposite ends of Europe. From the Edict of Rothari (643) onwards, virtually every Lombard decree had a prologue claiming royal responsibility for its issue.[8] Likewise, most English 'codes' after that of Aethelberht (597/616) were professedly royal work.[9] With the Burgundians, the position is less clear only because the manuscripts of their code leave it uncertain which king actually promulgated it, but those who observed it were in subsequent centuries known as *Gunbadingi* after King Gundobad (474–516), who thus emerges as the founder of Burgundian lawmaking.[10] It is also a reasonable guess, though no more, that the Visigothic codes of Euric (466–84) and Liuvigild

---

[8] *Ed. Roth.*, Pr., p. 1; *L. Gr.*, Pr., p. 91; *L. Liut (713)*, Pr., pp. 107–8; *L. Liut. (717)*, Pr., pp. 109–10; *L. Liut. (720)*, Pr., p. 113; *L. Liut. (721)*, Pr., p. 116; *L. Liut. (723)*, Pr., pp. 121–2; *L. Liut. (724)*, Pr., p. 128; *L. Liut. (725)*, Pr., pp. 133–4; *L. Liut. (734)*, Pr., p. 169; *L. Liut. (735)*, Pr., pp. 171–2; *L. Ra (746)*, Pr., pp. 185–6; *L. Ah. (750)*, Pr., p. 195; *L. Ah. (755)*, Pr., pp. 197–8.

[9] *L. Hl.*, Pr., p. 9; *L. Wi.*, Pr., p. 12; *L. In.*, Pr., pp. 88–89; *L, Af.*, Intr., 49:9, 10, pp. 46–7; *L. Ew. I*, Pr., pp. 138–9; *L. Ew. II*, Pr., pp. 140–1; *L. As. I*, Pr., pp. 146–7; *L. As. V*, Pr., pp. 166–7; *L. As. IV*, Pr., pp. 170–1; *L. As. VI*, cc. 10, 11, p. 182; *L. Em. I*, Pr., pp. 184–5; *L. Em. II*, Pr., pp. 186–7; *L. Eg. II*, Pr., pp. 194–5; *L. Eg. IV*, Pr., pp. 206–7; *L. Atr. I, Pr.*, pp. 216–7; *L. Atr. III*, Pr., pp. 228–9; *L. Atr. V*, Pr., pp. 236–7; *L. Atr. VI (Lat.)*, Pr., p. 247; c. 40:2, p. 257; *L. Atr. VII*, Pr., p. 260; *L. Atr. VIII*, Pr., p. 263; *L. Atr. IX*, Pr., p. 269; *L. Atr. X*, Pr., p. 269; *L. Cn. I*, Pr., pp. 278–9.

[10] *L. Burg.*, Pr: 1, p. 30. Some MSS give Gundobad, and some his son Sigismund (516–24); cf. Beyerle 1954, pp. 24–27. For *Gunbadingi*, cf. Wallace-Hadrill 1964, p. 37.

(568–86) had official royal prologues. The extant Visigothic *Liber Iudiciorum* opens with a book of general comments on the law without reference to a specific king, but its contents include laws in which responsibility for the whole collection is claimed by Kings Reccaswinth (652–72) and Erwig (680–7); and those laws in the code which were promulgated by the successors of Liuvigild were all attributed to their royal authors: in these respects (and in others) the Visigothic lawbook resembled the Theodosian Code more closely than other barbarian legislation.[11]

But when we turn to the Franks and their associates, we find a rather different picture. The researches of Karl August Eckhardt, whose achievement it has been finally to unravel the complexities of *Lex Salica*, have revealed that at least the third, fourth and fifth recensions of this text emanated from the royal chancery: the third can be connected with Guntchramn (561–92) or Childebert II (575–96), the fourth with Pippin (751–68) and the fifth with Charlemagne himself (768–814, probably in 798).[12] It is thus a good assumption that the same goes for the most important versions, the first (probably 507–11) and the sixth, or Karolina (probably 802). In fact, the 'Epilogue' to *Lex Salica*, which is not an original feature of the text, and was perhaps never an 'official' production at all, does ascribe the first set of titles to, *'primus rex francorum'*, and the legislative activity of Charlemagne in and around 802 is described both by Einhard and by the *Annals of Lorsch*.[13] *Lex Salica* was thus indeed, 'royal law'. And yet the original version of the *Lex* seems to have had no prologue, and the earliest, 'shorter' prologue, associated with the third recension of the code, gives the credit for it not to Clovis, but to four mysterious gentlemen who were apparently not kings, whatever else they were.[14] The 'longer' prologue, which Eckhardt has traced to the chancery of Pippin, refers in passing to the legislation of Clovis and his immediate successors, but oddly says nothing of the Carolingians themselves, and Charlemagne's versions of the text, like that of Clovis, had no special prefaces of their own.[15] The position is similar with the codes issued by the Franks for their subject peoples. *Lex Ribuaria* has no record of royal authorship in any of its versions, though Eckhardt and others have attributed it with some certainty to King Dagobert (622–38), and one manuscript refers to its renovation in the times of Charlemagne.[16] Likewise, the codes promulgated by Charlemagne for the Frisians, Saxons and Thuringians (?802) were totally anonymous.[17] Only the Alaman and Bavarian codes are more forthcoming. The first version of the Alaman

---

[11] *L. Vis.*, II i 4, 5, pp. 47–8. For the possibility of royal prologues to *Cod. Eur.* and to Liuvigild's *Antiquae*, cf. Zeumer 1898, pp. 427–38.

[12] Eckhardt 1953, pp. 43–78; Eckhardt 1954, pp. 170–2.

[13] *L. Sal. (K)*, Ep., p. 253 (and, for its date, Eckhardt 1954 pp. 146–50); Einhard, *V.C.*, c. 29, p. 33; *Capitularia*, I, p. 105; and cf., also, Eckhardt 1954, pp. 220–1.

[14] *L. Sal. (C)*, Pr., p. 2.

[15] *L. Sal. (D, E)*, Pr: 3, pp. 6–7.

[16] Beyerle-Buchner 1951, pp. 21–9, 34; Eckhardt 1959a, pp. 36–144; cf., also, Beyerle 1928, pp. 264–378; Beyerle 1935, pp. 1–80.

[17] On the date, cf. Buchner 1953, pp. 40–1, 44.

law (the *Pactus*) seems to have had a prologue claiming the authority of Chlothar II (613–29, for these purposes), and in the second (the *Lex*) its place was taken by a preface in the name of the Alaman duke Lantfrid (712–30).[18] The Bavarian Law has a remarkable preface, which is also found associated with other texts, describing the legislation for Franks, Alamans and Bavarians alike of a series of Frankish kings from Theuderic I (511–33) to Dagobert, but this has no obvious relevance at least for the extant version of the text which seems to date to the eighth century.[19] Even with Alamans and Bavarians, the revised Carolingian versions for which there is textual evidence have left no record of their authorship.[20] Finally, and perhaps most surprising for reasons that we shall soon see, the 'Capitularies' which supplemented the *Leges* are also sometimes anonymous in both Merovingian and Carolingian periods, quite unlike the similar decrees of Lombards or Anglo-Saxons.[21] It is thus not surprising that the *Rechtsschule*, whose horizons, like those of many historians of early medieval Europe, rarely extended beyond the Frankish realm, saw the barbarian laws as manifestations of the *Volksgeist*, promulgated by the king only (if at all) as his people's mouthpiece and only with their consent.[22] Even though we can be quite confident about royal responsibility for the Frankish laws, we need to explain why this is less obvious than elsewhere in Europe; and to this point, I shall return.

In spite of its wide variety, it is difficult, as I said, to classify Germanic legal texts into neat and exclusive categories. The *Rechtsschule* sought to distinguish *Lex* from *Capitulare* (pl. *Capitularia*): *Lex* was seen as traditional and customary, as comprehensive in range and as essentially popular in inspiration: in short as a code like *Lex Salica* itself; capitularies consisted of a series of individual regulations in chapters *(capitula)* covering problems as and when they arose, were innovative or administrative in character, and represented the policies and judgements of the king and his immediate advisers; and whenever the king wished to alter or add to the *Lex*, this could be done only with popular consent.[23] Now this distinction is not entirely unreal. There is a considerable and obvious difference between a text like *Lex Salica*, with its long lists of thefts and injuries, its crude and direct style and its air of belonging to a community of peasants on the one hand, and a solemn capitulary like *Admonitio*

---

[18] Eckhardt 1958, pp. 43–93; Eckhardt 1962a, pp. 7–10.

[19] *L. Bai.*, Pr., pp. 201–2; on this preface and its date, cf. Beyerle 1929, pp. 373–86; Eckhardt 1959a, pp. 128–39; for summary of the various views on the date of *L. Bai.*, cf. Buchner 1953, pp. 26–9.

[20] Eckhardt 1962a, pp. 9–10; Eckhardt 1927, pp. 9–28.

[21] *L. Sal. Capitularia*, I, pp. 238–50, III, pp. 254–61, V, pp. 263–7, are all anonymous. For the authorship of a considerable proportion of the Carolingian capitularies, we are indebted to scribal colophons rather than the text itself: cf., e.g., *Capitularia* no. 138, I, pp. 275–80; no. 139, I, pp. 281–5; no. 140, I, pp. 287–8; no. 141, I, pp. 289–91; no. 142, I, pp. 292–3.

[22] cf. Brunner 1906, p. 406. It is worth emphasising that, though we know of Æthelberht's responsibility for his code from Bede, *H.E.* II 5, p. 90, and from *L. Af.*, Intr., 49:9, pp. 46–7, the rubric asserting as much, p. 3, is probably not an original feature of the text.

[23] Brunner 1906, pp. 406–12, 418–20, 540–51; Buchner 1953, pp. 4–5, 45–6. But these scholars, unlike some of their predecessors, were aware of the difficulties, which are emphasised by Stein 1926, pp. 289–301; and Ganshof 1957, pp. 46–8, 61–9, 216–41.

Generalis (789), with its rhetorical and homiletic style, its Roman and Hebraic inspiration, and its concentration on the major issues of the Christian life on the other.[24] The king is indeed more prominent in the latter than the former; and when, as in 802/3 or 818/9, he issued *Capitularia Legibus Addenda*, a real effort does seem to have been made to secure some form of popular assent.[25] It is thus possible, and will prove useful for the rest of this paper, to distinguish between what one might call *primary* legislation, the original statement of a people's law in writing, taking the form of a code covering a wide range of eventualities; and *secondary* legislation, concerned either to amend, reinforce or supplement the first statement, or with merely administrative matters.[26] For the sake of convenience, I shall continue to call these respectively *Lex* and *Capitulare*.

But we have already seen that there is no reason, appearances apart, to suppose that primary legislation was any less royal than secondary; and this is not the only respect in which the classical distinction between *Lex* as *Volksrecht* and *Capitulare* as *Königsrecht* falls down.[27] It has no obvious relevance outside the Frankish sphere of influence. In Lombard Italy, the laws of Grimoald (662–71), Liutprand (713–44), Ratchis (744–9) and Ahistulf (749–56) were longer and more complex in syntax than most of those in Rothari's original edict, and clearly represent royal reforms and judgements mostly on points of private law, where Rothari had been mainly concerned to list the fines and compensations for a long series of crimes. But all this legislation, including the edict, seems to have involved exactly the same sort of collaboration between king, 'judge' and 'people'.[28] In England, it is impossible to see any difference between the legislative procedures followed by Ine, whose code (688/94) formed the basic *Lex* of the West Saxons, and those of Alfred, whose own laws (887/99) look like *Capitularia Legibus Addenda*, or those of Aethelstan (925–39) and Eadgar (957–75), whose decrees do resemble administrative regulations, or those of Cnut, who incorporated into one huge edict (1018–23) statutes by all of these kings and much else that was new.[29] Even in Francia, it would be truer to say that *Capitulare* merged into *Lex* than that each stood apart. *Lex Salica* and *Admonitio Generalis* might differ markedly, but there is no obvious difference in style or subject-

---

[24] *Capitularia*, no. 22, I, pp. 52–62.

[25] *Capitularia*, no. 39, I, pp. 111–4; no. 139, I , pp. 280–5.

[26] Ganshof 1957, p. 217–29.

[27] Cf. the passages of Brunner and Buchner cited in no. 23.

[28] Cf., e.g. *Ed. Roth.*, c. 386, pp. 89–90; *L. Gr.*, Pr., p. 91; *L. Liut. (713)*, Pr., pp. 107–8; *L. Liut. (717)*, Pr., pp. 109–10; *L. Liut (720)*, Pr., p. 113; *L. Liut. (721)*, Pr., p. 116; *L. Liut. (723)*, Pr., pp. 121–2; *L. Liut. (724)*, Pr., p. 128; *L. Liut. (725)*, Pr., pp. 133–4; *L. Liut. (726)*, Pr., p. 135; *L. Liut. (727)*, Pr., p. 141; *L. Liut. (728)*, Pr., pp. 146–7; *L. Liut. (729)*, Pr., p. 150; *L. Liut. (731)*, Pr., p. 155; *L. Liut. (735)*, Pr., pp. 171–2; *L. Ra. (746)*, Pr., pp. 185–6; *L. Ah. (750)*, Pr., p. 195.

[29] *L. In.*, Pr., pp. 88–9; *L. Af.*, Intr., 49:9, 10, pp. 46–7; *L. As. II*, Ep., pp. 166–7; *L. As. V*, Pr.:1, pp. 166–7; *L. As. III*, Pr., p. 170; *L. As. IV*, Pr., p..171; *L. As. VI*, cc. 10, 12:1, pp. 180–3; *L. Eg. II*, Pr., pp. 194–5; *L. Eg. IV*; cc. 1, pp. 206–7; 2; 1a, pp. 210–11; 14, pp. 214–15; *L. Cn. I*, Inscr., Pr., pp. 278–9; *L. Cn. II*, Pr., pp. 308–9.

matter between Charlemagne's Capitulary of Herstal (779) and his *Capitulare Legibus Additum* (803).[30] Above all, neither among the Franks nor among their neighbours is it true that *Lex* consisted purely of traditional custom. And since it is with this primary legislation, these codes, that I am mainly concerned, I will discuss their contents in a little more detail.

Anthropologists have taught us that custom is not a constant, though commitment to writing can make it so.[31] Only very rarely do we have evidence for the existence of a custom *before* it is found recorded in a legal code.[32] Thus we can never be sure that a provision found in a barbarian legal text is genuinely traditional. Nevertheless, there are indirect indications that much of what we find in Germanic codes does represent the custom of the relevant people as it was conceived at the time, even when the legislating authority was not in fact native to that people. When we find marked variations in content and emphasis between the laws of the Frisians, Saxons and Thuringians, though these were all probably issued by Charlemagne in 802, it is a reasonable conclusion that what is being reflected is customary diversity. A common fallacy in the interpretation of barbarian legislation is that the various compensations decreed for killing, wounding, rape, insult or theft represent attempts by the legislator to, 'limit the feud' by substituting monetary composition for the shedding of blood. Given the evidence of Tacitus that such compensation were established among the Germans of the first century A.D., we should never have needed anthropologists to demonstrate that the principle of compensation is an inherent part of any feuding system, and cannot represent an innovation by christianized authority.[33] It is true that Rothari declared that he was raising the sums payable for physical injury in order to encourage the peaceful settlement of feud; and it may be that the actual *monetary* assessment is new in other cases also.[34] But it should also be noted that Ine of Wessex nowhere stipulated in his code that the *wergild* of a nobleman was 1200 shillings, and that of a ceorl, 200, yet he does refer to *twelfhynde* and *twyhynde* men.[35] In general, the *wergilds* and compensations of the Germanic laws are likely to be among the oldest elements in them; indeed, in some cases, they may already have become archaic at the time they were committed

---

[30] *Capitularia*, no. 20, I, pp. 47–51; no. 39, I, pp. 111–14.

[31] Clanchy 1970, and the references there cited. Commitment to writing certainly had this effect in Irish law: what had always been immutable in theory became so in fact; cf. Binchy 1943, pp. 225–6.

[32] One possible example is the Ribuarian age of Majority, attested in *L. Rib.*, c. 84, p. 130; and previously, in Greg. Tur., *Hist. Franc.*, VII 33, p. 353: cf. Beyerle 1935, p. 12. Another possibility, pointed out by Dr. N. P. Brooks in his forthcoming study of *The Early History of Christ Church Canterbury*, is the Mercian royal wergeld, recorded in *L. Mirc.*, cc. 2, 3:1, pp. 462–3, and previously hinted at in Sawyer no. 1436.

[33] *Germania*, c. 12, pp. 280–1; Gluckman 1956, pp. 1–26; Wallace-Hadrill 1962, pp. 121–47.

[34] *Ed. Roth.* c. 74, pp. 22–23. One's conclusions on this point will be affected by whether one accepts or rejects the arguments of Grierson 1961.

[35] E.g. *L. In.* c. 70, pp. 118–19; cf. cc. 19, pp. 96–7, 34:1, pp. 104–5; cf. the much fuller social classification of *L. Af.* cc. 10, pp. 56–7; 18–18:3, pp. 58–61; 29–31, pp. 64–5; 39–39:2, pp. 72–3; 40, pp. 72–3.

to writing, as they must certainly have been later when they were still faithfully reproduced by the scribes of ninth century Francia or twelfth century England.[36]

Nevertheless, there is also something in every Germanic law-code that must represent innovation. I am not referring here to the influence of Roman Vulgar Law which can be exaggerated except for the Ostrogothic, Visigothic and to some extent the Burgundian texts.[37] Not do I mean the tendency described by Professor Wallace-Hadrill for one barbarian law-maker to copy another; on the whole, this imitation took the form of a declaration of local custom or policy on a topic suggested by another code rather than the exact reproduction of alien usage.[38] I am thinking particularly of laws which look from their content and style like changes in traditional law motivated by policy, or judicial decisions on points of dispute, such as one would have expected to find in secondary legislation if the classical theory were right. Laws on the defence of the Church must of course be innovations, and they are found in nearly all codes (though not in the first recension of *Lex Salica*).[39] The same is probably true of laws on kingship itself at least in some codes: Alfred's law on treason has no counterpart in the laws of Ine or Aethelberht, and the savage treason law of *Lex Saxonum* is most unlikely to be ancient custom for this sturdily conservative people, considering that they seem to have had no kingship at all in the early eighth century (the Korvey MS of the code does actually call this law 'Lex Francorum')[40]. Franz Beyerle showed how *Lex Salica* was made up partly of *Weistum*, descriptive, systematic, comprehensive and concerned with criminal law, and partly of *Satzung*, prescriptive, *ad hoc*, specific and often procedural in character: a classification that corresponds more or less exactly with the alleged distinction between *Lex* and *Capitulare*. The same elements may be isolated in the Edict of Rothari.[41] Most other codes contain clauses which seem to have been prompted by particular eventualities. *Lex Burgundionum* actually names names on two occasions, like the imperial novels attached to the Theodosian Code.[42] Two different provisions in *Lex Ribuaria* seem to correspond with known behaviour of Chlothar II and Dagobert.[43]

[36] Their archaic character may explain the absence of an aristocratic *wergild* in most of the *Leges*, including L. Abt.; for an alternative explanation, cf. Irsigler 1969. As examples of later compilations containing blatantly archaic material, I would cite the K-text of L. Sal., or Leg. Hen. Prim.

[37] Levy 1942; Levy 1943; Levy 1951; Levy 1956; Levy himself, the master of the subject, was anxious that the significance of his conclusions be not exaggerated: Levy 1962.

[38] Wallace-Hadrill 1971, pp. 33–37. I hope to return to the issue of Æthelberht's 'sources' on a future occasion.

[39] On the contrary, cf. L. Sal. (A), c. 2:16, p. 26! On this topic, see Würdinger 1935; Imbert 1967; Vismara 1967b.

[40] L. Af., c. 4–4:2, pp. 50–1; L. Sax. cc. 24–26, pp. 62–4. But to Alfred's law, cf. Leg. Capit. (786), c. 12, pp. 23–4: in a future paper on, 'The "Loss" of King Offa's lawbook', I hope to demonstrate that this capitulary may be the laws of Offa to which King Alfred referred, L. Af., Intr., 49:9, pp. 46–7.

[41] Beyerle 1924, pp. 220–30; Besta 1951, p. 51 & ff.; cf., also, Brunner 1906, p. 417–19.

[42] L. Burg., cc. 51–2, pp. 82–6.

[43] Cf., L. Rib., cc. 70:2, p. 124; 91, p. 133, with Fredegar, *Chron. IV*, cc. 54, pp. 44–5; 58, p. 48.

King Alfred, whom we encounter (in a rare vignette of daily life as a Germanic king) giving a judgement while washing his hands, included the following clause in his laws:

> If anyone have a spear over his shoulder, and a man is transfixed upon it, the wergeld is to be paid without a fine; if he is transfixed before his eyes, he is to pay the wergeld; if anyone accuses him of intention in the act, he is to clear himself in proportion to the fine, and by that oath do away with the fine, if the point is higher than the butt of the shaft. If both are level, that is to be considered without risk.

As Maitland saw, this clause conceals a shrewd assessment of the probabilities in cases of accidental injury; but, as he also saw, its bizarre arrangement suggests that it arose from a particular case.[44]

Several barbarian legislators, including Alfred, introduced their codes with a paraphrase of the Emperor Justinian's seventh novel to the effect that they were renovating and amending existing law, adding what was lacking and removing what was superfluous.[45] We can now see that this is almost exactly what they did. In Maitland's words, 'new resolves are mixed up with statements of old custom in these *leges barbarorum*'.[46] But before we draw any conclusions from this, we must note two other features of our texts. The first, to revert to my quotation from Maitland, is that the operative words are, 'mixed up'. The Visigothic, Lombardic and to some extent the Burgundian codes do distinguish with relative clarity between what was old and what was new, but such signposts are quite rare in barbarian legislation as a whole, and non-existent in the laws of Alfred. The authors of the northern law-codes, in other words, do not care to draw the attention of the users of their decrees to the respects in which they desire to see custom reinforced or modified. Only guesswork and stylistic analysis can tell the modern historian what is old and what is new. Secondly, and more striking, much northern legislation is highly selective. Here again, we must make an exception of Lombards and Visigoths, whose massive law-books covered a wide range of legal problems, and whose rulers regularly sought to plug such gaps as did become apparent. But elsewhere there are baffling omissions. *Lex Salica*, for example, had plenty to say about rape and adultery, and included a clause on the re-marriage of widows, but it said almost nothing of the problems of ordinary marriage, like dowry.[47] The Anglo-Saxon codes left the subjects of kindred structure and property inheritance to become the battleground of modern scholarship.[48] We can scarcely suppose that these topics

---

[44] Sawyer, no. 1445; *L. Af.* c. 36—36:2, pp. 68—71; Pollock & Maitland 1968, pp. 53—4, & p. 54, n. 1., whose argument I still prefer to that of Liebermann 1916, p. 58, n. to *L. Af.*, c. 36.

[45] Justinian, *Nov.* VII, Pr., III, p. 48; Isidore, *Hist. Goth.*, c. 51, pp. 287—8; *Ed. Roth.*, Pr., pp. 1—2; *L. Af.*, Intr., 49:9 pp. 46—7; cf. Zeumer 1898, pp. 428—30; Wallace-Hadrill 1971, pp. 34—5.

[46] Pollock & Maitland 1968, p. 12.

[47] *L. Sal. (A)*, cc. 13, pp. 59—63; 25, pp. 93—6; 45, pp. 173—6; *L. Sal. Capitularia*, 67, p. 238; 69, pp. 239—40; 100, pp. 256—7; 101, pp. 257—8.

[48] Compare Charles-Edwards 1972 with Loyn 1974; and Charles-Edwards 1976 with John 1960.

were unimportant or taken for granted; quite apart from anything else, they were discussed in comparable codes.[49] Nor is it easy to see why Alfred should have included in his laws a judgement on accidents with spears, but said nothing about cases involving a sword, a knife, a shield-boss or a spade for that matter: such accidents were presumably no less common, at least in some walks of society. Even major policy initiatives seem to have been omitted from both primary and secondary legislation, and to turn up in our texts only some time after their introduction. This was true of Charlemagne's reforms in the administration of justice.[50] Similarly, in England, there is good reason to suppose that the oath of allegiance to the king was introduced by Alfred under Carolingian inspiration; but the Carolingian type formula first featured under Eadmund (944—6), and the Carolingian provision that the oath be taken by all over the age of twelve appeared only as late as the laws of Cnut.[51] We may of course be dealing with lost laws here, but such *conditions de conservation peu satisfaisantes* (to quote Professor Ganshof) are themselves significant, as we shall see; and in any case our extant texts occur in enough manuscripts, at least in Francia, to make the hypothesis of extensive losses of major written legislation somewhat doubtful.[52] Throughout northern Europe, the issues selected for legislative record sometimes seem to have been dictated by arbitrary obsession rather than rational choice.

And this analysis of the content of barbarian legislation brings us to the rationale of the whole exercise. Germanic kings did not produce written law-codes, in order to codify existing law, as Justinian had done in his *Digest*.[53] Nor did they legislate in order to revise the whole range of law, like Napoleon. (The parallels are not entirely frivolous; the nineteenth century *Rechtsschule*, which first interpreted these texts, was dominated intellectually by the influence of Savigny and politically by the legacy of Napoleon). The barbarian codes consist of a mixture of both elements, of both tradition and change. Now what was the point of all this? It was one thing for the Emperor Justinian, whose model some barbarian kings followed, to codify, prune and amend a *Corpus Iuris*, whose traditions stretched back nearly a thousand years, and which was universally acknowledged to represent all the 'Grandeur that was Rome'. It was another to carry out a codification involving both conservation and innovation against a background that knew nothing at all of written law. One can see the value of secondary legislation, assuming that primary legislation had established the use of lawbooks, although we shall see that there are problems about capitularies also. One can even rationalize the primary legislation of Visigoths and Lombards, as an attempt

---

[49] e.g. *Ed. Roth.* 153—92, pp. 35—47, on kindred, succession and marriage; *L. Sal. (A)*, c. 59, pp. 222—3, on inheritance; *L. Abt.* cc. 75—84, pp. 7—8, on problems of betrothal as well as widows.

[50] Ganshof 1957, pp. 207—8.

[51] *L. Af.*, c. 1—1:1, pp. 46—7, supported by Sawyer, no. 362; *L. Ew. II*, c. 5, pp. 142—3; *L. As. V*, Pr:3 pp. 166—7; *L. Em. III*, c. 1, p. 190; *L. Cn. II*, c. 21, pp. 324—5; cf. Campbell 1975, pp. 46—7.

[52] See below, pp. 120—21, and nn. 86, 89.

[53] Justinian, *Constit. 'Tanta'*, pp. 13—24; on this tendency in Justinian's codifications; cf. Pringsheim 1940, and Archi 1968.

to convert their people to the use of *lex scripta*, by codifying basic custom on most issues and amending it where appropriate;[54] although one wonders about the immediate impact of a code like Rothari's on judges who were presumably illiterate, who must have known the customs already, and who might well resent their being changed. But the *raison d'etre* of the northern codes, involving a selection of custom, policy and judgement mixed up together, is far less obvious. Much barbarian legislation, in fact, gives the impression that its purpose was simply to get something into writing that *looked like* a written law-code, more or less regardless of its actual value to judges sitting in court. And this impression is reinforced by considering some other features of our texts.

III

The first feature to which I would like to draw your attention has been appreciated, though not explained, by nearly every student of the subject. Our codes are in Latin. It is true that qualifications must at once be made. The English laws, like those of the Irish and the Scandinavians, are of course in the vernacular. On the continent, the number of technical vernacular terms in the Lombard edict make it a primary source of Lombardic philology, while *Lex Salica* was equipped with a set of vernacular glosses.[55] But these qualifications only make it harder to understand why Latin was the chosen language of most continental Germanic legislators. It is no answer to say that the Germanic languages were insufficiently developed on the continent, since the native language was adequate in England; and if vernacular words and glosses were possible, why not whole clauses? Apart from the Visigothic and Burgundian codes, the content of barbarian legislation had little to offer the Roman provincial; but its language can have offered little to the Germanic settler, whom we can scarcely suppose to have been familiar with Latin in early sixth century Gaul or at any time across the Rhine.[56] Yet Latin was the deliberate choice of continental legislators, presumably because Latin was known to be the only appropriate language for written law to appear in, whatever other problems this caused. One may suspect that it was not used in England not because English lawyers were more competent or self-confident, but because in England (as in Ireland) there was no one with the knowledge of Latin to bridge the gap between local custom and Latin vocabulary. This is not the last paradox that we shall be encountering.

Less obvious, perhaps, are certain problems in the presentation of our texts. Some legal manuscripts make arrant nonsense. The provision in Bavarian law on striking a

---

[54] Paradisi 1971 has suggested that the codification of Lombard custom and its amendment were distinct processes carried through by Rothari on different occasions; this seems to me to involve too literal a reading of *Ed. Roth.*, Pr., pp. 1–2, which, as we have seen, was under strong literary influence from Rome, and perhaps elsewhere.

[55] For the 'Malberg glosses', cf. Eckhardt 1954, pp. 178–86, and Keller 1964. The Alaman and Bavarian laws also contain numerous vernacular terms and glosses.

[56] Cf. Gamillscheg 1970, pp. 21–3; and, for the Lombards, Gamillscheg 1934, p. 202. But Gothic in Spain was probably in full retreat by the time of the compilation of the *Liber Iudiciorum*: Abadal 1958, pp. 545–51.

woman, *'ictu quolibet'* appears in some manuscripts as, *'coitu quolibet'*(!), or even, *'coitu ictu quolibet'*(!!).[57] This is obviously the blunder of a scribe, though it casts a lurid light on general knowledge of the law. Less easy to dismiss are cases where blunders are perpetuated by scribe after scribe: the glosses to *Lex Salica* were reproduced long after they had evidently become gibberish, and the scribe who omitted them on the grounds (literally) that they were all Greek to him was not entirely typical.[58] As Eckhardt admitted, the whole science of *textkritik* whereby the complex relationship of various laws and their manuscripts was worked out by himself and others depended on the willingness of those who were responsible for our knowledge of the texts to repeat errors which must have had hair-raising results if their work was ever produced in court.[59] Nor is it always the scribe who should take the blame for the confusion which sometimes confronts one. A few codes, like those of southern Europe, or that of Aethelberht, seem to follow a recognizable plan. But Servatus Lupus, who was apparently responsible for an important collection of laws made at Fulda in the 830s, evidently considered that the traditional organization of *Lex Salica* left something to be desired;[60] and both Ine and Alfred wandered haphazardly from judgement to judgement (in Ine's case repetitively) without any apparent principle of organization at all. Moreover, many legislators strikingly failed to assist a persevering judge with accurate chapter-headings. Rather than interfere with the original division of *Lex Salica* into sixty-five titles, the author of its third recension incorporated his additional material into titles which had little or nothing to do with the subject in question.[61] *Lex Ribuaria* may never have been officially divided into chapters at all, since there is no regularity (and little logic) in the chapters we find in the manuscripts.[62] The combined laws of Alfred and Ine were divided into 120 chapters in a way that often makes nonsense of the contents, and since this arrangement is found in all versions it is arguably original, *pace* Liebermann, who was outraged by the suggestion.[63] Most striking of all are cases of blatant contradiction for which the original law-maker was evidently responsible. The *Karolina* version of *Lex Salica* which we owe to Charlemagne (no less) was apparently designed to produce a uniform version of the text out of the late sixth century third recension and that issued by his father, Pippin. In the process, he reproduced at different points in the code two penalties for placing a corpse on an

---

[57] Eckhardt 1927, p. 19. Cf. the important MS, Paris B.N.Lat.4404, where, in c. 47, the R. Loire has become the verb, *eligere: L. Sal. (A)*, p. 182.

[58] Buchner 1953, p. 18

[59] Eckhardt 1954, pp. 114–16.

[60] Beyerle-Buchner 1951, pp. 34–35; Eckhardt 1954, pp. 18, 39, 228–9. It is edited by Eckhardt 1969, pp. 198–230.

[61] Cf. *L. Sal. (A, C)*, cc. 7:11–13, pp. 42–3; 13:10–11, pp. 62–3; 55: 6–7, pp. 208–9.

[62] Beyerle-Buchner 1951, pp. 11–14; Eckhardt 1959a, pp. 23–32. Paris B.N. Lat. 4404 reduced the number of titles to 63 (an attempt to match L. Sal.?); the two MSS of Servatus Lupus' collection (for which see n. 90) expand the number to 124 or 127; neither makes much sense of the content.

[63] Liebermann 1916, p. 40

altar, one of which was almost twice the other; and he included the full text of a law which, only four years before, had been dismissed as obsolete![64] Connected with this is the problem of superseded texts. In Spain, Chindaswinth, Reccaswinth and Erwig all ordered that their codes were to replace earlier law-books, which were under no circumstances to be used in future; to judge from the manuscript evidence, they were successful.[65] But *Lex Salica* is still extant in five different versions, and was perhaps once extant in a sixth, because the earlier recensions continued to be copied after the production of Charlemagne's standardized *Karolina*; and Alfred actually appended the code of Ine to his own laws, though he had superseded many of its provisions.[66] What was a judge to make of this?

Some scholars have certainly sought to confront these problems. Brunner, perhaps the greatest of the *Rechtsschule*, suggested that all versions of *Lex Salica* after the first were private work; but, as we saw, Eckhardt demolished this view with his convincing demonstration that at least three recensions of the text emanated from official circles, and it does not seem likely that the Karolina could be extant in over sixty manuscripts without some kind of governmental impetus behind it.[67] As regards individual manuscripts, Bischoff has shown that some, including a post 802 MS of a pre-*Karolina* text, originated at court.[68] Others can be ascribed to such religious houses as Rheims, Tours, Corbie, Fulda, St. Gallen or Reichenau, places closely connected with the court whose inmates we cannot suppose to have been ignorant of, or uninterested in, the law.[69] The fact is that many barbarian governments themselves made remarkably little effort to organize their legislation in the sort of way we would expect. Again, the Visigoths and Lombards were out in front. The Visigothic lawbook even fixed its own price (which rocketed topically in the twenty-five years between Reccaswinth and Erwig!).[70] Rothari concluded his edict

[64] *L. Sal. (K)*, cc. 17:3, p. 69; 57:4, p. 209; 61, pp. 219, 221; cf. *L. Sal. (A, C)*, 55:5, p. 208; 58, pp. 218–21; *L. Sal. (D, E)*, 19:2, p. 60–1; 100, pp. 170–1. cf. Eckhardt 1953, pp. 18–19, 37; Eckhardt 1957, pp. 302–4.

[65] *L. Vis.* II i 4, 10, 11, 13, 14, pp. 47, 58–61; the effect of these laws may be gauged by the fact that *Cod. Eur.* is preserved in only a single MS, and *Lex Romana Visigothorum* in only one of Spanish provenance; and both are palimpsests: Paris B.N. Lat. 12161 (*C.L.A.* V, 626); and Cod. Legion 15 (*C.L.A.* XI, 1637). Cf. *L. Burg.*, Pr: 10. The Lombard legislators left *Ed. Roth.* intact, even when they had modified its conclusions; but they were always careful to clarify the relationship between the old law and the new.

[66] Cf. the datings supplied with the list of MSS in Eckhardt 1962b, pp. xiii–xvii; for Alfred and Ine, cf. Liebermann 1916, pp. 35–6.

[67] Brunner 1906, pp. 423–4; Eckhardt 1957, pp. 299–304.

[68] Bischoff on Paris B.N. Lat. 4627, cited by Eckhardt 1962b, p. xv–xvi; and on Paris B.N. Lat. 4418, ibid., p. xix; cf., also, Buchner 1940, p. 88 on Vat. MS Reg. Christ. Lat. 991. The point was noted by Stein 1947, p. 413.

[69] Eckhardt 1958, pp. 19–20; Eckhardt 1962b, pp. xiii–xxvi. In England, similarly, a high proportion of MSS have connections with Canterbury, Winchester and Worcester or York; several of the latter seem to have been connected with Archbishop Wulfstan (1002–23), who was actually the author of legislation in the early eleventh century: Whitelock 1955a, pp. 329, 331, 333; Bethurum 1966, with bibliography of Professor Whitelock's and her own discoveries.

[70] *L. Vis. V* iv 22, p. 226.

by ordering that, to prevent fraud and dispute, only copies written, 'recognized' or sealed by his notary Ansoald were to be used; the Lombard laws followed Roman diplomatic protocol in being carefully dated, and so did some of the Burgundian.[71] But in Francia and England there is no such consistent pattern. The *Decretio* of Childbert was 'recognized' and dated (596) by the referendary Asclepiodatus, of whom more anon; but authentication was unusual in the capitularies of both Merovingian and Carolingian periods, and non-existent in the Frankish family of *Leges*, while dating was relatively rare until the ninth century.[72] Provisions for the publication and archival recording of capitularies appear for the first time late in the reign of Charlemagne, and become quite common under Louis the Pious and Charles the Bald, but are not universal even then.[73] On the whole, the Frankish material lacks regular legislative form, unlike royal charters. Professor Ganshof, in his very important study of the capitularies, has in fact suggested that it was oral pronouncement, the *verbum regis*, which actually gave them legal force; by this, he does not apparently mean that there was no officially produced text, but that the precise form of the text was not important in the way that it would become in later medieval (or modern) statutes, or presumably was in ancient Rome. In practice, we owe our texts to the records kept by the king's *missi*, and deposited by them in the religious houses of which the clerics among them were members.[74] Whatever the demands of ninth century Frankish kings, the limitations of their court archive are brought out by the fact that the most important collection of early capitularies was made *for* the king by abbot Ansegisus acting on his own initiative (827), and that in the process he missed a number of major decrees.[75] The position in England was much the same. There is no trace of authentication, and dating is extremely rare.[76] As I have pointed out elsewhere, Aethelstan's legislation was so heterogeneous in

---

[71] Ed. Roth., c. 388, p. 90.

[72] *L. Sal. Capitularia,* VI, pp. 267–9; this, the Edict of Guntchramn (585) and the Edict of Chlothar II (614) are the only dated Merovingian capitularies. Notable undated Carolingian capitularies are *Capitularia*, nos. 13, I, pp. 31–2; 15, I, pp. 37–9; 16, I, pp. 39–41; 22, I, pp. 52–62; 26, I, pp. 68–70; 32, I, pp. 82–91; 33, I, pp. 91–9; 39, I, pp. 111–14; 41, I, pp. 117–18; 43–4, I, pp. 120–6; 45, I, pp. 126–30; 46, I, pp. 130–2; 50, I, pp. 136–8; 61–3, I, pp. 147–51; 64–5, I, pp. 152–4; 68–9, I pp. 157–9; 77, I, pp. 170–2; 88–97, I, pp. 187–204 (contrast Lombard usage); 137–42, I, pp. 273–93; 150, I, pp. 303–7; 185–90, II, pp. 3–11; 260, II, pp. 270–6; such dating becomes common only under Charles the Bald. For examples of sealing and attestation, cf. Schneider 1967; again, most of his relevant examples are late.

[73] *Capitularia*, nos. 50:8, I, p. 138 (808); 67:6, I, p. 157; 137, I, p. 275 (818/19); 150:26, I, p. 307 (823/5); 260:11, II, p. 274 (853); 273:36, II, p. 327 (864) — in sophistication of legislative form, this last, the Edict of Pitres, represents the climax of Carolingian law-making. For the failings of the Frankish chancery, cf. Brunner 1906, pp. 424–5, Buchner 1953, pp. 16, 47–8, Ganshof 1957, pp. 206–12. For a significant example of a private capitulary collection, see Eckhardt 1955.

[74] Ganshof 1957, pp. 50–61, 69–85, 196–212.

[75] *Capitularia*, I, p. 394; Ganshof 1957, pp. 210–12.

[76] The only dated Anglo-Saxon codes are *L. Wi*, pp. 12–14; and *L. Atr. V*, pp. 236–46.

[77] Wormald 1977, p. 112.

form, that the king appears in three codes in the first person, in two in the third person, and in one in the second.[77] On the other hand, Eadgar's fourth code (962/3 or 973) does conclude with arrangements for the dissemination of the text.[78] But this belated evidence, in England as in Francia, for an interest in the integrity of the written text of legislation only sets off the puzzling failure of earlier legislators to make similar arrangements.

These, then, are some of what one migh call warts on the face of barbarian legislation. They are what prompted Boretius to make the remarks I quoted at the outset, and they have inspired patronising, not to say rude, comments from other scholars about, *'la caractére superficielle de l'époque'* (de Clercq), or, *'barbarische Sorglosigkeit'* (Liebermann); the latest in this line of comments on the Anglo-Saxon laws come (naturally) from Dr. Richardson and Professor Sayles.[79] An alternative approach was offered by S. Stein, who came to dismiss almost every text he encountered as a forgery. Stein's solution was quite literally a *reductio ad absurdum*, but many of his observations on the Frankish texts, as distinct from his conclusions, have never been adequately rebutted.[80] If we are not to resort to his own hypotheses, or to the almost equally improbable hypothesis that Charlemagne, Hincmar, Alfred and Wulfstan did not know what they were doing, we need an account of the context and purposes of Germanic legislation which can accommodate the apparent flaws we have looked at. It may be that our error is to think too much in terms of the practical application of our texts.

In fact, we ought now to consider this problem more directly, instead of firing observations at it from a sceptical distance. What is the evidence that Germanic law-codes and capitularies were meant to be used in court and were so used? Common sense may not be entirely applicable here. We do of course find instructions in the laws that they are to be used in court, but such instructions, as distinct from mere demands for obedience, are not found consistently in all areas. The standards are once again set in the south of Europe. The Visigothic lawbook enjoined its own use in strident terms, and ordered that cases which it had not covered should not be settled locally, but referred to the king for judgement.[81] The Burgundian and Lombard codes said much the same, and so also did the Bavarian *Lex*, which can be shown to have copied Visigothic legislation in other respects.[82] The surviving influence of Roman models is clear here, as it was in the dating and authentication of most of these same texts.[83] Similarly,

---

[78] *L. Eg. IV*, c. 15—15:1, pp. 214—15

[79] de Clercq 1958, p. 40; Liebermann 1903, p. xviii; Richardson & Sayles 1966, pp. 15—24.

[80] Stein 1926; Stein 1941; Stein 1947; cf. Wallace-Hadrill 1962, pp. 95—120.

[81] cf. n. 65.

[82] Cf. *L. Burg.*, Pr: 10—11, p. 33; *Ed. Roth.*, c. 388, p. 90; *L. Liut. (713)*, Ep., p. 109; *L. Liut. (717)*, Ep., p. 113; *L. Liut. (721)*, Ep., p. 121; *L. Liut (726)*, Ep., p. 144; *L. Liut. (727)*, Ep., p. 146; *L. Liut (731)*, Pr., p. 155; *L. Ah. (755)*, Pr., pp. 197—8; *L. Bai.*, c. 2:14, pp. 308—9. For the influence of *Cod. Eur.* on *L. Bai.*, cf. Brunner 1906, p. 423; Eckhardt 1927, pp. 19—35; Beyerle 1929, pp. 278—87.

[83] Cf. *Cod. Theod.* I i, pp. 27—9.

from Charlemagne's time, we find increasingly frequent demands that counts, *scabini* and all others involved are to learn and use *lex scripta*.[84] And, as one might by now expect, tenth century England offers the same evidence in Edward the Elder's famous command (899—924) that reeves judge, 'as it stands in the lawbook'.[85] But it needs to be appreciated that this law of Edward's is unique in an English context. Neither in the rest of Anglo-Saxon legislation, nor in that of the peoples east of the Rhine and north of the Danube, nor in the Frankish laws before Charlemagne do we encounter what one might expect to find in any law-code. We can scarcely say that the point was taken for granted, because it is made explicit in the other texts we have considered.

The legal manuscripts of barbarian Europe, taken as a whole, tell a similarly ambivalent story. There are a very large number of manuscripts of the *Leges* and of most important capitularies, including Ansegisus, from Francia itself and from southern Germany; the vast majority of these date to the ninth century, when, as we have seen, kings did regularly demand that the written law be used by judges.[86] There are also a good number, considering the circumstances of foreign conquest, of the Visigothic and Lombardic texts. Professor Buchner has pointed out that the majority of these manuscripts consist of secular laws and little else; many contain more than one *Lex*, but this is what one would expect when the suitors in a Frankish court might well profess different tribal laws.[87] Here, then, is presumptive evidence of the use of legal texts in court. Perhaps we should not expect similar quantities of material from the Merovingian period, since Merovingian manuscripts of all types are much rarer than their Carolingian counterparts. But it is striking that, quite unlike the south German *Leges*, those of northern Germany are so ill-attested. *Lex Saxonum* survives only in two manuscripts, *Lex Thuringorum* in one and *Lex Frisionum* in none at all.[88] England offers a picture closer to that of the areas east of the Rhine than their western neighbours. Alfred's *domboc* survived in six manuscripts, and no other Anglo-Saxon legal text, apart from the *Quadripartitus* and the twelfth century collections, occurs in more.[89] Nor, even in ninth century Francia let alone elsewhere, is it actually true that all manuscripts are of a strictly practical

---

[84] *Capitularia*, nos. 22:63, I, p. 58; 33:26, I, p. 96; 40:4, I, p. 115; 57:4, I, p. 144; 58:2, I, p. 145; 60:3, 4, I, p. 147; 85:Pr., I, p. 184; 116:11, I, p. 235; 266:4, II, pp. 286—7; 273:34, II, pp. 325—7. This is to exclude the Italian evidence.

[85] *L. Ew. I*, Pr., pp. 138—9.

[86] Cf., for the most up-to-date lists (but, in some cases, in need of supplement and modification): Beyerle 1926, pp. xcii—xciii *(L. Bai.)*; Christ 1937, pp. 313—18; (Ansegisus); Beyerle-Buchner 1951, pp. 32—40 *(L. Rib.)*; Eckhardt 1958, pp. 11—37 *(L. Al.)*; Eckhardt 1962b, pp. xi—xxvii *(L. Sal.)*. For Lombard MSS, cf. Bluhme 1868, pp. xli—xlvi; for Visigothic, cf. Zeumer 1902, pp. xix—xxv; for Burgundian, cf. de Salis 1892, pp. 14—19.

[87] Buchner 1955, pp. 396—7.

[88] von Richthofen 1863, pp. 631—2 *(L. Fris.)*; von Richthofen 1875—89, pp. 1—5 *(L. Sax.)*; von Richthofen 1875—89, pp. 103—4 *(L. Thur.)*. On the MS situation in general, cf. Brunner 1906, pp. 413—14.

[89] Liebermann 1903, pp. xviii—xlii; palaeography was not Liebermann's *forte* and this list is badly in need of revision in the light of the work of Sisam, Jost, Whitelock, Bethurum and Ker.

type. Some of the most interesting associate their legal texts with historical material. A number of manuscripts of the Lombard laws include not only Rothari's king-list, but also a bizarre account of Lombard origins, and we can tell from Paul the Deacon that the association goes back at least as far as his day.[90] Two important collections of Frankish texts, Paris B. N. Lat. 10758, from Hincmar's Rheims, and its copy, Paris 4628a, from St. Denis, also contain Einhard's *Life of Charlemagne*.[91] The earliest manuscript of Alfred's law-book was bound up from very early in its existence with the famous 'Parker' MS of the Anglo-Saxon Chronicle; as with the Rheims and St. Denis MSS, we can tell that the connection was not entirely fortuitous, because, at the end of the tenth century, the whole manuscript was copied, and appended to the translation of Bede's *Ecclesiastical History*.[92] In fact, the association seems, for some reason, to have been natural: Widukind implies as much negatively, when beginning an account of Saxon custom, and then breaking it off on the grounds that *Lex Saxonum* is written down elsewhere. Even in far off Scandinavia, the lawbook of Gotland was supplemented by the *Historia Gotlandiae*.[93] I shall return to this persistent tendency. For the moment, we may note that it argues priorities in some legal collections that were not solely practical.

Unfortunately, the kind of research which would really settle this question, the close examination of all available accounts of judicial proceedings in the Barbarian West, has never been carried out, and I certainly do not possess the specialist knowledge to give a conclusive answer. All the same, I think that I can detect here the pattern which is already becoming familiar. In the trial of Count Paul for treason against the Visigothic king Wamba, to which Mr. Collins refers, the lawbook was cited by book, title and verse; and although, as Mr. Collins says, we lack the Spanish charters which would tell us in more detail about the application of the Visigothic code, we do find citations similar to that in the case of Paul in the charters and monastic histories of Visigothic southern France during the ninth century.[94] The surviving prestige of the *Liber Iudiciorum* in this area is dramatically highlighted by an extraordinary incident at the Council of Troyes (878): the Bishop of Narbonne arrived complaining that there was nothing in the lawbook about sacrilege, yet it also stipulated that judges should not use their own initiative in cases for which it did not provide; 'thus the rights of holy church are suffocated by the inhabitants of the Gallic and Spanish provinces'.[95] Likewise, north Italian charters stick relatively closely to *lex scripta*. In one case, a manumission was denied

---

[90] For MSS containing both the Lombard Edict and the *Origo Gentis Langobardorum* in various versions, cf. Bluhme 1868, pp. xxvi–xxviii, xxx–xxxiii, xxxviii–xxxix, xl–xlii, xlii–xliii; and Lowe 1914, pp. 10–11. For Paul's evidence on the link, cf. Paul. Diac., *Hist. Lang.*, I, 21, pp. 59–60.

[91] On these MSS, cf. Stein 1941, pp. 34–8, 49–54, 60–2; Stein 1947, pp. 130–2; Carey 1938, pp. 57–8; Eckhardt 1959b, pp. 130–3; Parkes 1976, pp. 167–8.

[92] Ker 1957, nos. 39, pp. 57–9; 180, pp. 230–4; cf. Parkes 1976, *passim*.

[93] Widukind, *Res. gest. Sax.*, I, 14, p. 24; von Amira 1960, p. 108.

[94] Julian, *Hist. Wamb.*, *Iudicium*, c. 7, p. 534; cf. *Formulae*, p. 593; Thevenin 1887, no. 88, pp. 118–19; and, for other references, Brunner 1906, p. 426.

[95] Mansi, XVII, col. 351.

validity on the grounds that the relevant charter predated the law of Liutprand's in which this form of manumission was first allowed.[96] On the other hand, I have (I hope) read all the Anglo-Saxon charters recording judicial decisions, and even on matters of criminal law where written law might have helped there is not a single direct reference to, still less a quotation from, the extant texts.[97] The picture in northern and central Germany is apparently equally blank. Between the two poles, the Frankish and south German evidence is more ambiguous. The formularies of the Merovingian and Carolingian periods, and Carolingian royal diplomata, did refer to the *lex*, and sometimes specifically to Salic or Alaman law, but only very rarely, even in the ninth century, did they cite it explicitly, like the equivalent southern material. Moreover, some of these references are bewildering. In Marculf's formulary, we find that manumission by throwing a penny at the candidate was according to 'Lex Salica'; but although the extant text of the code refers to this procedure in passing, it nowhere *decrees* it.[98] Even more remarkable, three other formularies describe betrothal with *solidus* and *denarius* as, 'secundum legem Salicam', but although we do have late chronicle evidence that Clovis himself offered Chrotechildis 1/1d, 'ut mos erat Francorum', we have already seen that Lex Salica itself says nothing of these matters.[99] Similarly, the references to Lex Alamannorum in the formularies of Reichenau and St. Gallen also fail to correspond with the actual provisions of the written text.[100] One must conclude, I think, from this that when the documents refer to *lex*, they mean custom (among many other things), and they do not necessarily mean the written law. In later eighth and ninth century private charters, there are some exceptions, for instance in those of Freising (significantly in Bavaria) and Lorsch (a great royal monastery).[101] But, on the whole, in spite of the efforts by Carolingian kings that we have noted, custom seems to have remained primary. My conclusion for Europe as a whole is thus unsurprising, but nonetheless suggestive. In those areas where the use of *lex scripta* was not only ordained but made easy, *lex scripta* was indeed used. In the areas where we find similar ambitions, but more marginal assistance to the judge, there are signs of a move in this direction, but no

---

[96] *Cod. Dipl. Longob*, I, no. 81, pp. 237–8; cf. *L. Liut (721)*, c. 23, p. 118; and *L. Liut. (727)*, c. 91, pp. 144–5; this reference, which I used in Wormald 1977, p. 113, I originally owed to Dr. C. J. Wickham. Cf. also, Brunner 1906, pp. 426–7.

[97] cf. Sawyer, nos. 254/443, 877, 883, 886, 892, 893, 896, 901, 926, 927, 934, 937, 1377, 1445, 1447, 1501; on the continent, one might well find reference to *lex* in such contexts: cf., e.g., nos. 926 or 937, and *Traditionen Freising*, no. 49, pp. 77–8.

[98] *Form. Marc.*, I, 22, p. 57; *Cart. Senon.*, no. 12, p. 190; *Cart. Senon.*, no. 42, p. 204; *Form. Sal. Bignon.*, no. 1, p. 228; *Form. Sal. Merk.*, no. 40, p. 256; *Form. Imp.*, no. 1, p. 288; no. 34, p. 312; cf. *L. Sal. (A)*, c. 26, pp. 96–7; *L. Rib.*, cc. 60, pp. 107–8; 65, p. 117.

[99] *Form. Sal. Bignon.*, no. 6, p. 230 (with f/n.); *Form. Sal. Merk.*, no. 15, p. 247; *Form. Sal. Lind.*, no. 7, p. 271; *Form. Extrav.*, no. 12, p. 541.

[100] *Form. Aug.*, no. 25, p. 357; *Form. Aug.*, no. 40, p. 362; *Form. Sangall.*, no. 22; p. 389; *Coll. Sangall.*, no. 18, p. 407; *Form. Aug. Coll.* B 46, p. 725; cf. *L. Al.*, c. 52, pp. 110–11.

[101] cf. *Traditionen Freising*, as in n. 97; and *Cod. Lauresham.*, no. 423, II, p. 106; no. 3006, III, p. 254. Cf., also, *Form. Imp.*, no. 15, p. 297; *Diplom. Karol.*, nos. 12, p. 18; 77, p. 111; 138, p. 189; 216, pp. 288–9.

more. In the parts of Europe where both instructions on, and manuscripts of, the law are rare, there is scarcely a trace of the use of written texts in actual cases.

It is time to suggest some conclusions about the use of Germanic legal texts in the administration of justice. We are faced with a paradox in that we have a considerable quantity of legislation, much of it implying its relevance to the preservation of law and order; yet the texts themselves have features which, taken together, do argue against their applicability, and there is remarkably little evidence for their application.[102] If we are to explain the situation I have described, we need to take account, first, of the fact that early medieval Europe was a big place, where, in spite of similarities of experience, the pattern was not everywhere the same; and, secondly, of the point that, as I have already argued elsewhere, there was a fundamental tension in the attitude of the conquering barbarians towards their inheritance in the Romano-Christian West, a dialectic between respect for the Roman example, and attachment to their own traditional culture.[103] It is well-known that northern continental Europe from the tenth century until well on in the Middle Ages was a *pays du droit coutumier*, and Glanville, somewhat surprisingly, attests as much for twelfth century England.[104] It is not honestly likely to have been anything else in the even less literate world of the early Middle Ages. I suggest that many of the problems we have been considering become less bewildering if we adapt Professor Ganshof's conclusions on the capitularies to the legislation of the northern barbarians as a whole. What mattered in the promulgation and enforcement of law remained the *word*, whether of the king, his wise men, the judges or the local legal experts. The use of writing, which the invaders had inherited from their victims, continued to belong, as Ganshof says, to the margins of the administration of justice.[105] This is, as we have seen, the impression that we derive from the cases we know about. It is even hinted at for legislation itself. Both the preface to the *Lex Baiwariorum* and the longer prologue to *Lex Salica* describe the *dictation* of the Law.[106] A regular formula in tenth century Anglo-Saxon law-codes was, '*we cwaedon* (we say)'.[107] To suggest that, like normal judicial procedure, the formal process of making law by the king or the legal specialist was oral, and that, in the *administration*

---

[102] There is, of course, little evidence for the application of Roman Law; but, the papyri apart, very few 'documents' survive from the Roman period, whereas we do have charters from the early medieval West.

[103] Wormald 1977, p. 100.

[104] *Glanville*, Pr., pp. 2–3; surprising, because *Quadripartitus*, and *Leg. Hen. Prim.* had ostensibly made a lot of ancient English custom available in Latin.

[105] Ganshof 1957, p. 201.

[106] *L. Bai.*, Pr., pp. 201–3; *L. Sal. (D)*, Pr:2, pp. 4–5; but, in the first of these cases, Theuderic was dictating, and ordering the law to be written.

[107] *L. Ew. I*, cc. 1:2, 3, 5, pp. 138–41; 2, pp. 140–1; 3, pp. 140–1; *L. As. I*, Pr., pp. 146–7; c. 5, pp. 148–9; *L. As. II*. cc. 2, pp. 150–1; 4, pp. 152–3; 6, pp. 152–3; 7, pp. 154–5; 8, pp. 154–5; 11, pp. 156–7; 12, pp. 156–7; 13, pp. 156–7; 19, pp. 160–1; 25, pp. 164–5; *L. As. V*, Pr., pp. 166–7; *L. As. IV*, c. 6:1, p. 171; *L. As. VI*, cc. 6:3, p. 176; 7, p. 177; 8:6, p. 180; 9, p. 181; 10, p. 181; 12:1, pp. 182–3; *L. Em. I*, c. 5, pp. 186–7; *L. Em. II*, Pr., pp. 186–7; cc. 4, pp. 188–9; 6, pp. 188–9; *L. Em. III*, cc. 4, 6, p. 191; *L. Eg. I*, c. 4, pp. 192–3.

of justice (my emphasis), its commitment to writing was marginal, albeit simultaneous, helps to explain the imprecision of many legal texts, the profusion of error and contradiction, both scribal and official, and the remarkable lack of attention to publication and preservation; it also, obviously, explains why only a proportion of laws demand their own application in court. It means that it misses the point to criticize barbarian kings for inefficiency when their legislation seems to leave something to be desired, or to assume that an absence of legislation argues an absence of effective government. Charlemagne and Alfred were certainly not incompetent in other respects. There is a correspondence between the cessation of Frankish legislation soon after the death of Charles the Bald and the decline of Carolingian government, and one might say the same of England after the death of Cnut; but Lombard kings not notorious as effete did without written law for seventy-five years after the technology of writing became available to them in Italy, and the mighty Otto the Great, who did occasionally give his judgements general validity, never felt the need to incorporate them in a single capitulary supplementary to *Lex Saxonum*.[108]

But this picture is not universally accurate. Southern Europe in the twelfth century was a *pays du droit écrit*, and we have already seen good evidence that it was in our period also, at least to a far greater extent than the areas to the north. The Visigothic, Lombard, Burgundian and even Bavarian material looks much more like legislation as we would understand it (more so in the first two cases); and there is much better evidence for its actual employment in court. There can be no doubt that the reason for this was that the Roman example was more alive in southern than in northern Europe. In Italy, Spain and southern Gaul, written *acta* remained central to legal procedure.[109] Roman law was not here a 'ghost story', as, in Vinogradoff's words, it was to the north.[110] Roman culture survived generally in the form, for example, of much more extensive lay literacy.[111] It was thus the environment that made the crucial difference to the scope and character of legislation in the southern Germanic kingdoms. Secondly, however, we have also seen striking evidence for more literate standards of law-making in the ninth century Frankish Empire, and, to a lesser extent, in tenth century England. The written instrument was becoming more important in Frankish legal procedure by the ninth century, and English judicial memoranda always allowed some role, if not a decisive one, to the evidence

---

[108] Widukind, *Res. gest. Sax.* II, 10, pp. 73–4. Glanville's words are worth quoting in this context: 'Leges autem Anglicanas licet non scriptas leges appellari non videatur absurdum, cum hoc ipsum lex sit, ''quod principi placet, legis habet vigorem'', eas scilicet quas super dubiis in concilio et principis accedente auctoritate, constat esse promulgatas': *Glanville*, p. 2.

[109] Cf. the Ravenna papyri, ed. G. Marini 1805; the Visigothic slates, for which cf. Diaz y Diaz 1966; and the *Tablettes Albertini*, ed. C. Courtois et al. 1952. For S. Gaul, cf. next note.

[110] Vinogradoff 1929, p. 13; references to Roman law and municipal *acta* are common in formulae of S. Gallic and Spanish provenance: *Formulae*, pp. 30, 142 & ff., 175–6, 535–6, 545, 589, 590–1; . for evidence of Roman Law in Lombard Italy, cf. Bognetti 1939.

[111] Wormald 1977, p. 99, and references.

of charters.[112] But we have seen that there was apparently no appreciable increase of citations of written law in Frankish legal records, and none at all in England, though the number of legal manuscripts did increase in Francia. Both in Francia and in England, moreover, the legislative tradition petered out after six generations. Here, then, standards seem to have been set from above, without concommittant growth in pragmatic literacy at 'grass-roots', by ascendant monarchies whose conquests had given them the confidence to claim to be Empires. This conclusion is of great importance, not only in accommodating the variations in the character of barbarian legislation that we have noticed, but also in resolving the paradox that in areas where we have no evidence for the use of written law, and evidence that argues against it, we yet have so many legal texts. We can now see that written law could represent an aspiration on the part of kings and their advisers, even when there was no obvious demand for it in normal legal procedure; the inspiration could be ideological rather than practical in origin. We can also see that, just as the survival of Roman practice in southern Europe permitted and inspired more sophisticated and comprehensive legislation for the Germanic peoples who settled there, so the establishment of Empires which resembled those of the Romans and Byzantines (at least in the eyes of their creators) could and did inspire a measure of emulation of the most famous Roman achievement, the tradition of written law. Legislation could be a matter of image-building, and one at least of the chosen images was that of Imperial Rome. It is in these terms that I would now like to try to account not only for the Carolingian interest in written law but also for much of the rest of Germanic legislation.

IV

First, then, the 'example of the Romans', to adapt Bede's phrase.[113] As Professor Wallace-Hadrill has often argued, the initial production of the barbarian law-codes in Latin must argue Roman assistance and even Roman influence. It is possible to suggest some names who might have helped their new masters in this respect, and I dropped some in an article last year. In Italy, the role of Cassiodorus as spokesman for a sequence of Ostrogothic rulers is well-known; if the *Edict of Theodoric* is indeed to be attributed to the great Ostrogoth, Cassiodorus cannot have written it, but he may stand as a type for a predecessor who did.[114] Under the Lombards, similar, if more retiring, figures may be detected;[115] something of what Maitland called the Lombard 'genius for law' must be credited, as we have seen, to the legacy of Roman

---

[112] Brunner 1906, p. 415. For the ambiguities of the English situation, cf., e.g., Sawyer, nos. 192, 1187, 1211, 1258, 1433, 1445, 1458, 1464; the fact that charters were important as evidence is indicated by the fact that they were both forged and stolen: Sawyer, nos. 885, 1258, 1429, 1434, 1457; and replacements were commissioned: nos. 227, 367—9, 371.

[113] Bede, H. E., II, 5, p. 90; whether Bede meant something abstract, or something more concrete (as Wallace-Hadrill 1971, pp. 37—9, suggests) by this phrase, the significant thing for our purposes is that he is thinking of 'Romani' in the context of written legislation.

[114] On *Ed. Theod.*, contrast Vismara 1967a with Sanchez-Albornoz 1962, pp. 155—6, n. 66. For discussion of the motives of Cassiodorus and his like, cf. Wormald 1976, pp. 221—5.

[115] Bognetti 1948, pp. 182—4; Bognetti 1948/9, p. 51.

officialdom, if not to Romans themselves. For the rulers of southern Gaul, the correspondence of Sidonius supplies us with counterparts to Cassiodorus. Leo of Narbonne, whom Sidonius compared to Appius Claudius, is described as preoccupied with declamations in the name of King Euric, whereby he restrained 'arms with laws'; there is a virtually irresistible temptation to ascribe to him the composition of the *Codex Euricianus*.[116] Similarly, Syagrius was a 'new Solon of the Burgundians in discussing the laws', and must somehow be associated with the emergence of *Lex Burgundionum*.[117] But the most striking case comes later among the Franks. We have already encountered Asclepiodatus, referendary and patrician, as the authenticator, and presumably in some sense the author, of Childebert II's *Decretio*. Even more important, it can be argued on stylistic grounds that he wrote the prologue, and perhaps some of the contents, for the third recension of *Lex Salica*.[118] Here is virtually direct evidence that Romans could be associated with emphatically barbarian legislation. The preface to the Bavarian *Lex* mentions Claudius, identifiable as a Roman, as one of those who assisted Dagobert in the issue of legislation, which does not seem to have been much Romanized.[119] If Asclepiodatus and Claudius could do it, we need not be afraid to postulate the role of similar figures in the production of the original *Lex Salica* or comparable codes. But I should like to enter a *caveat* against identifying 'Roman' influence with that of Senators or Bishops in all cases. Minds as impregnated with Roman cultural values as the friends of Sidonius might help to produce texts like the Eurician or Burgundian codes, which bear the stamp of Roman Vulgar Law, and even have some pretensions to style, but I cannot see them producing so inelegant and undilutedly Germanic a text as *Lex Salica*; and while the weight of ecclesiastical interests was soon felt in sixth century Frankish legislation, it is wholly absent here. This code and others like it must be attributed to less exalted figures, and, if I were looking for their authors, I would search the anonymous ranks of the provincial bureaucrats of curial class who transmitted Roman diplomatic protocols to the 'chanceries' of Germanic kings, and who were presumably responsible for the Latin seal-ring of Clovis's pagan father, Childeric.[120]

The motives of these Roman assistants to barbarian kings must, I think, have been ideological as well as practical. Romans were used to thinking of their ruler as a source of judgements;[121] it is easy to see why they should have wished barbarian kings to issue written regulations covering disputes between their Roman subjects

---

[116] Sidonius, *Carm.* 23, 447–9, I, pp. 312–13; *Ep.* VIII iii 3, II, pp. 408–11; the role of these individuals, which was first noticed by Mommsen, is discussed by Beyerle 1929, pp. 392 & ff; cf., also, Stroheker 1948, pp. 90–2, 98–9, 114, 123–7, and the relevant prosopography.

[117] Sidonius, Ep. V v, II pp. 180–3.

[118] Eckhardt 1954, pp. 170–2.

[119] L. Bai., Pr., p. 202; cf. Fredegar, *Chron. IV*, c. 28, p. 19; and discussion in Beyerle 1929, pp. 381–2, and Eckhardt 1959a, pp. 136–7.

[120] Classen 1955–6.

[121] See now Millar 1977, pp. 228–72, and 507–49.

and their own peoples, and this helps to account for much of the character of early Visigothic and Burgundian legislation.[122] But it does not explain *Lex Salica*. Here, we must make some allowance simply for the professional habits of hereditary government officials who were used to working for a legislating master. But, more generally, the Roman contribution to the production of very un-Roman laws seems to reflect the profound and ancient Mediterranean feeling that, as Cassiodorus put it, 'the true mark of *civilitas* is the observance of law; it is this ... which separates men from beasts'.[123] Traditionally, barbarians were like beasts in that they had no law; it was the role of the Romans to give them one. In the circumstances of the fifth and sixth centuries, there were understandably a good many Romans who wished to believe that the process was still going ahead on their own soil. One of the main points of Orosius' famous story of the Visigothic king Athaulf's change of heart about the substitution of *Gothia* for *Romania* was that one barbarian had apparently learned that a state could not do without laws.[124] The Byzantine Agathias reported that the Franks were not nomads like some other barbarians, 'but had a Roman polity for the most part, and their own laws'.[125] This conviction that barbarians would only seem civilized if they observed a visible law ran alongside the single most consistent principle of Roman dealings with barbarians: that they were best conducted with secure and permanent chieftains.[126] Barbarian kings were expected, as was Jimmy Thomas by Margot Asquith, to keep their men under control. Texts like *Lex Salica* might have little to offer the Roman in the way of law, but they were some sort of evidence that a king was carrying out this vital task. Gregory of Tours knew nothing of Frankish laws, but he did describe how Gundobad had, 'instituted milder laws among the Burgundians that there should be no undue oppression of the Romans'.[127] As a description of Gundobad's legislation, this leaves something to be desired, but it offers a revealing insight into what one Roman thought that barbarian law-making was for. Thus, one vital reason why Roman lawyers and administrators lent their aid to their new rulers, and perhaps encouraged them to go ahead with

---

[122] *Cod. Eur.*, cc. 276, pp. 4–5; 277, pp. 5–6; 312, pp. 19–20; *L. Burg.*, Pr:5, 8, 13, pp. 31–3; cc. 4, pp. 44–5; 7, p. 48; 8, pp. 49–50; 9, p. 50; 10, pp. 50–1; 13, p. 52; 15, p. 54; 22, p. 60; 26, p. 63; 28, pp. 65–6; 31, pp. 66–7; 38, pp. 69–70; 50, pp. 81–2; 54, pp. 88–9; 55, pp. 90–1; 57, p. 91; 67, p. 95; 84, pp. 106–7; *L. Burg. Const. Extrav.*, 18, p. 118; 20, p. 119; 21:11, 12, pp. 121–2. The character of early Visigothic legislation has been much discussed: for bibliography, see King 1972, pp. 6–11, 13–14, 17–19; I have not seen Dr. King's own discussion of the subject, but, *pro tem.* it seems to me that *Cod. Eur.* will have been similar to *L. Burg.*, i.e. Romanized law with a strong Germanic core, designed to apply to Goths, and to cases of dispute between Goth and Roman, and leaving the Roman population secure in the possession of their own law for dealings between themselves.

[123] Cassiodorus, *Ep. Var.* IV 33, pp. 128–9.

[124] Orosius, *Historia*, VII 43, pp. 559–60. It is surely in this general sense that one should take the passage in Jordanes, *Getica*, c. 25, p. 92, on Gothic submission to the Emperor's laws: D'Ors 1956, p. 383, is too literal.

[125] Agathias I ii, p. 17. On this theme in general, see Messmer 1960, pp. 32–43.

[126] Thompson 1965, pp. 72–108; Wallace-Hadrill 1971, pp. 7, 17, 20.

[127] Greg. Turon., *Hist. Franc.* II 33, p. 81.

written legislation, was that even a wholly barbarian law-code helped the Roman to believe what he devoutly wished to believe: that as little as possible had changed.

One reason, therefore, for the existence of barbarian law-codes, especially from the period immediately following the establishment of Germanic kingdoms on Roman soil, was that Romans wished to project this image onto Germanic kingship. Hence the use of Latin, and the influence, to a lesser or greater extent, of Roman Vulgar Law. But the barbarian legislative tradition was perpetuated at dates (after the mid seventh century) and in places (like England or across the Rhine) where Roman influence was remote. Moreover, if *Lex Salica* is, to quote Professor Wallace-Hadrill, 'inconceivable without the help of professionals trained in Roman Vulgar Law', it is equally inconceivable without the assistance of men to whom Salic custom was directly familiar. The name of the referendary who authenticated Rothari's edict, Ansoald, is Germanic, and so are the names of two of Dagobert's other assistants.[128] We therefore need to appreciate and understand the contribution of the barbarians themselves. In a famous passage, Einhard described how Charlemagne,

> after receiving the imperial name, noticed that much was lacking in the laws of his people — for the 'Franks have two laws very different in many places — and pondered how to fill the gaps, reconcile the discrepancies and correct the mistakes and flaws of expression. But none of this was achieved by him except that he added a few *capitula*, and these unfinished, to the laws. Yet the laws of all the peoples under his dominion which were unwritten he had written and committed to letters.[129]

Einhard's words are based on those of Suetonius, but, up to a point, they are accurate enough. We know that Charlemagne instituted enquiries into the customs of his various peoples, and it was probably as a result that the *Leges* of the Frisians, Saxons and Thuringians were produced. We have seen that he did merge the two divergent recensions of *Lex Salica*, and he may also have begun a reconciliation of Salic and Ribuarian laws.[130] We know that he did improve the language of many of the *Leges* already in existence, and that he added chapters to the Salic, Ribuarian, Bavarian and even Lombard laws, though without bringing the content of the original texts up to date.[131] But Einhard's most interesting phrase is, *'post susceptum imperiale nomen'*, because it is also true that much of this activity post-dated 800, and one is strongly tempted to conclude, *post hoc, propter hoc:* Charlemagne, as well as Einhard, knew what Suetonius had written about Augustus.[132] There is no reason to

---

[128] *Ed. Roth.*, c. 388, p. 90; *L. Bai.*, Pr., p. 202; the names are Chadoind and Agilulf; cf. Eckhardt 1959a, pp. 135–6.

[129] Einhard, *V.C.*, c. 29, p. 33; my translation is loosely based on that of Thorpe 1969.

[130] For the reconciliation of C & E texts, cf. pp. 116–7 and n. 64 above; for the possibility that Einhard was, after all, talking about Salic and Ribuarian laws, cf. Eckhardt 1955, pp. 22–3; for evidence on the Frisian, Saxon and Thuringian laws, cf. n. 13 above.

[131] For the *Emendata* texts, cf. nn. 16, 20, 64 above, and Beyerle-Buchner 1951, pp. 37–8; the relevant capitularies are, *Capitularia*, nos. 39, I, pp. 111–14; 41, I, pp. 117–18; 68–9, I, pp. 157–9; I, 98, pp. 204–6.

[132] But Suetonius does not feature in what Bischoff has argued to be the catalogue of the Court-Library: Bischoff 1965, pp. 57–60.

doubt that Charlemagne's capitularies, like those of his Merovingian predecessors, represented serious attempts to deal with serious problems, and that the greater use of writing by his government was inspired in part by concern with administrative efficiency.[133] Nevertheless, it is very striking that such a huge proportion of his capitulary output dates to the last fourteen years of his reign; and the practical advantages of much of his legislation, especially of the *Leges* which he issued or reissued, are not, as we have seen, entirely obvious. It would seem that written legislation represented an aspect of his new imperial dignity, because it was *par excellence* the function of a Roman Emperor; and this must also have been an element in the efforts which he, and still more his successors, made to improve the arrangements for the publication and recording of their capitularies.

We can explain a great deal of barbarian legislation in the same sort of way. The *Codex Euricianus* was probably issued in the extremely significant year of 476.[134] Liuvigild, the author of the revised Visigothic Code, adopted much of the Roman panoply of monarchy, and even indulged the supremely Roman habit of founding a city.[135] The promulgation of Rothari's great edict may well be connected with a campaign to seize the whole of Italy from the heretical Byzantines, and recreate the kingdom of Theodoric.[136] I feel myself that Clovis's issue of the Latin but religiously neutral *Lex Salica* is better linked to the new sub-imperial status he acquired in 508 than to his conversion.[137] The preface to the Bavarian law shows Clovis's successors, like Charlemagne later (and, according to the Dialogue of the Exchequer, William the Conqueror) fulfilling the Roman function of giving laws to subject peoples.[138] The enhanced interest in *lex scripta* which we find in tenth century England, if not in Ottonian Germany, and which was reflected both in the issue of capitulary-style codes and in some emphasis on the use and publication of written legislation, should be explained in part by the fact that, as Dr. Nelson stresses, they considered themselves Emperors; though here the model is more likely to be Carolingian than Roman.[139] In all these cases, imitation of the Roman, and specifically imperial, tradition of *lex scripta* reflected and raised the status of barbarian peoples and their

---

[133] Ganshof 1951, pp. 125—42. It may be noted that the Merovingians, Theudebert I (whom Beyerle 1956, pp. 125—7, plausibly suggests to have been confused with Theuderic I in *L. Bai*, Pr's list of Frankish legislators), and Chilperic, author of *L. Sal. Capitularia*, IV, pp. 261—3, showed strongly 'Romanizing' features in other aspects of their government and life-style: Stroheker 1948, pp. 124—7.

[134] Sidonius, *Ep.* VIII iii (q.v. n. 116) seems to date to 477.

[135] Isidore, *Hist. Goth.*, c. 51, pp. 287—8; cf. Claude 1971, pp. 61—75.

[136] Bognetti 1957, pp. 115—35; I share the doubts of Paradisi 1971 about the more 'Germanist' of Bognetti's suggestions.

[137] cf. Hauck 1967, pp. 30—3; Wolfram 1970, pp. 12—14.

[138] *L. Bai.*, Pr., pp. 201—2; Einhard, *V.C.*, loc. cit.; *Dialogus de Scaccario*, I 16, p. 63; 'decrevit subiectum sibi populum iuri scripto legibusque subicere' — this, of course, was virtually complete fiction, except, perhaps, in the context of Domesday Book.

[139] cf. Nelson, in this volume p. 68. cf also Campbell 1975, pp. 43—50. I hope to discuss the Carolingian inspiration behind tenth-century English monarchy further in a projected book on English legislation between Alfred and Cnut.

kings. And imitation of Rome is indicated in other ways. Codes were in Latin. The significance of the prologues to barbarian laws in which Justinian is paraphrased may lie in the fact that this was an established legislative formula as much as in the precise relevance of his words to what the barbarian kings were actually doing. The Visigoths arranged their code in twelve books, although this meant a first book which was almost wholly philosophical and an eleventh containing only a few miscellaneous laws; but they had Isidore to tell them that Roman law began with the Twelve Tables, even if they were unaware that Justinian had done the same.[140] The longer Prologue to *Lex Salica* expanded Asclepiodatus' shorter prologue into a strident reproduction of a basic Roman *topos*, balancing Frankish excellence in war by excellence in law; and the same equation may underlie that family of legal manuscripts we have considered in which legal material was associated with historical works describing the military achievements of a people and its rulers.[141] Thus, Roman example seems to explain in part both the production and the appearance of barbarian laws. It was not just that the surviving Romans wished their new masters to seem civilized; barbarian kings and their advisers had the same ambitions for themselves, and therefore committed to writing in Latin a selection of the relevant popular custom, and of their own decisions, or reissued and revised an established text. These motives are not exclusive of practical considerations, especially, as we have seen, in southern Europe; but even when we have reason to believe that legislators meant their work to be used, an ideological inspiration that was Roman in origin seems also to be involved, and this type of inspiration was perhaps the decisive factor in the original production of laws for which no practical explanation seems to be available.

But the Roman imperial example was not the only stimulus to legislation; it will hardly account for Aethelberht, for example. A second source of inspiration was Christianity, the Church and the Bible. Churchmen were involved in barbarian legislation as scribes and preservers of manuscripts, as a pressure-group on royal policy, and even as the actual authors of legal texts: we have already considered the role of Ansegisus in compiling the first formal capitulary collection and of clerical missi in transmitting the texts of capitularies and *Leges* via the great religious houses of the Frankish Empire; Archbishop Wulfstan is securely identified as the author of a great deal of later Anglo-Saxon legislation, and similar figures must lie behind much of the continental material.[142] Thus we could say that the Church, with its commitment to, and its effective monopoly of, literacy, played the same part with later barbarian

---

[140] Isidore, *Etym.* V i 3.

[141] L. Sal. (C), Pr:1, p. 2; L. Sal. (D: E), Pr:1, pp. 2–5. For the Roman *topos*, cf. Justinian, *Const. Imperatoriam*, Pr., I, p. xxiii; *Const. Deo Auctore*, Pr., I, p. 8; *Const. De Codice Confirmando*, Pr., II, p. 2. cf., also, Cassiodorus, *Ep. Var.* IV 12, p. 119; Sidonius, *Ep.* VIII iii 3 II, pp. 410–11; and *Glanville*, Pr., pp. 1–2.

[142] For Wulfstan, cf. n. 69 above. Cf. Lynch 1938, pp. 137–40 on *L. Vis.*; Beyerle 1926, pp. liii–lxxiv, and Eckhardt 1927, pp. 56–68, on *L. Bai*; Hincmar was almost certainly the author of some capitulary legislation, eg. *Capitularia*, no. 272, II, pp. 302–10.

legislation as did Roman government officials earlier. But if we say that, we need to make the same provisoes as we did with the Romans. In the first place, whatever the case with the inauguration rituals discussed by Dr. Nelson, there can be no question that legislation was pressed by churchmen on a disinterested or reluctant kingship. St. Augustine may well have wished to see King Aethelberht equipped with a written law-code, but both its content and its language argue that Aethelberht's code was the work of the king and his *sapientes*, not of the Roman missionaries.[143] Secondly, it is a mistake to confuse *interest* with *interests* in legislation. Much of the later Frankish and English material was obviously of vital importance to the encouragement of Christian behaviour and the protection of clerical rights. But primary legislation especially, like that of Aethelberht, contains much besides christian and clerical matters, and only a proportion of legal manuscripts mix canonical with secular legislation.[144] The contribution of Christianity to the emergence of the Germanic legislative tradition was also ideological and cultural, like the Roman contribution. Christianity was a religion of the Book. The Bible was the law-book of the heavenly kingdom, and Christ was of course regularly depicted as a judge holding a book. Moreover, the Bible contained, in the Pentateuch, what King Alfred called *seo ae* (*the* Law), the model legislation which Moses had derived from God.[145] Thus barbarian *lex scripta* could emulate Moses, could testify to the new status of kings as Christian rulers, and could identify their subjects as another holy people like the Israelites.

Like the Roman example, the Christian inspiration behind barbarian legislation is revealed by its contexts and by features of its presentation. It was Bede's view that, just as Darius had issued an edict of toleration to the Jews, so, even nowadays, when earthly powers are converted to the faith, they issue public edicts on the Church's behalf.[146] This is rather less than Aethelberht did, but there is an obvious connection between Aethelberht's law-code and his entry into the community of Christians. This *may* also have been a factor with Clovis: even if there is little evidence of Christian influence in *Lex Salica*, the very act of adopting a religion of the Book constituted an invitation to set down in writing customs in many ways similar to those of the ancient Hebrews. The Irish saw the point when they quite mendaciously connected the compilation of the *Senchas Mor* with the coming of St. Patrick (in the Annals they significantly dated it as contemporaneous with the Theodosian Code!).[147] Subsequent to their conversion, barbarian legislators were moved by religious considerations in other aspects of their activity. Charlemagne's conflation of the two texts of *Lex Salica* had its flaws for practical purposes, but it did create an

---

[143] cf. n. 22 above.

[144] cf. Buchner, cited in n. 87.

[145] Alfred, *Translation of the Pastoral Rule*, Pr., pp. 4–5; *L. Af.*, Intr., 49–49: 6; pp. 42–5.

[146] Bede, *In Ezram*, II 349–54, p. 296.

[147] Binchy 1943, p. 209; this legend appears already in the eighth-century *Corus Bescna*: for translation, cf. Donahue 1965, p. 70. For the Annalistic dating, cf. *Annals of Ulster*, I, pp. 6–7; the date given is 438. But cf. now Binchy 1975/6.

impression of uniformity in the most important Frankish *Lex*, and uniformity was a target which he pursued in liturgy, in canon law and in the monastic life.[148] Pauline and Augustinian theology certainly did more than concern for the convenience of judges to inspire Agobard's famous onslaught on the multiplicity of customary laws in the Frankish realm.[149] Above all, Moses was a dominant influence in the production and appearance of much barbarian legislation. The preface to the Bavarian Law which I have often referred to opens with a quotation from Isidore putting Moses first among the law-makers of the ancient world (including Solon, Lycurgus, Numa Pompilius and Caesar), and it concludes, in its own words, 'thus each people chooses its own law out of its custom'.[150] Mosaic example had a great deal to do with the developing conviction in early medieval Europe that every people should have its own *Lex*, and this is perhaps one reason why Frankish 'imperialist' law-giving for subject peoples was acceptable to its recipients. The Bavarian law itself follows the Ten Commandments for part of its extant course, and then that of the late Roman *Comparison of Mosaic and Roman Law*.[151] Charlemagne's *Admonitio Generalis* also aped the Decalogue.[152] But the impact of Moses is clearest of all, of course, in the lawbook of King Alfred. His 120 chapters might make legal nonsense, but 120 was well-known to be the age at which Moses died, and the number of disciples upon whom the Holy Ghost descended at Pentecost; it was thus a highly appropriate number of chapters for a law-book that was prefaced by a selection of Mosaic law, and an account of its modification by the early Church at Jerusalem.[153] In my view, Alfred's legislation constituted a remarkable attempt to set out the relationship between Divine Law and the laws of the Anglo-Saxons, who were thus invited to fuse as a new holy people. Indeed, it may be that we should explain the association between the *domboc* and the Anglo-Saxon chronicle in two early manuscripts, and perhaps also similar connections on the continent, as an attempt not to mirror the Roman diptych of laws and wars, but to present a sort of West Saxon counterpart to the book of Exodus, in which an account of the people's victorious wanderings is follows by a record of its law. We can thus see that some barbarian kings and churchmen were thinking of Divine Law when they issued and presented their *leges scriptae*. Again, it would seem that an important reason for the existence of barbarian legislation was that it projected an image of society which corresponded to the ideological aspirations, as well as the practical needs, of what we might call its articulate classes.

[148] Semmler 1960, pp. 37—65; Bullough 1975, pp. 23—6.
[149] Agobard, *Ep. adv. leg. Gundobad.*, pp. 150—239: esp. cc. 3, 4, p. 159; cf. Boshof 1969, pp. 39—54.
[150] L. Bai., Pr., pp. 198—200; cf. Isidore, *Etym.* V i.
[151] Beyerle 1926, pp. lvii—lxi.
[152] *Capitularia*, no. 22; cc. 61—9, I pp. 58—9.
[153] Isidore, *Quaest. in Exod.* xviii 1, *P.L.* 83, col. 300; Isidore, *Lib. numerorum*, xxv, 104, *ibid.*, col. 199; Bede, *In Templ. Sol.*, I 410—17, p. 157; Bede, *Expos. Act. Apost.* I, 15, p. 12; Hraban Maur, *In Exod.* II xi, *P.L.* 108, cols. 91—2. One should also mention in this connection the Irish *Liber ex lege Moysi*, for which, cf. Fournier 1909, and Kottje 1964, pp. 7—40; in Paris B.N. Lat. 3182, a Breton MS, *Lib. ex leg. Moys.* is associated with *L. Sal.*, and a mass of other insular canonical material.

We should consider, finally, motives for making written law which, while still involving the projection of an image rather than the practical application of law, might be better described as political than as ideological. The point made by the *Codex Euricianus*, if it was promulgated in 476 — that here was a new legislating authority now that there was no longer a Roman Emperor in the West — was obviously political as well as ideological in its significance. Similarly, Liuvigild's *Codex Revisus* coincided with the refoundation of the Visigothic monarchy and major steps towards the unification of Spain;[154] and Rothari had very concrete objectives as well, perhaps, as ideological ambitions. The major reorganizations of the Visigothic code were undertaken by two kings, Chindaswinth and Erwig, who had reason to feel insecure on their throne, and the second of these at least involved relatively little new legislation.[155] Similar considerations may underlie the reissue of *Lex Salica* by the upstart Pippin; the code was redistributed in 100 titles, and given a new and more assertive prologue, but there was no substantive revision to justify the new version.[156] Perhaps they also explain Alfred's failure to dispense with Ine's laws in his *domboc* though he had superseded many of them. Most obviously, Cnut's massive codes, which again reproduce much that was traditional, can be seen as a political gesture by an alien king to his new subjects, though it was a gesture which needed the whole-hearted cooperation of those subjects.[157] It has also been suggested that the abbreviated collections of Roman law put together by the Visigothic and Burgundian kings were designed to reconcile their Roman subjects to themselves;[158] and that Dagobert's *Lex Ribuaria* was a concession to a now ascendant part of his realm which he was entrusting to his infant son.[159] All this legislation seems to occur at politically sensitive moments, which argues that there was some political mileage in it. Following on from this, we might suggest that a further motive for the production of a code like *Lex Salica* was that it would identify as one people the disparate elements which made up Clovis's new kingdom, and bind them to the Merovingian dynasty.

There are some difficulties here. One can see the appeal to Romans of a text like *Lex Romana Visigothorum*, although the Romans of southern Gaul were presumably already living by Roman law, and since this collection could not have been made without Roman assistance, it looks more like a gesture by the Romans to King

---

[154] Stroheker 1939; Thompson 1969, pp. 57—91.

[155] For Chindaswinth as the original author of the *Liber Iudiciorum*, and for the extent of Erwig's alterations, cf. King 1972, pp. 18—21; for their political insecurity, which, in the light of Mr. Collins's remarks, should be stressed more than the dubious nature of their claims, cf. Thompson 1969, pp. 190—9, 231—42; Claude 1971, pp. 117—33, 166—84.

[156] Eckhardt 1953, pp. 17—32.

[157] Whitelock 1948; Whitelock 1955b.

[158] cf. Wallace-Hadrill 1962, p. 41; King 1972, pp. 10—11; and the references there cited, esp. Bruck 1953.

[159] Beyerle 1928, pp. 338—42, 349; Beyerle 1935, pp. 4—6; Eckhardt 1959a, pp. 112—27.

Alaric than *vice-versa*.[160] One can also see that the Anglo-Saxons might wish to have their traditional law confirmed by Cnut.[161] But it is not so easy to understand the appeal of texts like *Lex Salica* and *Lex Ribuaria* to peoples who were neither literate nor familiar with Latin; and neither these texts nor the Carolingian reissue of the former were made in the king's name, as we have seen. But eventually, *Lex Salica* did come to identify the Franks as a people, and we have also seen that, in retrospect at least, it was ascribed to Clovis, just as those who observed the Burgundian law were called *Gunbadingi* after its author. Moreover, many Frankish legal manuscripts contain king-lists, and those of the Carolingian recensions do take care to accommodate Carolingian claims. King-lists are also found in association with the Visigothic and Lombard legislation; indeed, some manuscripts of Lombard legal material contain splendid *pictures* of kings;[162] Alfred's law-book was accompanied not only by the Chronicle, but also by West Saxon king-list and genealogy, and West Saxon royal genealogies are also to be found in two twelfth century legal manuscripts, both going back to a common pre-conquest source. Thus, to judge from the manuscripts, kings did succeed in perpetuating the link between themselves and their dynasty on the one hand, and their legislation on the other. Manuscripts were of course clerical work; but clergymen were also, for the most part, Germanic aristocrats, and, in spite of what I have said about the Christian inspiration of barbarian legislation, it does not follow that their manuscripts reflect only a clerical perspective. A third and final explanation for the association between legal and historical material which we find in many of them may be that it testifies to a Germanic instinct that popular traditions about the past belonged with popular custom.[163] If so, it is highly significant from a royal point of view that regnal records were so prominent in connection with legal texts. It would seem that a people's *Lex* could develop symbolic significance even for those who could not read it; and that,

---

[160] cf. The *Commonitorium Breviarii*, printed by Mommsen in *Prolegomena* to *Cod. Theod.* (1904), pp. xxxiii—xxxv, for the Roman role in the production of *Lex Rom. Vis.* The Visigothic and Burgundian kings would naturally represent their codes as of great benefit to their subjects, like Justinian later; but it must be stressed that the view which sees them as major *concessions* makes sense only if we suppose *Cod. Eur.* and *L. Burg.* to have been strictly territorial and exclusive in their application, and few of the relevant scholars do so. Permission for bishops to hold a church council was another matter; but, in my view, scholars have been too ready to see the secular Roman population of S. Gaul as panting for Frankish liberation from their Arian yoke: Wormald 1976, pp. 222—3.

[161] A regular keynote in the legislation of Charles the Bald is the concession to each of his subjects of their *Lex: Capitularia*, nos. 204, II, p. 71; 205, II, p. 74; 254, c. 3, II, p. 255; 256, c. 3, II, p. 259; 262, c. 10, I, p. 281; 269, II, p. 296; 270, B., c. 3, II, p. 299; 275, c. 3, II, pp. 333—4; 276, II, p. 339; 283, II, p. 365 etc.

[162] For the versions of the Frankish king-list, cf. *L. Sal. (A, C)*, pp. 253—4 (where there is no reference to a Carolingian), and *L. Sal. (D, E)*, pp. 192—5 (where Grimoald and Charles Martel are both given a position in the E-text). For discussion, cf. Eckhardt 1953, pp. 60—1, Eckhardt 1954, pp. 162—3. For the Visigothic king-list, cf. Zeumer 1902, pp. 457—61; for the Lombard, *Ed. Roth.*, Pr., p. 2 (and, for the pictures, Bluhme 1869, pp. xxvii—xxxiii, xl—xli); for the important suggestion that Bede, *H.E.* II 5 indicates that thelberht's code may have been accompanied by a king-list, cf. Wallace-Hadrill 1971, pp. 39—40. For the contents of the MSS of Alfred's laws, cf. Ker 1957, nos. 39, pp. 57—8; 65, pp. 110—13; 180, pp. 230—3; 373, pp. 443—7.

[163] Hauck 1955, pp. 204—5.

by issuing it, barbarian kings secured their memory for posterity, and perhaps loyalty to themselves and their dynasty. In any event, both the historical context and the textual presentation of much barbarian legislation suggest that it could have political as well as ideological importance.

V

It is high time that I summed up what I have been trying to argue in this paper, but in doing so, I would like to consider a final problem. It is supremely difficult to get inside the mind of the secular barbarian of the early Middle Ages. We have too little material to establish the necessary cultural context, and so much of what we have is dressed up in the language and values of an admired, but in origin totally alien, Romano Christian thought-world. Usually, we have to guess motivation from what barbarians actually did, rather than what they said. In this paper, I have argued that the external features of much barbarian legislation make it quite difficult to understand its production simply in terms of the administration of justice, whatever the texts themselves say. The primary legislation of northern Europe is generally too selective, too confused and too carelessly produced and reproduced (by modern standards) to have been much use to a judge sitting in court, even supposing that they could have read texts which were nearly always written in Latin. I have suggested that the reason for this is not that the northern barbarians were stupid or primitive, but because here the pronouncement and enforcement of law remained essentially an oral process, a matter of the *verbum regis* and of local custom. *Lex scripta*, as the various contexts of its issue seem to hint, was not so much practical as ideological in its inspiration; many of the odder features of the texts make sense in literary, even if they make nonsense in legal, terms, and others would not have jarred as much if codes were designed to make an overall literary type of impression, rather than to be applied in legal detail. This certainly does not mean that we may not use Germanic legislation as evidence for Germanic law or for the policies of Germanic kings. In southern Europe, as we have seen, the barbarians inherited and perpetuated to some extent a culture of written law. Barbarian kings everywhere were naturally willing to respond to the Roman expectation, passed on to the Christian Church, that a ruler would guarantee law and order and give judgement on complex or urgent matters of dispute. It is impossible to read Fredegar's account of how Dagobert came to Burgundy, causing alarm to magnates but bringing joy to the poor, and never eating or sleeping, 'lest anyone should leave his presence without having obtained justice', without being reminded of a later Roman imperial *adventus*.[164] The capitularies of the Lombard kings subsequent to Rothari, of the sixth century Merovingians and the ninth century Carolingians, and the *Satzungen* and judgements incorporated into many barbarian codes, indicate the acceptance by Germanic kings of the responsibilities which their new station had laid upon them. And the prologues to barbarian legislation may well reflect the conscious objectives

[164] Fredegar, *Chron. IV*, c. 58, p. 48.

of its authors, even if their subconscious reluctance to adapt their traditional oral methods to the demands of literate legislation is also revealed by the flaws of presentation that we have considered. But because of this reluctance, at least in northern Europe, the barbarian codes represent *indirect* evidence, evidence at one remove, of barbarian custom and barbarian royal decisions. And because written law itself seems to have been inspired by ideological or symbolic considerations even for kings who certainly had strictly practical and legal objectives, and especially for the authors of primary legislation in northern Europe, it is also *direct* evidence for the image which Germanic kings and their advisers, Roman or clerical, wished to project of themselves and their people: an image that might be immediate and political, or abstract and ideological; the image of king and people as heirs to the Roman Emperors, as counterparts to the Children of Israel, or as bound together in respect for the traditions of the tribal past. I use the word image rather than propaganda, because propaganda implies an audience, and we can neither know nor imagine enough about the circulation of our texts to talk confidently about their audience; whereas an image can be sufficient unto itself, and whoever else they were trying to impress I see barbarian legislators as concerned primarily to impress themselves. We must be careful here not to fall into the archaeologist's trap of ascribing ritual symbolism to any object whose function we cannot understand. But as Dr. Nelson stresses, the Germanic barbarians of the early Middle Ages were, like many another basically illiterate culture, profoundly impressed by the ritual gesture, and writing can itself have great symbolic significance in such societies.[165] I am therefore content to assert bluntly, though not without the qualifications that I have made throughout, that Germanic kings made laws, first and foremost, partly in order to emulate the literary legal culture of the Roman and Judaeo-Christian civilization to which they were heirs, and partly in order to reinforce the links that bound a king or dynasty to their people. I would not like to be dogmatic about which image was uppermost in the mind of any one legislator.

Instead, I would like to conclude by seeking to answer, very briefly, the other half of the question I asked at the outset: how far did the making of written law increase the status and authority of Germanic kingship; or, to put it another way, how far was the making of law a royal function in Germanic society before Roman and Christian example introduced its kings to the ideal of written legislation? There are very considerable difficulties here. In other Indo-European peoples, the law was the jealously guarded preserve of a professional lawyer-class, although the Indians, the Romans and the Irish all believed also in presumably mythical royal law-makers.[166] The Germanic position, however, is very obscure. In Tacitus, judgement is in the hands of *principes* who were appointed by the popular assembly, but a proportion of

---

[165] Goody 1968, esp. pp. 11–19, 205–6, 226–37.
[166] Binchy 1943, p. 207; Binchy 1970, pp. 1–2, 15–17; Schulz 1953, pp. 5–37; cf., also, Benveniste 1973, pp. 307–12, 379–84.

the compensation for lighter offences goes, *'regi vel civitati'*.[167] In Scandinavia, to judge from admittedly much later evidence, law was the speciality of local experts, and the king's role seems to be a late development.[168] To come closer to the peoples who concern us, Athanaric the Visigoth insisted on being called a judge, *not* whatever it was that the Greek sources translated *basileus* and the Romans *rex*, 'because kings have power, but judges wisdom'; as the (theoretically) temporary leader of the Visigothic war confederation, he apparently had judicial powers, like a similar figure in Caesar's Gaul, but such powers were not wielded by the Gothic rulers whom Roman sources dignified with the title of king.[169] Jordanes ascribes the *belagines* of the Goths, which they keep, he says, to this day, to Dicineus, a contemporary of Caesar, who had, *'pene regiam potestatem'*, who ruled not only the common people, but also kings, who ordained priests, and whose son, by reason of his *peritia*, was accounted both *rex* and *pontifex*, and judged the people. Since Cassiodorus, Jordanes' source, was, by his own confession, concerned above all to plug the line that the Goths had been ruled by kings since ancient times, it is very significant that Jordanes does *not* call Dicineus a king; in some ways, he reminds one of the status of Athanaric, though in others he does look rather like a sort of Druid.[170] Finally, we have seen that almost no Frankish or Frankish inspired *Lex*, as opposed to the capitularies, was ever ascribed in its prologue to the king who produced it; the shorter Prologue to *Lex Salica* gives the credit to four named *rectores*, and the Prologues to *Lex Salica* generally seem to be more concerned to celebrate the Frankish people as a whole than any of their kings.[171] One manuscript of *Lex Ribuaria* attributes it to a certain Eddana, to whom I have found no other reference, ancient or modern, but who is not described as a king.[172] As far as I can see, the only conclusion that we can draw from this evidence is that ancient Germanic kingship as such was *not* closely associated with the 'finding', promulgation or enforcement of law. If Athanaric and Dicineus were temporary overseers of kings, vested with judicial powers, the *principes* of Tacitus and the *rectores* of *Lex Salica* may be local legal experts, somewhat on the Scandinavian model; the point is that none of them were considered kings in the normal sense, and the sources specifically distinguish them from kings.

---

[167] Tacitus, *Germania*, c. 12, p. 280.

[168] Albani 1969: for the Scandinavian legal texts and their character, cf. von Amira 1960, pp. 82—126.

[169] Themistius, *Or.* x 134, I, p. 204; cf. Thompson 1966, pp. 44—8, with further references, but especially Wolfram 1975. In connection with the Gallic evidence, it is interesting that the Irish Cormac mac Airt, whom Professor Binchy appears to think mythical, but Professor Byrne perhaps historical, was remembered in Irish legend both as King of Tara and as law-giver extraordinary.

[170] Jordanes, *Getica*, c. 11, pp. 73—5. For Cassiodorus' objectives, cf. *Ep. Var.* IX 25, pp. 291—3; and Momigliano 1955.

[171] *L. Sal. (C)*, Pr., pp. 2—3; *L. Sal. (D, E)*, Pr., pp. 2—9. But it may be significant that, when *Lib. Hist. Franc.* (727), p. 244, takes up the story of the origins of *Lex Salica* from the shorter Prologue, it connects it with the first Frankish decision to have a king, like other peoples.

[172] Modena Ord. I 2, described by Bluhme 1868, p. xli; the MS, which gives pictures of both Eddana and the four *rectores*, is one of the two that seems to derive from Servatus Lupus at Fulda.

But by the time Germanic society emerges into the light of our legal texts (if we can call it light), this situation seems to have changed. On the one hand, Germanic kings are now much more prominent. Quite apart from the fact that most codes *are* ascribed to kings, fines go not to the *civitas* but to the king, and judicial officials are responsible not to the people but to him; this is not so true in *Lex Salica* as in subsequent legislation, but the king has important legal functions even here.[173] On the other hand, the importance of local legal experts seems to have receded. Kings regularly made law with the advice of *sapientes* or *witan*, and our texts refer to *deman*, *rachinburgii* or *legislatores*, but it is striking that, if we except portions of the rather eccentric *Lex Frisionum*, we cannot put a name to any of them as such.[174] No society can operate without some members learned in custom, and people of this type must have supplied kings with a knowledge of the genuinely customary elements in their laws. But Germanic legal specialists never constituted a powerful and exclusive class, as their counterparts did in Irish, and to some extent in Scandinavian, society. It seems unlikely that we can explain these developments simply in terms of the cultural stimuli which I have been considering throughout most of this paper. Like Mr. Wood, I would emphasise the contribution made by the process of migration. It naturally boosted the importance of military leadership in matters of peace as well as war, and some confederate leaders of Athanaric's type will have been able to make their supremacy permanent and to add the title of king to their judicial power. Correspondingly, it will have destroyed any Germanic counterpart to the Irish professional classes who will have been lacking in the ability to acquire plunder by fighting or sustenance by farming, and whose prestige may well have been undermined by the trauma of migration. Thus Germanic kings appear in the aftermath of the invasion as vested with the legal functions which they do not seem originally to have had.

At the same time, the persistent ambiguities of the Frankish evidence indicate that the process was barely complete. In the light of what we can see of the primitive Germanic situation, and of the failure of the greatest barbarian people to publicize the royal role in legislation, we can see the supreme importance of the Romano-Christian tradition of monarchical and literate legislation in setting the seal on what the experience of migration seems to have begun. By making written law in the image of Moses and the Roman Emperors, barbarian kings gradually consolidated their apparently new status as peacetime rulers of their people, just as some kings appear to have secured their individual position by issuing or reissuing established law. It seems unlikely that they were unaware of this, and that this was not itself a major reason why they did so. In the age of the migrations, Germanic kings may already have assumed primary responsibility for law and order. But it was the appeal to all parties of the Romano-Christian image of the legislating monarch which set European kingship firmly on the path towards Frederick II and Edward I.

[173] cf. Wallace-Hadrill 1962, p. 180; Wallace-Hadrill 1971, p. 36.

[174] *L. Fris. Addit. Sapient.*, pp. 682–98; no. xi, pp. 696–7 is the single most spectacularly pagan piece of Germanic legislation.

6

Kings and Merchants

P. H. SAWYER

One of the prerogatives claimed by English kings in the thirteenth and fourteenth centuries was the right to regulate merchants and commerce.[1] They freed particular groups of merchants from various obligations, they licensed markets, granted charters of privilege to boroughs and to guilds of merchants or craftsmen, they levied customs and controlled the coinage. One obvious motive was to increase revenue; charters of privilege were not so much granted as sold, and customs could yield large sums of cash. The regulation of trade was sometimes also an instrument of foreign policy, as when Edward III attempted to influence Flanders by interfering with wool exports. This aspect of royal authority became, in time, a cause of constitutional conflict but in the twelfth century it appears to have been accepted without question and the development of this prerogative is clearly a matter of some importance to anyone seeking to understand the growth of kingship in medieval Europe. This lecture is an attempt to trace the connection between kings and merchants in the centuries after the collapse of Roman imperial authority in western Europe, a period in which which the power and functions of kings were not so extensive as they later became and in which commerce was relatively unimportant. The early medieval history of the connection between kings and merchants can teach us much about the development of both kingship and commerce.

In the thirteenth and fourteenth centuries the historian has a relative abundance of material on which to draw, thanks partly to the dependance of royal governments on written records: in the Dark Ages, when government was by the spoken word, we only have the writings produced and preserved by churchmen. This limitation has two main consequences; first, there is little or no evidence for pagan areas before their conversion and secondly, in Christian Europe we tend to see the world through the eyes of churchmen. Merchants and markets therefore only occur in our sources if they were relevant to the spiritual or ecclesiastical purpose of the writers, for example if they played some part in demonstrating the power of a saint or of his relics. The saints' lives and collections of miracle stories written in the Dark Ages contain many references to merchants but these are only incidental and can give little information about the scale of the commercial activity they mention. The ninth-century life of St Anskar is unusual in its emphasis on merchants and markets but that was because Anskar's missionary work was largely undertaken in the

---

[1] Unwin 1918

Scandinavian trading places Ribe, Hedeby and Birka.[2] There were, of course, many other types of source which occasionally refer to commerce; sermons, works of exegesis and of instruction, letters and charters. Ælfric's *Colloquy*, written about A.D. 1000, describes many types of specialist, including a merchant who risked loss of his goods and even his life to bring 'precious things which are not produced in this land'.[3] Charters preserved by religious communities normally granted land or legal privileges but there are a few grants of freedom from tolls for particular churches and these provide welcome information about the places at which tolls were gathered.[4] Even the law codes, which are especially valuable because they contain many clauses regulating traders and markets, were increasingly compiled and preserved by churchmen, as Patrick Wormald has emphasised in his lecture.

Historians of Dark-Age commerce have naturally attempted to supplement these limited, ecclesiastical sources by using numismatic, archaeological and even linguistic evidence, but all pose difficult problems of interpretation. To consider the material evidence first, there is a natural temptation to treat any evidence of the movement of goods from one place to another as a sign of trade, especially when the objects were of high value. In 1959 Professor Grierson pointed out that there were many other explanations for the movement of valuables in Dark-Age Europe; plunder, tribute, ransoms, mercenary pay, compensations, the exile of nobles and, possibly most important of all, gift.[5] The temptation to assume commercial transactions and to ignore, or dismiss, the other explanations is, however, strong, as may be seen in the recent official publication on Sutton Hoo in which the coin hoard found in the burial is boldly described as 'exceptional in that it is not a merchant's hoard'.[6] Professor Grierson has elsewhere emphasised the essentially uncommercial character of Dark-Age society by demonstrating that in seventh- and eighth-century England coins had a social rather than a commercial significance.[7] To underline the difficulties is, however, not to deny the potential value of numismatic and archaeological evidence for the study of early trade. In many parts of Europe coins were certainly used in trade long before the eleventh century and modern excavations have greatly enlarged our knowledge of trading places and workshops as well as of ships.

Linguistic evidence provides very different kinds of information. Much can be learned about contacts, including commercial contacts, between different linguistic groups by a study of loan words and, more fundamentally, the comparative study of related languages can provide valuable clues to the prehistory of some important social institutions. Analysis of the related words for king; Latin *rex*, Irish *rí* and Sanskrit *raj-* has, for example, illuminated the early concept of kingship in Indo-

[2] *Vita Anskarii*
[3] lines 153–7
[4] see below, pp. 143–44
[5] Grierson 1959
[6] Bruce-Mitford 1975, p. 587
[7] Grierson 1961

European society[8], and similar studies have lead to significant conclusions about the early history of commerce.[9] Here too there are difficulties. While the borrowing of a word by one language from another may reflect some contact, the lack of such verbal borrowing cannot prove that there was no contact; such an argument from silence would be wrong. There are also chronological problems; prehistoric borrowings cannot be dated and although comparative linguistics may help interpret the development of early society, other evidence is needed to set those developments in a time scale.

Some important contributions to our understanding of early medieval society have also been made by social anthropologists. It is, of course, impossible to argue solely from analogy; what is true of the Trobriand Islands in the twentieth century is not necessarily true of fifth-century Kent or the seventh-century Hebrides. The observations of anthropologists are, however, particularly important for the present discussion in two respects. First they have drawn attention to the fundamental importance in many societies of the institution of gift-exchange. In these societies social relationships are expressed or created by gifts, and a gift can create the obligation to make a counter-gift. This discovery, given coherence by the French anthropologist Marcel Mauss,[10] has provided a key to the interpretation of many features in early Germanic and Celtic society, for when we do have written evidence in the form of literature or laws, or even written evidence of language itself, it is possible to recognise that these societies were also fundamentally reciprocal, and that consequently the opportunity, or need for commerce was relatively limited. Anthropology has also shown how very inappropriate many of our assumptions about commerce are when applied to societies with simple technologies. The distinctions between long-distance and local trade, or between gift-exchange and barter are hardly adequate to describe the complex transactions that occur in societies with different values and priorities from ours, in which competitive acquisitiveness is not necessarily a virtue.[11]

One of the possible sources for the later medieval royal interest in markets and merchants was the system developed by the Roman imperial government to control and profit from commerce.[12] It is easy to exaggerate the scale and importance of Roman commerce; much of the traffic through the Mediterranean and elsewhere was by contractors working directly for the government, and the main industrial production was for the state. The wealth of merchants appears to have been insignificant compared with that of the landed aristocracy. Professor Jones was able to show that the total wealth of one of the leading merchants in Alexandria in the late antique period amounted at most to 275 pounds of gold, with which he compared

[8] Binchy 1970, pp. 3–14
[9] Benveniste 1973, pp. 53–120
[10] Mauss 1969
[11] see below, pp. 144–5
[12] For the following paragraph see Jones 1964, pp. 824–72

the annual *income* of between 1500 and 4000 pounds of gold that was normal for territorial magnates. It is even more significant that the vexatious taxation of merchants in the fourth and fifth centuries yielded no more than a tiny proportion of the imperial revenue. Relatively unimportant though commerce may have been, it was closely regulated by the imperial government. Tolls were levied at external and provincial frontiers, and after Constantine city tolls were rendered to the state. The external rate was very much higher, 12.5 *per cent*, than the internal, which was of the order of 2.5 *per cent*. External trade was also controlled by being restricted to a small number of specified frontier crossings, and the export of some commodities, such as arms and armour, was, in theory, prohibited. Merchants were freed from many of the normal restraints of citizenship so that they could do their work, but they were also taxed. Constantine imposed the *collatio lustralis*, a quinquennial tax on *negotiatores*, the term being interpreted very widely to include small craftsmen like cobblers, and apparently even prostitutes, as well as shippers and merchants engaged in long-distance trade. In 444 Valentinian III imposed an additional burden on trade, the *siliquaticum*, amounting to one *siliqua* per solidus, that is 1 in 24, paid equally by vendor and purchaser. He also ruled that all transactions had to take place before collectors on appointed days and at specified places. These regulations were obviously limited to the relatively small area then under the control of the western emperor but they illustrate very well the attitude of the imperial government to commerce as an activity to be regulated and taxed. There are many indications that this interest in commerce was one of the aspects of imperial authority that were taken over by the barbarian rulers in Gaul, Spain and Italy; in particular the tolls levied by Merovingian kings in Gaul appear to have been a continuation of imperial tolls.[13]

In order to understand what contribution, if any, the barbarians made to this connection between kings and commerce it is therefore necessary to look at the peripheral areas of Europe that never came under Roman rule, and of these Scandinavia and Ireland are, in very different ways, most revealing. Scandinavia was so distant from the Roman frontier that it escaped many of the influences that affected the German neighbours of the empire; Rome could exert little diplomatic or military pressure on the lands around the Baltic, but there were economic connections. Scandinavia produced some things that were much needed in the empire, notably leather, vast quantities of which were used in a great variety of military equipment, including tents. Cattle and leather were imported by Roman merchants or contractors from many parts of Germany and there are archaeological indications of the importance of this traffic as far north as Sweden. Many of the Roman period graves of the central Swedish provinces of Västergötland and Östergötland and the Baltic island of Öland contain fine leather working tools that show the importance of that craft in that society, and the relative abundance of Roman imports in the same areas at least show lively contact with the Empire.[14] The

[13] Ganshof 1962
[14] Hagberg 1967, pp. 115–28

importance of Germany as a source for cattle products is reflected in two of the few Germanic words used by Roman authors, *reno* 'skin, hide', not 'reindeer skin', and *sapo* 'soap'. Other words suggesting contact with the Baltic area are *ganta* 'goose' and *glaesum* 'amber'. In return Germanic languages borrowed Latin words for merchants; *mango* 'trader, slave-trader' occurs in Old English as *mangere*, used to gloss *negotiator* or *mercator* and it survives in Modern English in such words as fishmonger and ironmonger.[15] The Latin word *caupo* 'innkeeper, trader' spread even further afield and occurs not only in Old English as *ceapman*, Modern English *chapman*, but as a verb in Gothic *kaupon* 'to trade', as well as Modern German *kaufen* and Russian *kupit* 'to buy'.[16] The same word lies behind the English place-name element *chipping*[17] as well as such Scandinavian place-names as Linköping, København and the modern name for the Viking trading centre in southern Norway, Kaupang. Commerce with the Empire must have had some influence on Scandinavian society but it is unlikely to have had much direct effect on their kingship; the imperial attitude to trade and traders within the empire is unlikely to have been adopted by the kings of Scandinavia as a conscious borrowing. Nevertheless, Scandinavian kings appear to have had much the same interest in merchants and markets in the ninth and later centuries as the rulers of former Roman provinces, which suggests that the later medieval prerogatives cannot be simply explained as an inheritance from the empire. Ireland also escaped direct Roman rule but, thanks to its early conversion and the very conservative attitude of early Irish scholars, especially the *brehons*, the custodians and interpreters of the law, we are better able there than elsewhere to glimpse some features of a pre-Christian, non-Roman society, and for the present discussion this evidence is especially important because, although Ireland had many kings, whose authority and activities can be studied in some detail, it had little if any commerce. The early Irish sources say so little about trade or traders that it has been generally accepted that commerce was first introduced into Ireland on any scale by the Scandinavian invaders of the ninth and tenth centuries.[18]

Britain also provides valuable evidence for this subject. Most of the island had been part of the Empire, but after the withdrawal of imperial control early in the fifth century, power passed to native rulers and later, in large areas, to Germanic chieftains whose successors were the kings of Anglo-Saxon England. The transition from imperial province to Germanic kingdoms was therefore indirect and there is room for disagreement about the direct influence that Rome had on Anglo-Saxon institutions. So for example, the tolls levied by eighth-century English kings on ships at London and elsewhere may have been an adaptation of the Roman *portorium*, but they could also have been introduced sometime after the end of Roman Britain by

---

[15] Grierson 1977, pp. 24–5
[16] Benveniste 1973, p. 110
[17] Harmer 1950
[18] Dillon and Chadwick, pp. 124–44; Binchy 1970, p. 16

either British or English rulers. The fact that the English charters describe the tolls as *vectigal*, *censum* or *tributum*, but not *teloneum*,[19] the word which, under the influence of the Vulgate replaced *portorium* in Gaul,[20] suggests that the second alternative is more likely, but the possibility of Roman influence cannot be dismissed. The functions of English kings as revealed by the early law-codes do not appear to owe much to Rome and their dealings with traders are better explained as a development of Germanic kingship. Unfortunately, Welsh laws which might help our interpretation of possible Roman survivals are only preserved in late versions in which English influences have left their mark.

In all parts of Europe, both Roman and non-Roman, local exchanges of produce were probably a normal feature of life. They are well attested in the Roman Empire where the urban markets were supplemented by country fairs, some of which were on quite a large scale, like that described by Cassiodorus held in September, on St Cyprian's day, near Consilinum in Lucania at which produce from all parts of southern Italy could be bought, including cattle, clothes and children, offered as slaves by poor parents.[21] The imperial currency included coins of various denominations to serve a wide range of needs and goods could therefore often be sold for money, but some exchanges were probably by barter. Social anthropology has an especially important contribution to make here, for it shows how barter can take place in coinless societies. Malinowski described a process of barter, called *gimwali*, in the Trobriand Islands and emphasised that the natives distinguished it clearly from other forms of exchange; it was conducted without ceremony or magic, by a process of haggling, and was possible between complete strangers.[22] His description is worth quoting at some length for it shows how goods could be exchanged in a society in which most significant social relationships were based on, and expressed by an elaborate system of gift-exchange.

> This bartering, pure and simple, takes place mainly between the industrial communities of the interior, which manufacture on a large scale the wooden dishes, combs, lime pots, armlets and baskets and the agricultural districts of Kiriwana, the fishing communities of the West, and the sailing and trading communities of the South. The industrials, who are regarded as pariahs and treated with contumely, are nevertheless allowed to hawk their goods throughout the other districts. When they have plenty of articles on hand, they go to the other places, and ask for yams, coco-nuts, fish, and betel-nut, and for some ornaments, such as turtle shell, earrings, and spondylus beads. They sit in groups and display their wares, saying "You have plenty of coco-nuts, and we have none. We have made fine wooden dishes. This one is worth forty nuts, and some betel-nut, and some betel pepper." The others then may answer, "Oh, no, I do not want it. You ask too much". "What will you give us?" An offer may be made, and rejected by the pedlars, and so on, till a bargain is struck.

---

[19] Sawyer 1968, nos 29, 86, 87, 88, 91, 98, 143, 1612, 1788. *T(h)eloniarii* are named in some of these charters as royal agents
[20] Ganshof 1962, pp. 293—4
[21] Jones 1964, pp. 855—6
[22] Malinowski 1922, pp. 189—90

This bartering took place alongside a variety of other exchanges, notably the *kula*, an elaborate exchange of shell ornaments that took place around a great circle of island communities, over 250 miles across. *Kula* partners made other gifts to each other but if they engaged in barter it was always with others, not their partners. There was also a ceremonial exchange of fish and vegetables, called *wasi*, between inland and coastal villages, and Malinowski drew particular attention to a form of bartering of fish and vegetables that stood in sharp contrast to the *wasi*. 'It was called *vava* and took place between villages which had no standing *wasi* partnership and therefore simply *gimwali* their produce when necessary.' Such observed complexities should serve as a warning against over simple interpretations of historical or archaeological evidence of exchanges.

After the collapse of Roman imperial authority in the West, local exchanges by barter or otherwise continued, although rarely mentioned in our sources. A clause in Ine's law-code refers to the buying of beasts and one in Athelstan's second code prohibits the exchange of livestock except with the witness of a reeve, priest, landowner or royal official, which implies that such exchanges were both normal and might be made privately.[23] With the decline of urban markets the best opportunities were offered by fairs, which were probably in origin assemblies for some festival purpose. After the conversion to Christianity they were, in various ways, associated with particular saints. In Celtic society one important annual fair *(oenach)* was held in many districts at the start of the harvest season, the festival of Lughnasa, at the beginning of August. This survived in England as Lammas day (1 August), a word meaning 'loaf mass'; its absence from other Germanic parts of Europe shows its Celtic character.[24] The Irish laws show that, in Professor Binchy's words;

> the king of every tribe was bound to convene an *oenach* at regular intervals. The site of the fair was normally an ancient burial ground; indeed the tradition reflected in many poems and sagas that the *oenach* originated in the funeral games held for kings and heroes may have a kernel of truth. Doubtless many of the modern 'fairs' throughout Ireland are, or were formerly, held on the site of an old Irish tribal *oenach*. At such gatherings, besides the exchange of goods and the holding of games, horse-racing, and various athletic competitions, the 'public business' of the *tuath* (kingdom), including important lawsuits between different kindreds and the issue of special ordinances, was transacted.[25]

The most important of these assemblies was held at *Tailtiu* (modern Tailteann, anglicised as Teltown) near Kells, and was summoned by the king of Tara at the festival of Lughnasa. The *oenach Tailten* is well attested in historical sources from the sixth century and the annals note particularly when it was disrupted (an event reported eight times between 717 and 927) or not held at all.[26] Some of these assemblies developed into the cattle fairs of modern Ireland but they are always likely

---

[23] Ine 56, II Athelstan 10, ed Liebermann i. 114, 156; Attenborough 1922, pp. 54, 132
[24] MacNeill 1962, p. 1
[25] Binchy 1958, pp. 124
[26] Binchy 1958, pp. 115–27; MacNeill 1962, pp. 311–38

to have been occasions when some of those attending could barter, or sell, their produce or handicrafts.

Local exchanges at markets, fairs, or incidentally when the opportunity occurred should be distingusihed from long-distance commerce in goods of high value, offered for sale not by producers, but by middle men or merchants. Local fairs, did, of course, sometimes attract such men, one good example from the later Roman Empire being the annual fair held at Aegae in Cilicia which lasted 40 days free of toll and attracted western merchants even after the Vandals made the Mediterranean unsafe.[27] There was, however, a distinction between local exchanges and long-distance commerce, and linguistic evidence suggests that this distinction was basic in Indo-European society. The French linguist Emile Benveniste was even prepared to assert that 'there are in Indo-European no common words to designate trade and traders, there are only isolated words, peculiar to certain languages, of unclear formation, which have passed from one people to another'.[28] He emphasised that the terms for commerce have no linguistic connection with the words used in those languages for the activity of buying and selling; 'to sell one's surplus, to buy for one's own sustenance is one thing: to buy, to sell, for others, another'. Many of the words used to describe commerce present great etymological difficulties. One word apparently without an etymology is Latin *merx* 'merchandise, an object of trade' from which *mercor* 'to trade', *mercator* 'trader' as well as *commercium* all derive. Another Latin word for a trader, *caupo*, whose influence on Germanic and other languages has already been mentioned, may be a borrowing from an Oriental language. That such borrowings did occur is shown by Latin *arrha* 'pledge' which derived from Phoenician. Latin *emporium* came from a Greek word for a large-scale merchant *emporos* which 'simply indicates the fact of bringing into port after crossing the sea. It is not a specific term relating to a specific activity'.[29] The most remarkable of these Latin words for trade and traders is *negotium*, a negative construction *nec-otium* meaning literally 'absence of leisure' that, according to Benveniste's interpretation was influenced both in its original formation and its later development by Greek models.[30] His conclusion is that:

> Commercial affairs as such have no special term; they cannot be positively defined. Nowhere do we find a proper expression which denotes this specifically. The reason is that — or at least in the beginning — it was an occupation which did not correspond to any of the hallowed, traditional activities.[31]

The needs of most people both inside and outside the Roman Empire were normally met from local resources. Rulers and aristocrats had vast estates to feed their large households, and they also had servants and craftsmen to construct their

---

[27] Jones 1964, p. 867
[28] Benveniste 1973, p. 114
[29] Benveniste 1973, pp. 114–5
[30] Benveniste 1951
[31] Benveniste 1973, p. 118

buildings and to make the cloth, the tools, weapons and other equipment that they needed. Their dependant freemen also had rights in the varied common resources of these estates, sometimes in distant woodland or marsh. When necessary they probably helped each other in such major enterprises as building new barns, byres or houses. Some other needs might be supplied by travelling craftsmen, including smiths, or in local exchanges, whether at fairs or elsewhere. One commodity for which there was a general demand was salt, and the arrangements to meet it show how complex the methods of distributing commodities in early society could be. Although salt may have been less vital than is sometimes suggested — in Norway and Iceland the normal methods of preserving meat were by smoking or drying[32] — it was certainly widely used in Europe; in Ælfric's *Colloquy* the salter declares that without him the storehouses and cellars would be empty for butter and cheese could not be preserved without salt, nor could vegetables be seasoned.[33] Domesday Book shows that many rural estates had rights to salt from coastal *salinae*, 1195 of which are enumerated in that survey between Lincolnshire and Cornwall,[34] while many other places had similar rights to salt from inland brine-springs like those at Droitwich or in Cheshire. A network of saltways led great distances from these centres and can be reconstructed from incidental references to them in charter perambulations, some of which are of the tenth century.[35] By the eleventh century there was certainly an active trade in salt; in Domesday Book there are explicit references to the sale of salt, and it also records the tolls charged in Cheshire on waggon-, horse- and man-loads.[36] This trade can be traced back into the ninth century when the royal rights at Droitwich, then called *Saltwic*, included tolls described as waggon-shilling and load-penny *(wægnscilling* and *seampending)*.[37] Many of the features described in Domesday Book and by later writers such as John Leland suggest that this trade in salt developed out of, and supplemented, a system of distribution that had provided the needs of rural communities, near and far, long before pennies were available to be charged as toll. In the eleventh century many estates had as one of their appurtenances a well defined right to a certain quantity of salt, the implication being that if more was needed it would have to be obtained in some other way. Some entries in Domesday Book even suggest that the basis of this supply was an exchange, as at Bromsgrove which had a right to 300 *mitts* of salt in return for 300 waggon loads of wood.[38] As late as the sixteenth century production at Droitwich was deliberately limited, it was not made between Christmas and

---

[32] *Kulturhistorisk Leksikon for Nordisk Middelalder*, s.v. fisketilvirkning, kötträtter, rökning, saltning, speking, torkning
[33] lines 180–84
[34] Bridbury 1955, pp. 19–20
[35] Houghton 1932; Crump 1939; Finberg 1972, pp. 500–2
[36] Loyn 1962, pp. 106–9; DB i. 268
[37] Sawyer 1968, no. 223; Whitelock 1955, no. 99
[38] DB i. 172

Midsummer,[39] and it was only at the end of the seventeenth century that anyone attempted to tap new sources of supply there by digging new, and deeper, wells;[40] for centuries the old sources were enough. The antiquity of the arrangements is also indicated by the rituals associated with these wells. At Nantwich, as late as the eighteenth century, a hymn was sung on Ascension Day for the blessing of the brine and one pit was decked with flowers, green boughs and ribbons, and young people danced round it.[41] Leland described a similar festivity at Droitwich;

> Some say that this salt springe dyd fayle in the tyme of Richard de la Wiche Byschope of Chichester, and that aftar by his intercessyon it was restorid to the profit of the old course. Such is the superstition of the people. In token wherof, or for the honour that the Wichmen and saulters bare unto this Richard their cuntreman, they used of late tymes on his daye to hang about this sault spring or well once a yeere with tapestry, and to have drinking games and revels at it.[42]

An interesting example of the conversion into a Christian festival of what appears to have been a pre-Christian practice.

The king probably had rights to salt produced at Droitwich from a very early date, possibly even deriving from the period of Roman rule, and this would explain the entitlement of such places as Princes Risborough in Buckinghamshire, a royal estate in Domesday Book, to salt from Droitwich.[43] Former royal rights, whether granted away or usurped, may explain some of the other renders of salt described in Domesday Book, but others are likely to be survivals of earlier arrangements whereby communities obtained salt in return for wood and other supplies. Lords or communities that could not expect to receive salt as a due had to buy it and either send to the source of supply or wait for a travelling salter to come on foot or with waggons or horses. By the late ninth century Mercian rulers were taking toll on loads at Droitwich, and they may have done so two centuries earlier.[44] The right of rulers to some toll or tribute at the salt-springs may have been very ancient, or it could have been an extension of those rights to toll that eighth-century rulers certainly had in some of the coastal markets of England. It is, of course, possible that both had origins in Roman Britain. The use of the word *wic* to describe both coastal markets[45] and inland brine-springs points to some significant connection between such places. It may mean no more than that both were trading places, but there may be some implication of royal rights, including a right to toll.

---

[39] Leland, p. 94. I am indebted to Dr Margaret Gelling for drawing my attention to this passage.
[40] Nash 1781, pp. 298–9
[41] Tait 1916, p. 42 n.
[42] Leland, p. 93
[43] DB i. 143b
[44] Early eighth-century references to Droitwich as a place in which salt was sold, or to the render of a special royal tribute there, occur either in Evesham charters of doubtful authenticity, Sawyer 1968, nos 83, 97, or in a note of a Worcester charter that is too short for its authenticity to be tested, Sawyer 1968, no 1824
[45] see below, p. 152

The general obligation on all freemen in early Germanic and Celtic society to offer and receive gifts applied particularly to their leaders. The rulers and aristocrats were rich not only in land but also in treasure and one of the hall-marks of nobility was the ostentatious display of wealth, coupled with open-handed generosity to friends and followers who deserved it.[46] Like rich people nowadays they delighted in the possession of beautiful and exotic things, whose value was enhanced by rarity, and such things were also appropriate as gifts. Exotic goods came from many parts of the world, but for western Europe one especially important and relatively accessible source of many of the raw materials that were highly prized then, as now, was Scandinavia and the lands beyond the Baltic.

Animal skins and furs have always been an important element in clothing and although fur-bearing animals are found in all parts of Europe, the best furs come from the coldest regions. Towards the end of the eleventh century Adam of Bremen was well aware both of the abundance of furs in the Baltic lands and of the high value put on them by his German contemporaries.[47] He records that in Norway 'there are black foxes and hares, white martens and bears of the same colour who live under the water'. He describes the Sembi or Pruzzi as having 'an abundance of strange furs, the odour of which has inoculated our world with the deadly poison of pride. These furs they regard as dung, to our shame, I believe, for right or wrong we hanker after a martenskin robe as much as for supreme happiness', while the Swedes 'regard as nothing every means of vainglory: that is gold, silver, stately chargers, beaver and marten pelts, which make us lose our minds admiring them'. When, two centuries earlier, the Norwegian Ottar visited England, he told King Alfred about the tribute paid to him by the Lapps: 'that tribute is in the skins of beasts, in the feathers of birds, in whale-bone, and in ship-ropes which are made from whale-hide and seal-hide. Each pays according to his rank. The highest in rank has to pay fifteen marten-skins, five reindeer skins, one bearskin, and ten measures of feathers, and a jacket of bearskin or otterskin, and two ship-ropes. Each of these must be sixty ells long, one made from whale-hide and the other from seal'.[48] It is very likely that much of this tribute rendered in northern Norway eventually reached the royal and noble households of Christian Europe and beyond.

Ivory was another material in great demand for rings and other ornaments or as a beautiful and costly substitute for wood in making such objects as book covers or caskets. When elephant tusks became very scarce, whale-bone or walrus tusks were used instead, and until the discovery of Greenland the only source for the latter was northern Norway. These materials were used for some important objects; the Franks Casket is made of whale-bone and the eighth-century Gandersheim casket was made somewhere in England, Mercia probably, of walrus ivory.[49] Another highly prized

[46] Grierson 1959; Charles-Edwards 1976
[47] Adam of Bremen, iv. 18, 21, 31
[48] Ross 1940, p. 21
[49] Beckwith 1972, nos 1, 2

material was amber, and although deposits of this fossil resin are found in many parts of Europe, the most abundant sources are around the Baltic, especially in Samland and in Jutland.[50] The recent discovery of what appears to have been an eighth-century amber workshop at Ribe, with a large accumulation of discarded pieces suggests that significant quantities were being worked, and probably exported, at that time.[51] Most other northern exports are not so easily identified or studied, but Ottar's account of his wealth suggests that they included feathers and animal skins and it would not be unreasonable to add iron to the list; the rich Norwegian deposits were then being exploited and in western Europe supplies of iron appear to have been very limited.[52]

Some of the produce of the pagan north reached western Europe by way of gift, Ottar brought some walrus tusks to King Alfred, but much of the western demand for such things can only have been satisfied by merchants, by the men described in our sources as *negotiatores*, *mercatores*, or, in English, *ceapmen*. They did not, of course, deal exclusively in northern goods; slaves came from many parts and there was a return traffic to the North of high quality weapons, glassware and, especially from England, cloth. Merchants who traded in more than one kingdom were necessarily strangers somewhere, and as such they lacked the normal protection afforded in the Dark Ages by lords and kinsmen. They might group together for mutual support in a guild but such associations could do little if the hostility of the natives was aroused; even in Constantinople western merchants were massacred in 1182. It is small wonder that the Frisians in eighth-century York fled when one of their number killed a Northumbrian noble.[53] Traders therefore needed protection and although that might be provided by various people, as is shown by a late-seventh-century Kentish law dealing with the responsibilities of those who gave shelter for three nights to 'a stranger, a trader *(cepeman)* or any other man who has come across the frontier',[54] it was best provided by kings who could do so by extending their peace to cover such men. As late as the eleventh century the penalty for breaking the peace given by the king himself was far higher than if it had been given by one of his agents. The king's direct interest in men 'who came across frontiers' is made clear in another late seventh-century law, from Wessex, in which it is declared that the king should receive a large part of the wergeld of any stranger.[55] Several early English law-codes show some concern with the regulation of strangers, sometimes described as traders; they must keep to the road and take care to proclaim their presence should they leave it, on pain of being treated as thieves;[56] they must make their transactions before

[50] Beck 1970
[51] Bencard 1973, p. 42
[52] Blindheim 1963, Hauge 1946, Duby 1962, pp. 78–9
[53] Whitelock 1955, p. 725
[54] Hlothhere and Eadric, 15, ed. Liebermann, i. 11, Attenborough 1922, p. 20
[55] Ine 23, ed. Liebermann i. 98, Attenborough 1922, p. 42
[56] Wihtred 28, Ine 20, ed. Liebermann i. 14, 98; Attenborough 1922, pp. 30, 42

witnesses or the king's reeve,[57] a precaution against theft that was greatly elaborated in the tenth century; and in the laws of Alfred it was ordained that traders should bring before the king's reeve the men they intended to take with them when travelling through the country.[58] This responsibility of the king's agent for merchants provides the background for Æthelweard's account of the first Viking attack on Wessex: when Beaduheard, the king's *exactor*, heard that three ships had arrived he quickly rode 'to the port, thinking they were merchants rather than enemies, and commanding them imperiously he ordered them to be sent to the royal vill, but he and his companions were straightaway killed by them.'[59]

Some of the chapmen in Wessex may well have come from other English kingdoms, they would still have been strangers, but some certainly came from overseas. The presence of foreign merchants, especially Frisians, is well attested in many parts of northern Europe in the eighth and ninth centuries, and the evidence suggests that they tended to do their business not in the countryside but in special trading places that were easily accessible by boat.[60] Bede describes London as 'an emporium for many people who came to it by land and sea' and he described the intention of a Mercian to sell a Northumbrian captive as a slave to a Frisian merchant in London in 679.[61] There is good evidence, both literary and archaeological, for several coastal or riverside trading centres of the same kind in the eighth century; York, Ipswich, Fordwich in Kent, *Hamwih*, the predecessor of Southampton.[62] There are many similar places on the Continent and in the Baltic, notably Quentovic, Dorestad, Ribe, Helgö, and later Kaupang, Hedeby and Birka.[63]

It is, of course, archaeological evidence that is best able to reveal some of the things that were being traded, and where they came from. At *Hamwih* for example some material came from Mercia, fine glassware and pottery from Germany, other pottery from northern France, lava millstones from the Niedermendig region and there are many signs of contact with Frisia, including an inscription in Frisian runes.[64] There are similar indications of contact with Frisia at other sites and these agree well with the abundant literary evidence for the general importance of Frisians in the trade of the North Sea before the Viking raids began. Frisians had the great advantage that their territory not only formed part of the coastal route between the Baltic and western Europe, but that it also controlled the estuaries of the rivers Rhine and Meuse, leading into Germany and north-eastern France. Dorestad lay on a branch of the Rhine and its enormous scale, the site covers some 240 hectares

---

[57] Ine 25, Liebermann i. 100, Attenborough 1922, p. 44
[58] Alfred 34, ed. Liebermann i. 68, Attenborough 1922, p. 78
[59] Æthelweard, iii. 1
[60] Jellema 1955
[61] Colgrave and Mynors 1969, ii. 3; iv. 20
[62] Biddle 1974
[63] Jankuhn 1974
[64] Addyman 1972

compared with the 30 of *Hamwih* or Hedeby, confirms the commercial importance of Frisia and reinforces the impression that although these traders conveyed goods between many areas, it was the traffic with Scandinavia and the Baltic that was most valuable and important.[65]

Many of these coastal or riverside trading places were called *wics*. London occurs as *Lundenwic* in a seventh-century law-code, the modern form of the name York derives from *Eoforwic*, while others are more obvious; *Hamwih*, Ipswich, Fordwich, Quentovic, and possibly Wigford near Lincoln.[66] The word *wic* was borrowed very early by the Germans from Latin *vicus*, and like the Latin word it had many meanings. One of them was certainly a trading place. This view has recently been challenged by Dr Köbler who has suggested that the word only came to have this specialised meaning at a relatively late stage after some *wics* had developed into trading places.[67] That may be true, but the development of this specialised meaning occurred very early. Dr Biddle has drawn attention to the reference in a seventh-century law-code to a royal official in *Lundenwic* called a *wicgerefa*, a *wic* reeve.[68] Across the Channel Quentovic, which was variously described as an *emporium* and a *portus*, was also an important mint in the seventh and eighth centuries, producing coins with the legend *Wic in Pontio* or, simply, *Wicco fit*.[69]

Whatever these waterside trading places were called, they appear to have been under some special royal protection, like the traders who did their business in them. It was the king's privilege to grant freedom from toll and other dues at such places, and royal agents are often mentioned in connection with them. The king's *wicgerefa* in London has been mentioned, and there were royal *prefecti* in Quentovic and also, to judge by the Life of St Anskar, in Birka.[70] In several of the Scandinavian trading places, including Ribe and Hedeby, it was the king who granted land in the ninth century for the construction of churches.[71] It has been claimed that these Scandinavian trading places were in fact founded by Frisians.[72] The arguments against this view are compelling but it is worth emphasising here that even if it were true, it would hardly explain the royal interest in these places, unless the Scandinavian kings are cast in the implausible role of puppets or agents of western entrepreneurs. The indigenous character of this Scandinavian commercial activity has recently been confirmed by a comparative study of later Scandinavian and Baltic law-codes, especially those concerned with shipping, that has shown very clearly that

---

[65] van Es 1972
[66] Biddle 1974
[67] Köbler 1972
[68] Biddle 1976, note 118; Hlothhere and Eadric 16, ed. Liebermann i. 11, Attenborough 1922, p. 22
[69] Dhondt 1962, esp. pp. 185, 202–3
[70] *Vita Anskarii* 19
[71] *Vita Anskarii* 24, 31–2
[72] Stjerna 1909; Wadstein 1914; cf. Jankuhn 1953; Wessen 1923, 1925

they had a native basis, and were quite distinct from western legal systems: they were certainly not an import from western Europe.[73]

The royal protection seems normally to have been effective and many of these trading places were left undefended until the Viking period. Some had Roman walls, but non-Roman sites like *Hamwih*, Dorestad, Hedeby and Birka originally had no fortifications, suggesting that the royal sanctions were enough. In return kings gained great benefits, from tolls, rents, fines and other rights, including the right of pre-emption which was still maintained at Chester in the eleventh century where the king's agent had the first choice of any marten pelts that were landed.[74] Tolls were probably the most valuable source of revenue; the fact that many religious communities took care to obtain, preserve, sometimes have confirmed, charters granting freedom from toll on one or more ships at stated ports suggests that the payment of toll was a significant burden and therefore an important source of profit to kings.[75] Merchants had other liabilities, best revealed by grants of exemption as, for example, the remarkable list in a grant by Louis the Pious to two important Jewish merchants; *teloneum*, toll, comes first, and some of the others were specialised forms of it, *pontaticus*, at a bridge, or *trabaticus*, possibly at a bar on a road, as well as the more general *pulveraticum*. There were dues for moorings and harbours, *ripaticus* and *portaticus*, fishing dues, *cenaticus*, a traffic tax to cover damage to fields and meadows, *cespitaticus*, and they were also freed from liability to *paravereda* and *mansionaticus*, requisitioning for the post and for accommodation.[76] This list is not complete, it omits some dues such as the toll on salt, *salaticus*, but it does give a good idea of the kind of return that kings and their agents in Frankish Gaul expected from itinerant merchants.

In England tolls appear to have been levied first only at coastal markets. The charters granting freedom from toll were all produced in the period 733—764 and all concern toll on ships that were apparently owned by the religious communities themselves. By the end of the ninth century the ruler of Mercia had a well established right at Droitwich to toll on waggons and other loads, and he reserved the same rights for himself at Worcester. This suggests that in the course of the eighth and ninth centuries there was some extension of royal authority to cover local market transactions as well as those undertaken by strangers. What had begun as the protection of foreign merchants developed into a right to protect, and control, all buying and selling. It may even be that the enlargement of the meaning of the English word *port* to include all markets instead of the limited sense in its Latin source, *portus*, which referred only to harbours, was one of the by-products and signs of this enlargement of royal authority.[77]

[73] Hasselberg 1953, pp. 102—13
[74] DB i. 262b
[75] See above, p. 144, n. 19; early Frankish charters granting freedom from toll are listed and discussed by Ganshof 1962
[76] Verlinden 1955, pp. 707—8; cf. Doehaerd 1957
[77] Bosworth and Toller, *s.v.*

The archaeological and written evidence suggests that many of these trading places were especially active during the eighth century, no doubt prospering under the relative security provided by the Carolingians and the Mercians. It may well have been the growing demand for northern produce in these flourishing markets that led men to search even farther afield for fresh supplies. Ottar later explained that his journey around North Cape was undertaken partly out of curiosity but 'mainly for the walruses because they have very fine ivory in their tusks'.[78] It is therefore reasonable to suggest that it was this growing demand in western Europe that encouraged the penetration of the lands east of the Baltic in the eighth century.

The increase in the activity of coastal markets was followed, in England, by a growth of market towns in which local exchanges of a non-luxury kind took place. They were clearly well established by the tenth century and soon after 900 Edward the Elder adapted earlier laws by ruling that buying and selling could only take place in a market, a *port*, and this restriction was frequently repeated, with modifications, later in the century.[79] Many of these markets, also called *burhs*, flourished and later figure in Domesday Book as sizeable towns under royal lordship with special town-laws that were clearly distinguished from the law of the surrounding countryside. Many also had mints to produce the coin that was increasingly needed for market transactions, and numismatic evidence makes it possible to show how the English coinage grew both in volume and complexity during the tenth century.[80] By the middle of the following century market transactions in cash must have played a major part in English rural life for Domesday Book and other evidence shows that peasants were expected to pay most, if not all, their taxes and rents as well as church and other dues in silver pennies, which they could only obtain by selling their surplus labour or produce.

There appears to have been a significant increase in the amount of coinage in circulation in England in the late tenth century, most probably because of growing wool exports paid for in silver, some of which came ultimately from mines in the Harz mountains discovered in 960's.[81] The growth of the local markets can be traced back much earlier than that, and it is possible that they were in part stimulated by the expanding overseas trade. Merchants would need provisions for their journey home, which would have been obtained in the surrounding countryside, and they must sometimes have needed repairs to their ships and equipment: the workshops found in such places as *Hamwih* probably produced tools and other utilitarian goods as well as ornaments. Transactions in the coastal markets did not, of course, depend on coinage, but some of the earliest mints in England were associated with these places; and by the beginning of the ninth century coins were being or had been

---

[78] Ross 1940, p. 21
[79] 1 Edward I, ed. Liebermann i. 138, Attenborough 1922, p. 114; cf. Whitelock 1955, p. 72
[80] Loyn 1961, 1971
[81] Sawyer 1965

produced at or for *Hamwih*, London, York as well as somewhere in East Anglia.[82] It is probable that money and the habit of using it for buying and selling spread from the coastal markets during the eighth and ninth centuries. At the end of the ninth century new mints were established at Winchester and Exeter, the beginning of an extension of minting that was to continue throughout the tenth century until under Edgar there were more than 60.[83] One clear indication of the importance of coinage in rural society is the fact that when, early in the eleventh century, Æthelred needed to raise large sums of tribute to pay Viking raiders, he had to levy a monetary tax throughout the countryside; the wealth of England was dispersed.

Once Viking attacks began, the raiders quickly demonstrated the vulnerability of the undefended coastal markets. Some, including London, York, and possibly Lincoln, had the advantage of Roman defences, which may have been repaired, and one of the responses of both Frankish and English kings was to build new fortifications. Some of these were little more than forts for campaigning purposes, but in England others were large sites, with streets laid out in a regular pattern, and were clearly designed as more than simple refuges.[84] They were in fact *burhs* or *ports* in which markets could be held. The best known *burhs* were built by the West Saxons, at the end of the ninth century in Wessex itself, and later as one of the means by which the Danish areas of England were brought to submission. The West Saxons were however not the only rulers to build such fortifications. The Mercians had already done so long before, for example at Hereford, possibly because it was vulnerable to Welsh attacks.[85] One of the fortunate documents to survive from the late ninth century is a charter of Æthelred, ruler of Mercia and his wife issued after they had fortified Worcester.[86] They granted to the church of Worcester 'half of all the rights which belong to their lordship, whether in the market or in the street, both within the fortification and outside' but reserved to themselves the waggon-shilling and load-penny 'which are to go to the king's hand as it always did at *Saltwic* (Droitwich), but otherwise the land-rent, the fine for fighting, or theft, or dishonest trading, and contribution to the borough-wall, and all the (fines for) offences which admit of compensation, are to belong half to the lord of the church, for the sake of God and St Peter, exactly as it has been laid down as regards the market place and streets'.[87] The market may well have been a relatively new creation within the new fortifications. This was the view of Tait who wrote 'it seems fairly clear... that the market-place and the streets which led to it with the jurisdiction over them, the profits of which were to be shared with the church, were new, like the

---

[82] Dolley 1976, pp. 354–5; Metcalf 1974
[83] Dolley 1976, pp. 356–8
[84] Biddle 1976, pp. 124–34
[85] Biddle 1976, pp. 120–1
[86] Sawyer 1968, no. 223
[87] Whitelock 1955, no 99. For the interpretation of the clause about tolls, see Harmer 1950, p. 339 n. 4

tolls reserved to the king'.[88] Whether it was first established by Æthelred in the late ninth century or earlier, it is clearly an example of the kind of *burh* that flourished in the following century. They were either established by kings or brought under royal protection. Many housed mints, and were under the direct control of royal agents, the town reeves, who appear to have been men of great importance.[89] The burgesses, inhabitants subject to the laws of the *burh*, were often privileged tenants of the king.[90] These *burhs* were in fact new towns, many with planned lay-outs,[91] and their creation was an early stage in that process of urban expansion that spread through Europe in the eleventh and twelfth centuries.[92] In England the development was not only precocious, it was also firmly under royal control.

In these markets there was doubtless some trade in luxuries, but their main business was in basic commodities. This is shown very clearly by the list of commodities on which toll was paid at London early in the eleventh century.[93] It included timber, cloth, fish, *crapiscis* (probably whales), wine, hens, eggs, cheese and butter. Special mention is made of men from Rouen, Flanders, Ponthieu, Normandy, and *Francia*, as well as from Liège, Nivelles and Huy, the last probably bringing their speciality, metalwork. The subjects of the German Emperor were allowed the same privileges as the English and were allowed to buy wool that was offered for sale and to provision their ships with up to three live pigs. They had no right of pre-emption and paid their toll in the form of cloth, pepper, gloves and vinegar. This text is a useful reminder of the importance at that time of trade in bulk goods of an ordinary sort, and it also shows that London's links were with ports across the Channel and the North Sea. There were connections, economic as well as religious, with the Mediterranean, but these amounted to no more than a tiny proportion of the traffic across the northern seas.[94]

The light, fast craft that had been suitable for the earlier trade in light-weight luxury goods, were no longer suitable and they were consequently replaced by larger vessels, better designed for bulky cargoes. This change is illustrated very well by the newly discovered eleventh-century cargo boat from Lynæs in Roskilde fjord in Denmark, with a design that may be contrasted with the earlier craft discovered near the head of that fjord, at Skuldelev. These new ships had a deeper draught and they needed new harbours. In the eleventh and twelfth centuries the sheltered, shallow sites that had been preferred in earlier times were abandoned in favour of harbours with a greater depth of water; a shift that is possibly represented by the removal of

---

[88] Tait 1936, p. 20
[89] Whitelock 1955, p. 67
[90] Loyn 1971
[91] Biddle and Hill 1971
[92] Dhondt 1948
[93] IV Æthelred 2, ed. Liebermann i. 232–4, Robertson 1925, pp. 70–2
[94] Lopez and Raymond 1955, pp. 56–60

Hamwih from its original position on the shallow Itchen to the site of medieval Southampton on the River Test, with deeper wharves.

By the tenth century the royal responsibility for strangers engaged in distant commerce had been extended, in England, to cover and control local exchanges, and as these prospered so too did the kings. It is not fanciful to see behind the shifting fortunes of the English and French kings, a reflection of their ability to profit from the activity of merchants, local as well as distant. Thanks to England's importance in the trade of northern Europe, English kings were, in the eleventh century, relatively wealthy, while their French counterparts were less fortunate. In time this economic activity spread and increasingly influenced the Isle de France until, by the end of the twelfth century, Italian merchants found it worth their while to attend the Champagne fairs. As more traffic passed along the Seine and the Loire, and their tributaries, the wealth of the French kings grew, a prosperity that had architectural as well as political consequences.

These economic developments were even slower to reach Ireland. Whatever buying and selling, or bartering, took place at such assemblies as the *Oenach Tailten* there were no established markets there before the Viking invasions. The great monastic communities, or cities, of Ireland certainly resembled towns in many respects; they had large populations, including many craftsmen, and these people had to be fed, but the transactions that took place were governed more by social or religious considerations than commercial ones.[95] The first recognisable towns in fact grew in or near the Viking strongholds, notably Dublin, which produced the first native Irish coinage late in the tenth century.[96] The conversion of these strongholds into towns may have been partly due to the needs of the Vikings themselves, many of whom had become rich in treasure thanks to their plundering expeditions, but it was also affected by developments across the Irish Sea, where the growing towns like Chester and Bristol needed raw materials that could be conveniently supplied by boat.

The example of Ireland in fact confirms the general thesis put forward here. Commerce in exotic or luxury goods then, as now, depended not only on supply but also on demand, which had to be effective, that is, some acceptable exchange was needed. The nobles of Ireland probably coveted such luxuries as furs, ivory, amber beads, wine, fine weapons and high quality cloth as much as the nobles of England or Frankia, but they had little to offer in return that could not be obtained more easily elsewhere. Other parts of Europe were better suited in the Dark Ages to supply the demand for cattle and leather and although Ireland was a potential source of slaves, that potential was first exploited on any scale by the Vikings, who came not as traders but as raiders. Traders who carried goods across the sea, or across frontiers, were necessarily at some stage of their journeys strangers in need of protection, a protection best provided by kings. In Ireland there were many kings and many

[95] de Paor 1976
[96] Ó Ríordáin 1976

strangers under their protection, but those aliens were not merchants but exiles or pilgrims.[97] In those parts of northern Europe that attracted merchants, kings were more fortunate and were well rewarded for the protection that they gave, gaining both wealth and prestige. In time they were able to extend that protection, and control, to cover local transactions among their own peoples. In many parts of Europe that development occurred very early, thanks to Roman imperial authority but in those areas that never formed part of the empire, or, like Britain were abandoned to native rule at a relatively early stage, it happened more slowly, the rate depending less on the authority of kings than on the activity of merchants.

[97] Charles-Edwards 1976a

Bibliography

ABADAL, R. 1958: 'A propos du legs Visigothique en Espagne', *Settimane Spoleto*, 5, pp. 541–85
ADAM OF BREMEN: *Gesta Hammaburgensis ecclesiae pontificum*, ed. B. Schmeidler (1917); trans. F. J. Tschan (1959)
ADDYMAN, P. V. 1972: 'Saxon Southampton: a town and international port of the 8th to the 10th century', *Vor- und Frühformen der europäischen Stadt*, vol. 1, pp. 218–28
ADOMNAN, *Life of Columba*: edd. A. O. and M. O. Anderson (Edinburgh, 1961)
ÆLFRIC: *Colloquy*, ed. G. N. Garmonsway, 2nd edn (London, 1947)
ÆTHELWEARD: *The Chronicle of Æthelweard*, ed. A. Campbell (1962)
AGATHIAS: *Agathias Historiarum Libri Quinque*, ed. B. Niebuhr (Bonn, 1828)
AGOBARD, *Adv. Leg. Gundobad: Agobardi Lugdunensis Archiepiscopi Epistolae*, ed. E. Dümmler, *M.G.H.*, Ep. Kar. Aev., Vol. 3, pp. 150–239
ALBANI, C. 1969: *L'Istituto Monarchico nell'antica societa nordica* (Florence)
ALFRED, *Translation of the Pastoral Rule: King Alfred's West Saxon version of Pope Gregory's Pastoral Care*, ed. H. Sweet (Oxford, Early English Texts Society, 45; 1871)
VON AMIRA, K. 1960: *Germanisches Recht*, 2nd edn., ed. K. A. Eckhardt (Berlin)
AMMIANUS MARCELLINUS: ed. and trans. J. C. Rolfe, 3 vols (1963–4)
ANDERSON, M. O. 1973: *Kings and Kingship in Early Scotland* (Edinburgh)
ANDRIEU, M. 1953: 'Le sacre épiscopal d'après Hincmar de Reims', *Revue d'Histoire Ecclésiastique*, 48, pp. 22–73
ANGLO-SAXON CHRONICLE: ed. B. Thorpe (Rolls Series, 1861); trans. D. Whitelock (Cambridge, 1961)
ANNALES BERTINIANI: edd. F. Grat, J. Viellard and S. Clemencet (Paris, 1964)
ANNALES REGNI FRANCORUM: ed. F. Kurze, *M.G.H.*, S.R.G. in usum scholarum (1895)
ANNALS OF ULSTER: *The Annals of Ulster*, ed. W. M. Hennesy (Dublin, 1887), vol. 1.
ANONYMI VALESIANI PARS POSTERIOR: ed. and trans. J. C. Rolfe in *Ammianus Marcellinus*, vol. 3
ANTIPHONARIO VISIGOTICO MOZARABE: ed. L. Brou and J. Vives (Madrid, 1959)
ANTON, H. H. 1968: *Fürstenspiegel und Herrscherethos in der Karolingerzeit* (Bonn)
ARCHI, G. 1968: 'Le classicisme de Justinien', *Revue Historique de Droit français et étranger*, iv, 46, pp. 579–601

ARQUILLIÈRE, H. X. 1955: *L'Augustinisme politique* (2nd edn., Paris)
ARS IULIANI TOLETANI EPISCOPI: ed. M. A. H. Maestre Yenes (Toledo, 1973)
ASTRONOMUS, *Vita Hludovici Pii*: ed. W. Pertz, *M.G.H.*, SS. II
AVITUS: ed. R. Peiper, *M.G.H.*, A.A., VI (2) (1883); also U. Chevalier (Lyons, 1890)
BAK, J. 1973: 'Medieval Symbology of the State: Percy E. Schramm's contribution' in *Viator*, 4, pp. 33–63
BALANDIER, G. 1972: *Political Anthropology* (Harmondsworth)
BARROW, G. W. S. 1973: *The Kingdom of the Scots. Government, Church and Society from the Eleventh to the Fourteenth Century* (London)
BARTRUM, P. C. 1966: *Early Welsh Genealogical Tracts* (Cardiff)
— 1975: *Welsh Genealogies 300–1400* 8 vols (Cardiff)
BECK, C. W. 1970: 'Amber in Archaeology', *Archaeology*, 23, pp. 7–11
BECKWITH, J. 1972: *Ivory Carvings in early medieval England* (London)
BEDE, *Expos. Act. Apost.*: *Venerabilis Bedae Expositio Actuum Apostolorum*, ed. M. L. W. Laistner (Cambridge, Mass., 1939)
BEDE, H. E.: *Bedae Historia Ecclesiastica*, ed. C. Plummer (Oxford, 1896)
BEDE, *In Ezram: Bedae In Ezram et Nehemiam*, ed. D. Hurst (Turnholdt, Corpus Christianorum, 119A, 1969)
BEDE, *In Templ. Sol.: Bedae In Templo Salomonis*, ed. D. Hurst (Turnholdt, Corpus Christianorum, 119A, 1969)
BEESON, C. H. 1924: 'The *Ars Grammatica* of Julian of Toledo', *Studi e Testi*, 37, pp. 50–70
BENCARD, M. 1973: 'Ribes vikingetid', *Mark og montre*, 9, pp. 28–48
BENVENISTE, E. 1951: 'Sur l'histoire du mot latin *negotium*', *Annali della Scuola Normale Superiore di Pisa*, ser. 2, 20, pp. 21–5
— 1973: *Indo-European Language and Society*, trans. Elizabeth Palmer (London, 1973)
BERANGER, J. 1948: 'Le refus du pouvoir', *Museum Helveticum*, pp. 178–96
BERGIN, O. 1970: *Irish Bardic Poetry*, edd. D. Greene and F. Kelly (Dublin)
BEST, R. I. and O'BRIEN, M. A. 1957: *The Book of Leinster, formerly Lebar na Núachongbála*, vol. 3 (Dublin)
BESTA, E. 1951: 'Le Fonti dell'Editto di Rotari', *Atti del I° Congresso internaziolale di Studi Longobardi* (1952), pp. 51–69
BETHURUM, D. 1966: 'Wulfstan', *Continuations and Beginnings*, ed. E. G. Stanley (London), pp. 210–46
BEYERLE, F. 1924: 'Über Normtypen und Erweiterungen der Lex Salica', *Z.SS.R.G., g.a.*, 44, pp. 216–61
— 1926: *Lex Baiuvariorum* (München)
— 1928: 'Die Lex Ribuaria', *Z.SS.R.G., g.a.*, 48, pp. 264–378
— 1929: 'Die süddeutschen Leges und die Merovingische Gesetzgebung', *Z.SS.R.G., g.a.*, 49, pp. 264–434
— 1935: 'Das Gesetzbuch Ribuariens', *Z.SS.R.G., g.a.*, 55, pp. 1–80

— 1947: (ed.) *Die Gesetze der Langobarden* (Weimar)
— 1954: 'Zur Textgestalt und Textgeschichte der Lex Burgundionum', *Z.SS.R.G.*, *g.a.*, 71, pp. 23—54
— 1956: 'Die beiden süddeutschen Stammesrechte', *Z.SS.R.G.*, *g.a.*, 73, pp. 84—140
BEYERLE, F. and BUCHNER, R. 1951: *Lex Ribuaria*, *M.G.H.*, Legum Sectio I, Vol. 3, Pt. ii
BIDDLE, M. 1974: 'The Development of the Anglo-Saxon Town', *Settimane Spoleto*, 21, pp. 203—30
— 1975: 'Felix Urbs Winthonia; Winchester in the age of monastic reform', in D. Parsons, ed., *Tenth Century Studies*, pp. 123—40
— 1976: 'Towns', *The Archaeology of Anglo-Saxon England*, ed. David M. Wilson (London), pp. 99—150
BIDDLE, M. and HILL, D. 1971: 'Late Saxon planned towns', *Antiquaries Journal*, 51, pp. 70—85
BINCHY, D. A. 1943: 'The Linguistic and Historical Value of the Irish Law Tracts', *Proc. Brit. Acad.*, 29, pp. 195—227
— 1956: 'Some Celtic Legal Terms', *Celtica*, 3, pp. 221—31
— 1958: 'The Fair of Tailtiu and the Feast of Tara', *Ériu*, 18, pp. 113—38
— 1970: *Celtic and Anglo-Saxon Kingship* (Oxford)
— 1975: 'The Passing of the Old Order', in Brian Ó Cuív (ed.), *The Impact of the Scandinavian Invasions on the Celtic-speaking Peoples, c. 800—1100 A.D.* (2nd edn., Dublin)
— 1975/6: 'The pseudo-historical Prologue to the *Senchas Már*', *Studia Celtica*, 10/11 (1975—76), pp. 15—28
BINDING, K. 1868: *Das burgundish-romanische Königreich* (Leipzig)
BIRCH, W. G.: *Cartularium Saxonicum* (3 vols. 1885—93)
BISCHOFF, B. 1965: 'Die Hofbibliothek Karls des Grossen', *Karl der Grosse, Lebenswerk und Nachleben*, ed. W. Braunfels et al; vol. 2, *Das Geistige Leben*, ed. Bischoff (Dusseldorf), pp. 42—62
BLINDHEIM, C. 1963: 'Smedsgraven fra Bygland i Morgedal', *Viking*, 36, p. 28—81
BLOCH, M. 1924: *Les Rois Thaumaturges* (Paris)
BLONDEL, L. 1958: 'Le prieuré Saint-Victor, les débuts du christianisme et la royauté burgonde à Genève', *Bulletin de la societé d'histoire et d'archéologie de Genève*, pp. 211—58
BLUHME, F. 1868: *Leges Langobardorum*, *M.G.H.*, Leges in folio, vol. 4. There is a more convenient edition by F. Beyerle in the series, *Germanenrechte* (1962); and an English translation, Drew, 1973
BOGNETTI, G. P. 1939: 'Longobardi e Romani', *Studi . . . in onore di Enrico Besta . . .* (Milan), pp. 353—410; repr. in Bognetti 1966 I, pp. 85—141
— 1948: 'Santa Maria foris portas di Castelseprio e la storia religiosa dei Longobardi'; repr. in Bognetti 1966 II, pp. 13—673

— 1948/9: 'I ministri romani dei Re Longobardi . . .' *Archivio Storico Lombardo*, viii, 1, pp. 10—24; repr. in *L'Eta Longobarda* (Milan, 1967), vol. 3, pp. 49— 66
— 1957: 'L'Editto di Rotari come espediente politico di una monarchia barbarica', *Studi in onore di G. de Francesco*; repr. in *L'Eta Longobarda*, Milan (1968), vol. 4, pp. 115—35
— 1966: *L'Eta Longobarda*, 2 vols, Milan
BOHANNAN, L. 1952: 'A genealogical charter', *African Journal of the International African Institute*, 22, pp. 301—315
BOSHOF, E. 1969: *Erzbischof Agobard von Lyons* (Köln)
BOSTON, J. S. 1969: 'Oral tradition and the history of Igala', *Journal of African History*, 10, pp. 29—43
BOSWORTH, J. and TOLLER, T. N.: *An Anglo-Saxon Dictionary* (Oxford, 1882)
BOUMAN, C. A. 1957: *Sacring and crowning* (Groningen)
BOYLE, A. 1971: 'The Edinburgh synchronisms', *Celtica*, 9, pp. 169—179
BRACKMANN, A. 1967: *Gesammelte Aufsatze* (Darmstadt)
BRIDBURY, A. R. 1955: *England and the salt trade in the later middle ages* (Oxford)
BRUCE-MITFORD, R. 1976: *The Sutton Hoo ship-burial* (London)
BRUCK, E. 1953: 'Caesarius of Arles and the *Lex Romana Visigothorum*', *Studi . . . Arangio-Ruiz* (Naples)
BRÜHL, C. -R. 1962: 'Frankischer Krönungsbrauch', *Historische Zeitschrift*, 194, pp. 265—326
— 1973: *Codice diplomatico longobardo*, vol. 3 (1). (Fonti per la storia d'Italia, vol. 64, Roma Istituto Storico Italiano per il Medio Evo)
— 1975: *Palatium und Civitas* (Köln)
BRUNNER, H. 1906: *Deutsche Rechtsgeschichte*, 2nd edn. vol. 1 (Leipzig)
BUCHNER, R. 1940: *Textkritische Untersuchungen zur Lex Ribuaria* (Leipzig)
— 1953: *Die Rechtsquellen*: Beiheft to Wattenbach-Levison, *Deutschlands Geschichtsquellen im Mittelalter* (Weimar)
— 1955: 'Plan einer Geschichte der Quellen und Literatur des weltlichen Rechts von 450 bis 900', *Aus Verfassungs — und Landesgeschichte: zum 70ten Geburtstag Th. Mayer* (Konstanz), vol. 2, pp. 391—401
BÜTTNER, H. 1952: 'Aus den Anfängen des abendlandischen Staatsdenkens', *Historisches Jahrbuch*, 71, pp. 77—90
BULLOUGH, D. A. 1965: 'Anglo-Saxon institutions and early English society', *Annali della Fondazione Italiana per la storia amministrativa*, 2, pp. 647—59
— 1975: 'The continental background of the reform', *Tenth Century Studies*, ed. D. Parsons (London), pp. 20—36
BYRNE, F. J. 1971: 'Tribes and tribalism in early Ireland', *Ériu*, 22, pp. 128—66
— 1973: *Irish Kings and High-Kings* (London)
CAMPBELL, A. 1959: *Old English Grammar* (Oxford)
CAMPBELL, J. 1975: ''Observations on English Government from the tenth to the twelfth century', *Trans. Roy. Hist. Soc.*, 5th ser. 25, pp. 39—54
CAMPOS, J. and ROCO, I. 1971: ed. *Santos Padres Espanoles* (Madrid)

CAPITULARIA: A. Boretius, *Capitularia Regum Francorum*, *M.G.H.*, Legum Sectio II, vol. 1 (1883), vol. 2 (1890—1901)
CAREY, F. M. 1938: 'The Scriptorium of Rheims during the archbishopric of Hincmar', *Classical and Medieval Studies in honour of E. K. Rand* (New York), pp. 41—60
CARNEY, J. 1973: 'Society and the bardic poet', *Studies*, 62, pp. 233—50
CART. SENON: *Cartae Senonenses*, ed. in *Formulae*
CASSIODORUS, *Ep. Var.*: *Cassiodori Senatoris Epistolae Variae*, ed. T. Mommsen, *M.G.H.*, A.A., vol. 12 (1894)
CHADWICK, H. M. 1905: *Studies in Anglo-Saxon Institutions* (Cambridge)
— 1907: *The origin of the English nation* (Cambridge)
CHAPLAIS, P. 1965: 'The Origin and Authenticity of the Royal Anglo-Saxon Diploma', *Journal of the Society of Archivists*, pp. 48—61
CHARLES-EDWARDS, T. M. 1971: 'The heir-apparent in Irish and Welsh Law', *Celtica*, 9, pp. 180—90
— 1971a: 'The seven bishop-houses of Dyfed', *Bulletin of the Board of Celtic Studies*, 24, pp. 247—62
— 1972: 'Kinship, Status and the Origins of the Hide', *Past and Present*, 56, pp. 3—33
— 1974: 'Native political organization in Roman Britain and the origin of the MW *brenhin*', *Antiquitates Indogermanicae. Studien zur indogermanischen Altertumskunde und zur Sprach- und Kulturgeschichte der indogermanischen Völker. Gedenkschrift für Herman Güntert zur 25 Wiederkehr seines Todestages*, edd. Manfred Mayrhofer, et al. (Innsbruck), pp. 35—45
— 1976: 'The distinction between land and moveable wealth in Anglo-Saxon England' *Medieval Settlement: Continuity and Change*, ed. P. H. Sawyer (London), pp. 180—7
— 1976a: 'The Social Background to Irish *Peregrinatio*', *Celtica*, 11, pp. 43—59
CHERRY, B. 1976: 'Ecclesiastical architecture', *The Archaeology of Anglo-Saxon England*, ed. D. M. Wilson (London), pp. 151—200
CHRIST, K. 1937: 'Die Stiftsbibliothek von Nickolsberg und die Überlieferung der Kapitulariensammlung des Ansegis', *Deutsches Archiv*, 50, pp. 281—322
CHRONICON ADEFONSI IMPERATORIS: ed. L. Sánchez Belda (Madrid, 1950)
C.L.A.: E. A. Lowe, *Codices Latini Antiquiores* (Oxford, 1931—71)
CLANCHY, M. T. 1970: 'Remembering the Past and the Good Old Law', *History*, 55, pp. 165—76
CLASSEN, P. 1955—6: 'Kaisserreskript und Königsurkunde', *Archiv für Diplomatik*, (1955), pp. 1—87; and (1956), pp. 1—115
CLAUDE, D. 1971: *Adel, Kirche und Königtum im Westgotenreich* (Sigmaringen)
DE CLERCQ, C. 1958: *La legislation religieuse franque* (Anvers), vol. 2
COD. DIPL. LONGOB.: *Codice Diplomatico Longobardo*, ed. L. Schiaparelli and C. R. Brühl (Milan, Fonti della Storia Italica, 1929, 1933, 1974)

COD. EUR.: *Codex Euricianus*, ed. Zeumer, 1902
COD. LAURESHAM.: *Codex Laureshamensis*, ed. K. Glöckner (1929—36)
COD. THEOD.: *Codex Theodosianus*, ed. T. Mommsen and P. M. Meyer (Berlin, 1904—5)
COLGRAVE, B. 1956: ed. and trans. *Felix's Life of St. Guthlac* (Cambridge)
COLGRAVE, B. and MYNORS, R. A. B. 1969: *Bede's Ecclesiastical History of the English People* (Oxford)
COLL. SANGALL.: *Collectio Sangallensis*, ed. in *Formulae*
CONGAR, Y. M. J. 1966: 'Ordinations *invitus, coactus* de l'église antique au canon 214', *Revue des Sciences Philosophiques et Theologiques*, 50, pp. 169—97
COPLEY, G. J. 1951—3: 'The tribal complexity of Middle Anglia', *Archaeological News Letter* 4, pp. 152—6 and 160
— 1954—5: 'The tribal complexity of the early Kentish kingdom', *Archaeological News letter* 5, pp. 24—8 and 35
CORIPPUS, *In Laudem Iustini*: ed. and trans. A. Cameron (London, 1976)
CORPUS SCRIPTORUM MUZARABICORUM I: ed. J. Gil (Madrid, 1973)
DE COULANGES, F. 1888—92: *Histoire des Institutions politiques de l'ancienne France*, 6 vols (Paris)
COURTOIS, C. 1955: *Les Vandales et l'Afrique* (Paris)
COVILLE, A. 1928: *Recherches sur l'Histoire de Lyon du ve siècle au ixe siècle (450—800)* (Paris)
CRUMP, W. H. 1939: 'Saltways from the Cheshire Wiches', *Transactions of the Lancashire and Cheshire Antiquarian Society*, 54, pp. 84—142
D.A.C.L.: *Dictionnaire d'Archéologie chrétienne et de Liturgie*, ed. F. Cabrol and H. Leclercq (Paris, 1903—53)
DALTON, O. M. 1927: *Gregory of Tours: History of the Franks* (Oxford)
DAVIES, W. 1973: 'Middle Anglia and the Middle Ages', *Midland History*, 2, pp. 18—20
DAVIES, W. and VIERCK, H. 1974: 'The contexts of *Tribal Hidage*: social aggregates and settlement patterns', *Frühmittelalterliche Studien*, 8, pp. 223—93
D.B.: Domesday Book
DESHMAN, R. 1976: '*Christus rex et magi reges* Kingship and Christology in Ottonian and Anglo-Saxon Art', *Frühmittelalterliche Studien*, 10, pp. 367—405
DEVISSE, J. 1976: *Hincmar, archevêque de Reims 845—882*, (3 vols. Geneva)
DHONDT, J. 1948: 'Développement urbain et initiative comtale en Flandre au XIe siécle', *Revue du Nord*, 30, pp. 133—56
— 1962: 'Les Problèmes de Quentovic', *Studi in Onore di Amintore Fanfani*, vol. 1 (Milan), pp. 183—248
DIALOGUS DE SCACCARIO: *Dialogus de Scaccario*, ed. C. Johnson (London, Nelson's medieval texts, 1950)
DIAZ Y DIAZ, M. C. 1966: 'Los documentos hispano-visigoticos sobre pizarra', *Studi Medievali*, 7, pp. 75—107

DICKINS, B. 1952: ed. *The Genealogical Preface to the Anglo-Saxon Chronicle. Four texts edited to supplement Earle-Plummer* (Cambridge)

DILLON, M. 1947: *The Archaism of Irish Tradition* (London). Also in *Proc. Brit. Acad.*, 33 (1947)

DILLON, M. and CHADWICK, N. K. 1967: *The Celtic Realms*

DIPLOM. KAROL.: *Diplomata Karolinorum*, ed. E. Mühlbacher, *M.G.H.*, Diplomata (1906)

DOEHAERD, R. 1957: 'Impots directes acquittes par des marchands et des artisans pendant le Moyen Age', *Studi in Onore di Armando Sapori*, pp. 81—90

DOLLEY, M. 1973: 'The Eadgar Millenary — a Note on the Bath Mint', *Seaby's Coin and Medal Bulletin*, pp. 156—59

— 1976: 'The coins', *The Archaeology of Anglo-Saxon England*, ed. D. M. Wilson (London), pp. 349—72

DOLLEY, M. and METCALF, D. M. 1961: 'The reform of the English coinage under Eadgar', *Anglo-Saxon Coins*, ed. M. Dolley, pp. 136—68

DONAHUE, C. 1965: '*Beowulf* and Christian tradition: a reconsideration from a Celtic stance', *Traditio*, 21, pp. 55—116

DREW, K. F. 1972: Trans. *The Burgundian Code* (repr. Philadelphia)

— 1973: Trans. *The Lombard Laws* (Philadelphia)

DUBY, G. 1962: *L'economie rurale et la vie des campagnes dans l'Occident médiévale*, (Paris)

DUCHESNE, L. 1915: *Fastes Episcopaux de l'Ancienne Gaule*, vol. 3 (Paris)

DUMVILLE, D. N. 1973a: 'A new chronicle-fragment of early British history', *English Historical Review*, 88, pp. 312—14

— 1973b: 'Biblical apocrypha and the early Irish: a preliminary investigation', *Proceedings of the Royal Irish Academy*, 73 C, pp. 299—338

— 1976: 'The Anglian collection of royal genealogies and regnal lists', *Anglo-Saxon England*, 5, pp. 23—50

— 1977: 'Sub-Roman Britain: history and legend', *History*, N.S. 62, pp. 173—92

— 1978: 'The ætheling: a study in Anglo-Saxon constitutional history', *Anglo-Saxon England* 7

DUNCAN, A. A. M. 1975: *Scotland: The Making of the Kingdom* (Edinburgh)

DUPARC, P. 1958: 'La Sapaudia', *Comptes rendus de l'Académie des inscriptions et Belles lettres*, pp. 371—83

ECKHARDT, K. A. 1927: *Die Lex Baiuvariorum: eine kritische Studie* (Breslau)

— 1952: *Lex Salica: 100-titel Text, Germanenrechte*

— 1954: *Pactus Legis Salicae: Einführung und 65-titel text, Germanenrechte*

— 1955: *Die Kapitulariensammlung Bischof Ghaerbalds von Lüttich* (Göttingen)

— 1957: *Lex Salica: 70-titel text und systematische Verfassung, Germanenrechte*

— 1958 and 1962a: *Lex Alamannorum, vol 1: Einführung und Recensio Chlothariana*, Germanenrechte (1958); *vol. 2: Recensio Lantfridiana*, Germanenrechte (1962). This edition altogether supersedes the more generally available edn. by K. Lehmann in *M.G.H.*, Legum Sectio I, vol. 5, pt. i (1888), which it was necessary to cite here

— 1959a: *Lex Ribuaria, vol. 1: Austrasiches Recht in 7ten Jahrhundert, Germanenrechte*
— 1959b: 'Die von Baluze benutzten Handschriften der Kapitulariensammlung', *Mélanges C. Braibant*, pp. 123—40 (Brussels)
— 1962b: *Pactus Legis Salicae, M.G.H.*, Legum Sectio I, vol. 4, pt. i
— 1969: *Lex Salica, M.G.H.*, Legum Sectio I, vol. 4, pt. ii
— 1975: *Studia Merovingica*, (Bibliotheca Rerum Historicarum, 11, Aalen)
ED. ROTH.: *Edictum Rothari*, ed. Bluhme, 1868
EINHARD, *V.C.*: *Einhardi Vita Caroli*, ed. O. Holder-Egger, *M.G.H.*, *S.R.G.* in usum scholarum (1911)
EITEN, G. 1907: *Das Unterkönigtum im Reiche der Merovinger und Karolinger* (Heidelberg)
EKWALL, E. 1936: 'Some notes on English place-names containing tribal names', *Namn och Bygd*, 24, pp. 178—83
— 1953: 'Tribal names in English place-names', *Namn och Bygd*, 41, pp. 129—77
ELLARD, G. 1933: *Ordination Anointings in the Western Church before 1000 A.D.* (Cambridge, Mass.)
ENNODIUS, *Vita Epifani*: Ed. F. Vogel, in *M.G.H.*, A.A., VII (1885)
EPISTOLAE ARELATENSES GENUINAE: ed. W. Gundlach, *M.G.H.*, Epistolae Merowingici et Karolini Aevi I, Epistolarum Tomus III (1892)
EPISTOLAE AUSTRASIACAE: ed. W. Gundlach, *M.G.H.*, Epistolae Merowingici et Karolini Aevi I, Epistolarum Tomus III (1892); also Corpus Christianorum, vol. 117, 1957
EPITOME OVETENSIS: ed. T. Mommsen, *Chronica Minora*, vol. 2. *M.G.H.*, A.A., XI
ERDMANN, C. 1951: ed. *Forschungen zur politischen Ideenwelt des Frühmittelalters* (Berlin)
ERLANDE-BRANDENBURG, A. 1975: *Le Roi est mort* (Paris)
VAN ES, W. A. 1972: 'Die neuen Dorestad-Grabungen 1967—1972', *Vor- und Frühformen der europäischen Stadt*, vol. 1, pp. 202—17
EWIG, E. 1952: 'Die fränkischen Teilungen und Teilreiche (511—613)', *Akademie der Wissenschaften und der Literatur. Abhandlungen der Geistes- und Socialwissenschaftlichen Klasse, Jahrgang*, no. 9
— 1953: 'Die fränkischen Teilreiche in 7 Jahrhundert (613—714)', *Trierer Zeitzchrift*, 22, pp. 85—144
— 1956: 'Zum christlichen Königsgedanken im Frühmittelalter', *Das Königtum, Vorträge und Forschungen*, ed. T. Mayer, pp. 7—73
— 1958: Volkstum und Volksbewusstsein im Frankenreich des 7 Jahrhunderts', *Settimane Spoleto*, 5, pp. 587—648
— 1963: 'Residence et capitale pendant le haut Môyen Age', *Revue Historique*, 230, pp. 25—72
— 1973: 'Das Privileg des Bischofs Berthefrid von Amiens für Corbie von 664 und die Klosterpolitik der Königin Balthild', *Frankia*, 1, pp. 62— 114

— 1974: 'Studien zur merowingischen Dynastie', *Frühmittelalterliche Studien*, 8, pp. 15—59
FELIX, *Elogium Iuliani*: *Patrologia Latina*, 96
FINBERG, H. P. R. 1972: 'Anglo-Saxon England to 1042', *The Agrarian History of England and Wales*, I, ii, ed. H. P. R. Finberg (Cambridge), pp. 385—525
FLORENCE OF WORCESTER, *Chronicon*: ed. B. Thorpe (London, 1848)
FONTAINE, J. 1973: *L'Art pré-roman visigothique* (Paris)
FORMULAE: K. Zeumer, *Formulae*, *M.G.H.*, Legum Sectio V (1882—86)
FORM. AUG.: *Formulae Augienses*, ed. in *Formulae*
FORM. AUG. COLL.: *Formularum Augiensium Collectio*, ed. in *Formulae*
FORM. EXTRAV.: *Formulae Extravagantes*, ed. in *Formulae*
FORM. IMP.: *Formulae Imperiales*, ed. in *Formulae*
FORM. MARC.: *Marculfi Formulae*, ed. in *Formulae*
FORM. SAL. BINGNON.: *Formulae Salicae Bignonianae*, ed. in *Formulae*
FORM. SAL. LIND.: *Formulae Salicae Lindenbrogianae*, ed. in *Formulae*
FORM. SAL. MERK.: *Formulae Salicae Merkelianae*, ed. in *Formulae*
FORM. SANGALL.: *Formulae Sangallenses*, ed. in *Formulae*
FORTES, M. 1968: 'Of Installation ceremonies', *Proceedings of the Royal Anthropological Institute for 1967*, pp. 5—20
FOURNIER, P. 1909: '*Le Liber ex lege Moysi* et les tendences blbliques du Droit canonique Irlandais', *Revue Celtique*, 30, pp. 221—34
FRANKIS, P. J. 1973: 'The thematic significance of "enta geweorc" in *The Wanderer*', *Anglo-Saxon England*, 2, pp. 253-69
FREDEGAR, *Chron. IV.*: J. M. Wallace-Hadrill, *The Fourth Book of the Chronicle of Fredegar with its Continuations* (London, Nelson's medieval texts, 1960)
FREDEGAR, *Chronicarum Libri IV cum continuationibus*, ed. B. Krusch, *M.G.H.*, S.R.M. II (1888)
FREEMAN, E. A. 1887: *The History of the Norman Conquest of England*, vol. 1 (3rd edn., Oxford)
GAMILLSCHEG, E. 1934 and 1970: *Romania Germanica* (Berlin), vol. 1, 2nd edn., 1970; vol. 2, 1934
GANSHOF, F. L. 1951: 'The use of the written word in Charlemagne's administration' — originally published (French) in *Le Moyen Age*, 57; trans. J. Sondheimer, *The Carolingians and the Frankish Monarchy* (London, 1971), pp. 125—42
— 1957: 'Recherches sur les capitulaires', *Revue historique de Droit français et étranger*, iv, 35, pt. i, pp. 33—87; pt. ii, pp. 196—246. There is a revised edition, *Was waren die Capitularien?* (Darmstadt, 1961)
— 1962: 'A propos du tonlieu sous les merovingiens', *Studi in onore di Amintori Fanfani*, i (Milan), pp. 291—315
GARCIA GÓRRIZ, Fr. M. P. 1966: *La Basilica visigotica de S. Juan de Baños y el arte visigodo* (Palencia)
GARCIA MORENO, L. A. 1974a: *El fino del reino visigodo de Toledo: decadencia y catastrofe* (Madrid)

— 1974b: *Prosopographia del reino visigodo de Toledo* (Madrid)
GENICOT, L. 1975: *Les Généalogies* (Turnhout)
GERMANENRECHTE: *Germanenrechte*, neue folge (Göttingen)
GIBBON 1960: *Decline and Fall of the Roman Empire*, abridged by D. Low (Harmondsworth)
GLANVILLE: *The Treaties on the laws and customs of the realm of England, commonly called Glanville*, ed. G. D. G. Hall (London, Nelson's medieval texts, 1965)
GLUCKMAN, M. 1956: *Custom and Conflict in Africa* (Oxford)
GÓMEZ-MORENO, M. 1932: 'Las primera crónicas de la reconquista', *Boletín de la Real Academia de la Historia*, 100, pp. 562—623
GONSER, P. 1909: ed. *Das angelsächsische Prosa-Leben des heiligen Guthlac* (Heidelberg)
GOODY, J. 1968: *Literacy in Traditional Societies* (Cambridge)
GREGORY THE GREAT, *Regula Pastoralis: Patrologia Latina*, 77
GREGORY OF TOURS; GREG. TURON., *Hist. Franc.: Gregorii Turonensis Historiae Francorum Libri X, M.G.H.*, S.R.M., vol. 1, 2nd edn. B. Krusch and W. Levison (1951)
GRIERSON, P. 1941: 'Election and Inheritance in Early Germanic Kingship', *Cambridge Historical Journal*, 7, pp. 1—22
— 1959: 'Commerce in the Dark Ages: A Critique of the Evidence', *Trans. Roy. Hist. Soc.*, 5th series, 9, pp. 123—40
— 1961: 'La fonction sociale de la monnaie en Angleterre aux VIIe — VIIIe siècles', *Settimane Spoleto*, 8, pp. 341—62
— 1977: *The Origins of Money* (London)
HACKENBERG, E. 1918: *Die Stammtafeln der Angelsächsischen Königreiche* (Berlin)
HAGBERG, U. E. 1967: *The Archaeology of Skedemosse* (Stockholm)
HARMER, F. E. 1950: '*Chipping* and *Market*: a lexicographical investigation', *Early Cultures of North-West Europe* (H. M. Chadwick Memorial Studies) ed. Sir Cyril Fox and Bruce Dickins (Cambridge), pp. 335—57
HARRISON, K. 1973: 'The primitive Anglo-Saxon calendar', *Antiquity*, 47, pp. 284—7
— 1976: *The Framework of Anglo-Saxon History to A.D. 900* (Cambridge)
— 1976a: 'Woden', in G. Bonner (ed.), *Famulus Christi, Essays in commemoration of the thirteenth centenary of the birth of the Venerable Bede* (London), pp. 351—6
HART, C. 1973: 'Athelstan "Half King" and his family', *Anglo-Saxon England*, 2, pp. 115—44
HASSELBERG, G. 1953: *Studier rörande Visby Stadslag och dess källor* (Uppsala)
HAUCK, K. 1950: 'Rituelle Speisegemeinschaft im 10. und 11. Jht, *Studium Generale*, 3
— 1955: 'Lebensnormen und Kultmythen in germanischen Stammes- und Herrschergenealogien', *Saeculum*, pp. 186—223

— 1967: 'Von einer spätantiken Randkultur zum karolingischen Europa', *Frühmittelalterliche Studien*, 1, pp. 1—91
HAUGE, T. D. 1946: *Blesterbruk og Myrjern: Studier i den gamle jernvinna i det ostenfjelske Norge* (Oslo: Universitets Oldsaksamlings Skrifter, iii)
HEARNE, T. 1723: ed., *Hemingi Chartularium Ecclesiae Wigorniensis*, 2 vols (Oxford)
HENIGE, D. P. 1971: 'Oral tradition and chronology', *Journal of African History*, 12, pp. 371—89
HERICUS OF AUXERRE, *De Miraculis Sancti Germani*: Patrologia Latina, 124
HILLGARTH, J. N. 1966: 'Coins and chronicles: Propaganda in sixth-century Spain and the Byzantine background', *Historia*, 15, pp. 483—508
— 1970: 'Historiography in visigothic Spain', *Settimane Spoleto*, 17, pp. 261—311
— 1971: 'Las fuentes de San Julian de Toledo', *Anales Toledanos*, 3, p. 97—118
HODGKIN, T. 1895: *Italy and her Invaders*, vol. 6 (Oxford)
HODGKIN, R. H. 1952: *A history of the Anglo-Saxons*, 2 vols. (3rd edn., Oxford)
HÖFLER, O. 1954: 'Das Sakralcharakter des germanischen Königtums', *Das Königtum seine geistigen und rechtlichen Grundlagen*, ed. T. Mayer (Vorträge und Forschungen, iii, Konstanz), pp. 75—104
HOFFMAN, H. 1972: 'Zur Geschichte Ottos des Grossen', *Deutsches Archiv*, 28, pp. 42—73
HOHLER, C. 1975: 'Some service books of the later Saxon Church', *Tenth Century Studies*, ed. D. Parsons, pp. 60—83
HOUGHTON, F. T. S. 1932: 'Salt-ways', *Transactions and Proceedings of the Birmingham Archaeological Society*, 54, pp. 1—17
HÜBRICH, E. 1975: 'Fränkisches Wahl- und Erbkönigtum zur Merovingerzeit', *Königswahl und Thronfolge in fränkisch- karolingischer Zeit*, ed. E. Hlawitschka (Darmstadt), pp. 3—55
HUGHES, K. 1977: *The early Celtic idea of history and the modern historian. An inaugural lecture* (Cambridge)
ILDEFONSUS, *De Viris illustribus*: ed. C. Codoñer Merino (Salamanca, 1972)
IMBERT, J. 1967: 'L'influence du Christianisme sur la legislation des peuples Francs et Germains', *Settimane Spoleto*, 14, pp. 365—96
INSTITUTIONUM DISCIPLINAE: Ed. P. Pascal, *Traditio*, 13 (1957), pp. 426—7
IRSIGLER, F. 1969: *Untersuchungen zur Geschichte des frühfränkischen Adels* (Bonn)
ISIDORE, *Etym.*: *Isidori Hispalenisis Libri Etymologiarum* (Oxford, 1911)
ISIDORE, *Hist. Goth.*: *Isidori Hispalensis Historia Gothorum etc.*, ed. T. Mommsen, *M.G.H.*, A.A., Chronica Minora, vol. 2
JÄSCHKE, K. -U. 1970: 'Frühmittelalterliche Festkrönungen?', *Historische Zeitschrift*, 211, pp. 556—88
JANKUHN, H. 1953: 'Der fränkisch- friesische Handel zur Ostsee im frühen Mittelalter', *Vierteljahrschrift für Sozial- und Wirtschaftsgeschichte*, 40, pp. 193—243
— 1974: 'Frühe Städte im Nord- und Ostseeraum (700—1100 n. chr.)', *Settimane Spoleto*, 21, pp. 153—201

JELLEMA, D. 1955: 'Frisian Trade in the Dark Ages', *Speculum*, 30, pp. 15—36
JOHN OF BICLARO: Chronica, ed. T. Mommsen, *Chronica Minora*, vol. 2, *M.G.H.*, A.A., XI
JOHN, E. 1960: *Land Tenure in Early England* (Leicester)
— 1966: *Orbis Britanniae* (Leicester)
JONAS: *Vita Columbani*, ed. B. Krusch, *M.G.H.*, S.R.M. 4 (1902); also *S.R.G.* in usum scholarum (1905)
JONES, P. F. 1929: *A concordance to the 'Historia Ecclesiastica' of Bede* (Cambridge, Mass.)
JONES, A. H. M. 1962: 'The Constitutional Position of Odovacer and Theodoric', *Journal of Roman Studies*, 52, pp. 126—30
— 1964: *The Later Roman Empire 284—602* (Oxford)
JONES, D. H. 1970: 'Problems of African chronology', *Journal of African History*, 11, pp. 161—76
JONES, G. R. J. 1971: 'The multiple estate as a model framework for tracing early stages in the evolution of rural settlement', *Les Congrès et Colloques de l'Université de Liège*, 58, pp. 251—67
— 1972: 'Post-Roman Wales', *The Agrarian History of England and Wales, Vol. I, Part II, A.D. 43—1042*, ed. H. P. R. Finberg (Cambridge)
— 1976: 'Historical geography and our landed heritage', *University of Leeds Review*, 19, pp. 53—78
JORDANES, *Getica*: ed. T. Mommsen, *M.G.H.*, A.A., V (i) (1882); see also Mierow, 1915
JORDANES, *Romana*: ed. T. Mommsen, *M.G.H.*, A.A., V (i) (1882)
JULIAN, *Hist. Wamb.*: *Historia Wambae Regis auctore Iuliano*, ed. W. Levison, *M.G.H.*, S.R.M. 5 (1910); repr. Corpus Christianorum, vol. 115
JUSTINIAN, *Nov., Const.* etc.: *Justiniani Corpus Iuris Civilis*, vol. 1: *Institutiones, Digesta*, ed. P. Krüger and T. Mommsen (1872); *vol. 2: Codex*, ed. P. Krüger (1877); *vol. 3: Novellae*, ed. R. Schöll and G. Kroll (1895)
KANTOROWICZ, E. H. 1946: *Laudes Regiae* (Berkeley)
— 1955: 'The Carolingian King in the Bible of San Paolo fuori le Mura', *Late Classical and Medieval Studies in Honour of A. M. Friend* (Princeton)
KATZ, S. 1937: *The Jews in the Visigothic and Frankish Kingdoms of Spain and Gaul* (Cambridge, Mass.)
KELLEHER, J. V. 1963: 'Early Irish history and pseudo-history', *Studia Hibernica*, 3, pp. 113—27
— 1968: 'The pre-Norman Irish genealogies', *Irish Historical Studies*, 16, pp. 138—53
KELLER, R. E. 1964: 'The language of the Franks', *Bulletin of the John Rylands Library*, 47, pp. 101—22
KER, N. R. 1957: *A catalogue of manuscripts containing Anglo-Saxon* (Oxford)
KERN, F. 1954: *Gottesgnadentum und Widerstandsrecht*, 2nd edn. by R. Buchner (Darmstadt). There is an English translation of the superseded 1st edn., *Kingship and Law in the Middle Ages* by S. B. Chrimes (London, 1953)

KIENAST, W. 1968: *Studien über die französischen Volkstämme des Frühmittelalters* (Stuttgart)
KING, P. D. 1972: *Law and Society in the Visigothic Kingdom* (Cambridge)
KIRBY, D. P. 1963: 'Bede and Northumbrian chronology', *English Historical Review*, 78, pp. 514—27
KNOTT, E. 1922—6: ed. and trans. *The Bardic Poems of Tadhg Dall Ú Huiginn (1550—91)* (2 vols., London)
KÖBLER, G. 1972: '*Civitas* und *vicus, burg, stat, dorf* und *wik*', *Vor- und Frühformen der europäischen Stadt*, 1, pp. 61—76
KOTTJE, R. 1964: *Studien zum Einfluss des alten Testaments auf Recht und Liturgie des frühen Mittelalters* (Bonn)
KRÜGER, K. H. 1971: *Königsgrabkirchen der Franken, Angelsachsen und Langobarden bis zum Mitte des 8 Jahrunderts* (München)
L. AF.: *Laws of Alfred*, ed. Liebermann, 1903
L. AH.: *Leges Ahistulfi*, ed. Bluhme, 1868
L. AL.: *Lex Alamannorum*, ed. Eckhardt, 1958, 1962a
L. AS.: *Laws of Aethelstan*, ed. Liebermann, 1903
L. ATR.: *Laws of Aethelred II*, ed. Liebermann, 1903
L. BAI.: E. de Schwind, *Lex Baiwariorum, M.G.H.*, Legum Sectio I, vol. 5, pt. ii (1926)
L. BURG.: *Leges Burgundionum*, ed. de Salis, 1892
L. CN.: *Laws of Cnut*, ed. Liebermann, 1903
L. EG.: *Laws of Edgar*, ed. Liebermann, 1903
L. EM.: *Laws of Edmund*, ed. Liebermann, 1903
L. EW., *Laws of Edward the Elder*, ed. Liebermann, 1903
L. FRIS.: *Lex Frisionum*, ed. von Richthofen, 1863
L. GR.: *Leges Grimoaldi*, ed. Bluhme, 1868
L. HL.: *Laws of Hlothere and Eadric*, ed. Liebermann, 1903
L. IN.: *Laws of Ine*, ed. Liebermann, 1903
L. LIUT.: *Leges Liutprandi*, ed. Bluhme, 1868
L. MIRC.: *Mircna Laga*, ed. Liebermann, 1903
L. RA.: *Leges Ratchis*, ed. Bluhme, 1868
L. RIB.: *Lex Ribuaria*, ed. Beyerle-Buchner, 1951
L. SAL. (A, C, K): *Pactus Legis Salicae*, ed. Eckhardt, 1962b
L. SAL. CAPITULARIA: *Capitula legi Salicae addita*, ed. Eckhardt, 1962b
L. SAL. (D. E.): *Lex Salica*, ed. Eckhardt, 1969
L. SAX.: *Lex Saxonum*, ed. von Richthofen, 1875—89
L. VIS.: *Leges Visigothorum*, ed. Zeumer, 1902
L. WI.: *Laws of Wihtred*, ed. Liebermann, 1903
LEACH, E. 1966: 'Ritualisation in man in relation to conceptual and social development', *Philosophical Transactions of the Royal Society of London*, series B. Biological Sciences, no. 772, vol. 251, pp. 403—8
LEG. CAPIT. (786): *Legatine Capitulary (786)*, ed. E. Dümmler, *Alcuini Epistolae*, no. 3, *M.G.H.*, Epistolae Kar. Aevi, II (1895), pp. 19—29.

LEGES BURGUNDIONUM: *Leges Burgundionum*, ed. L. R. de Salis, *M.G.H.*, Leges 2(1), 1892; also trans. Drew, 1972
LEGES LANGOBARDORUM: *Leges Langobardorum*, ed. F. Beyerle, *Germanenrechte*, 1962; trans. Drew, 1973
LEGES VISIGOTHORUM: ed. K. Zeumer, *M.G.H.*, Leges I, 1902
LEG. HEN. PRIM.: L. J. Downer, *Leges Henrici Primi* (Oxford, 1972)
LELAND, J.: *Itinerary*, ed. Lucy Toulmin Smith, 2 (London, 1908)
LEVILLAIN, L. 1903: 'Le Sacre de Charles le Chauve à Orléans', *Bibliothèque de l'École des Chartres*, 64, pp. 31–53
— 1933: 'L'Avènement de la dynastie carolingienne', *Bibliothèque de l'École des Chartes*, 94, pp. 225–95
LEVISON, W. 1946: *England and the continent in the eighth century* (Oxford)
— 1952: *Deutschlands Geschichtsquellen im Mittelalter, Vorzeit und Karolinger, I, Die Vorzeit von den Anfangen bis zur Herrschaft der Karolinger* (Wien)
LEVY, E. 1942: 'Reflections on the first reception of Roman Law in Germanic States', *American Historical Review*, 48, pp. 20–29; repr. in his *Gesammelte Schriften* (Köln-Graz, 1963), 1, pp. 201–9
— 1943: 'The vulgarization of Roman Law in the early Middle Ages', *Medievalia et Humanistica*, 1, pp. 14–40; repr. in *Gesammelte Schriften*, 1, pp. 220–47
— 1951: *West-Roman Vulgar Law: the Law of Property* (Philadelphia)
— 1956: *Weströmisches Vulgarrecht: Das Obligationenrecht* (Weimar)
— 1962: Review of A. D'Ors, *El Codigo de Eurico* in *Z.SS.R.G.*, *romanistische Abteilung*, 79, pp. 479–88; repr. in *Gesammelte Schriften*, 1, pp. 305–13
LEWIS, I. M. 1962: 'Historical aspects of genealogies in Northern Somali social structure', *Journal of African History*, 3, pp. 35–48
LEX SALICA: ed. K. A. Eckhardt, *M.G.H.*, Leges IV (2) (1969)
LIB. HIST. FRANC.: *Liber Historiae Francorum*, ed. B. Krusch, *M.G.H.*, S.R.M., 2 (1888)
LIBER ORDINUM: ed. M. Férotin (Paris, 1904)
LIEBERMANN, F. 1903, 1916: *Gesetze der Angelsachsen* (Halle), vols. 1 and 3. There are English translations by F. L. Attenborough, *The Laws of the Earliest English Kings* (Cambridge, 1922), by Robertson, 1925, and selectively but most accurately, by Whitelock, 1955
LIVERMORE, H. 1971: *The Origins of Spain and Portugal*
LÖWE, H. 1963: 'Kaisertum und Abendland in ottonischer und frühsalischer Zeit', *Historische Zeitschrift*, 196, pp. 529–62
LOPEZ, R. S. and RAYMOND, I. W. 1955: *Medieval Trade in the Mediterranean World* (New York)
LOT, F. and HALPHEN, L. 1909: *Le Règne de Charles le Chauve* (Paris)
LOWE, E. A. 1914: *The Beneventan Script* (Oxford)
LOYN, H. R. 1953: 'The term *ealdorman* in the translations prepared at the time of King Alfred', *English Historical Review*, 68, pp. 513–25

— 1955: 'Gesiths and thegns in Anglo-Saxon England from the seventh to the tenth century', *English Historical Review*, 70, pp. 529–49
— 1961: 'Boroughs and Mints, A.D. 900–1066', *Anglo-Saxon Coins*, ed. R. H. M. Dolley (London)
— 1962: *Anglo-Saxon England and the Norman Conquest* (London)
— 1971: 'Towns in late Anglo-Saxon England: the evidence and some possible lines of enquiry', *England before the Conquest: Studies in Primary Sources presented to Dorothy Whitelock*, ed. P. Clemoes and K. Hughes (Cambridge), pp. 115–28
— 1974: 'Kinship in Anglo-Saxon England', *Anglo-Saxon England*, 3, pp. 197–209
LYNCH, C. H. 1938: *Saint Braulio of Saragossa* (Washington)
LYNCH, C. H. and GALINDO, P. 1950: *San Braulio de Zaragoza* (Madrid)
MACALISTER, R. A. S. 1938–56: ed. and trans. *Lebor Gabála Érenn. The Book of the Taking of Ireland*, 5 vols (London and Dublin)
— 1945: *Corpus Inscriptionum Insularum Celticarum*, vol. 1 (Dublin)
MAC CANA, P. 1970: 'The three languages and the three laws', *Studia Celtica*, 5, pp. 62–78
MAC NEILL, J. 1909: 'Notes on the distribution, history, grammar, and import of the Irish ogham inscriptions', *Proceedings of the Royal Irish Academy*, 27 C, pp. 329–70
— 1911: 'Early Irish population groups: their nomenclature, classification and chronology', *Proceedings of the Royal Irish Academy* 29 C, pp. 59–114
— 1915: 'On the reconstruction and date of the Laud synchronisms', *Zeitschrift für celtische Philologie*, 10, pp. 81–96
MAC NEILL, E. 1922: 'A pioneer of nations', *Studies*, 11, pp. 13–28, 435–46
— 1927: 'Miscellanea', *Journal of the Royal Society of Antiquaries of Ireland*, 57, pp. 150–8
MACNEILL, M. 1962: *The Festival of Lughnasa* (Oxford)
MADOZ, J. 1952: 'San Julian de Toledo', *Estudios Eclesiasticos*, 26, pp. 39–69
MALINOWSKI, B. 1922: *Argonauts of the Western Pacific* (London)
MALONE, K. 1962: ed. *Widsith*, 2nd. edn. (Copenhagen)
MANSI: *Sacrorum Consiliorum nova et amplissima collectio*
MARINI, G. 1805: *I papiri diplomatici* (Roma)
MARTÈNE, E. 1736: *De antiquis ecclesiae ritibus libri tres* (Antwerp)
MARTIN 1703: *Description of the Western Islands of Scotland* (London)
MARTINE, F. 1968: *Vie des Pères du Jura* (Sources Chrétiennes, vol. 142, Paris)
MARTÍNEZ DIEZ, G. 1966: *La Coleccion Canonica hispana* (Madrid)
— 1971: 'Los Concilios de Toledo', *Anales Toledanos*, 3, pp. 119–38
MATTHEW PARIS: *Chronica Majora*, ed. H. R. Luard (Rolls Series, 1872)
MAUSS, M. 1969: *The Gift: Forms and Functions of Exchange in Archaic Societies*, trans. I. Cunnison (London, repr.)
MENENDEZ PIDAL, R. 1956: 'Los godos y èl origen de la epopeya española', *Settimane Spoleto*, 3, pp. 285–322
MESSMER, H. 1960.: *Hispania-idee und Gotenmythos* (Zurich)

METCALF, D. M. 1974: 'Monetary Expansion and Recession: Interpreting the Distribution-patterns of Seventh- and Eighth-Century Coins', *Coins and the Archaeologist*, ed. J. Casey and R. Reece (British Archaeological Reports, 4, Oxford), pp. 206–23

MEYER, K. 1913: ed. 'The Laud synchronisms', *Zeitschrift für celtische Philologie*, 9, pp. 471–85

— 1913–14: ed. and trans. 'Über die älteste irische dichtung', I–II, *Abhandlungen der königliche Akademie der Wissenschaften zur Berlin, Phil-Hist. Klasse*: I, Jahrgang 1913, Nr. 6, II: Jahrgang 1914, Nr. 10

M.G.H.: *Monumenta Germaniae Historica*; A.A. — Auctores Antiquissimi; S.R.G. — Scriptores Rerum Germanicarum; S.R.M. — Scriptores Rerum Merovingicarum

MIEROW, C. C. 1915: *The Gothic History of Jordanes*, 2nd edn (Princeton)

MILLAR, F. 1977: *The Emperor in the Roman World* (London)

MILLER, M. 1970: *The Sicilian Colony Dates. Studies in Chronology*, I (New York)

— 1975a: 'Bede's use of Gildas', *English Historical Review*, 90, pp. 241–61.

— 1975b: 'Historicity and the Pedigrees of the Northcountrymen', *Bulletin of the Board of Celtic Studies*, 26 (1974–6), pp. 255–80

— 1976: 'Date-guessing and pedigrees', *Studia Celtica*, 10/11 (1975/6), pp. 96–109

— 1977: 'Date-guessing and Dyfed', *Studia Celtica*, 12

MISSALE FRANCORUM: ed. L. C. Mohlberg, in *Rerum Ecclesiasticarum Documenta*, Series Maior, Fontes I (Rome, 1957)

MITTEIS, H. 1944: *Die Deutsche Königswahl*, 2nd rev. ed. (Brünn)

MOMIGLIANO, A. 1955: 'Cassiodorus and the Italian culture of his time', *Proc. Brit. Acad.*, 41, pp. 207–45; repr. in *Studies in Historiography* (London, 1966), pp. 181–210

MORRIS, R. 1976: 'The Powerful and the Poor in Tenth-century Byzantium: Law and Reality', *Past and Present*, 73, pp. 3–27

MÜLLENHOFF, K. 1873: *Germania Antiqua*

MUNDÓ, A. M. 1964: 'La datación de los códices litúrgicos visigóticos toledanos', *Hispana Sacra*, 17–18, pp. 529–54

MURPHY, F. X. 1952: 'Julian of Toledo and the Fall of the Visigothic Kingdom in Spain', *Speculum*, 27, pp. 1–21

NASH, T. 1781: *Collections for the History of Worcestershire*, i (London)

NASH-WILLIAMS, V. E. 1950: *The Early Christian Monuments of Wales* (Cardiff)

DE NAVASCÚES, J. M. 1961: *La dedicacion de S. Juan de Baños* (Palencia)

NELSON, J. L. 1965: 'Ritual and Reality in the early medieval *ordines*', *Studies in Church History*, 11, pp. 41–51

— 1976: 'Symbols in context: rulers' inauguration rituals in Byzantium and the west in the early Middle Ages', *Studies in Church History*, 13, pp. 97–119

— 1977: 'Kingship, law and liturgy in the political thought of Hincmar of Rheims', *English Historical Review*, 92, pp. 241–79

— 1977b: 'On the limits of the Carolingian Renaissance', *Studies in Church History*, vol. 14, pp. 51–69

NITHARD, *Historiarum libri quattuor*: ed. E. Müller, *M.G.H.*, S.R.M., in usum scholarum
NOTITIA GALLIARUM: ed. T. Mommsen, *Chronica Minora*, vol. 1, *M.G.H.*, A.A., IX (1892)
O'BRIEN, M. A. 1976: ed. (Intro. by J. V. Kelleher), *Corpus Genealogiarum Hiberniae*, 1, (2nd edn., Dublin)
Ó CORRÁIN, D. 1971: 'Irish regnal succession: a reappraisal', *Studia Hibernica*, 11, pp. 7—39
— 1974: '*Caithréim Chellacháin Chaisil*: history or propaganda?' *Ériu*, 25, pp. 1—69
O'DONOVAN, J. 1844: ed. and trans. *The genealogies, tribes, and customs of Hy-Fiachrach, commonly called O'Dowda's Country* (Dublin)
OEXLE, O. G. 1967: 'Die Karolinger und die Stadt des heiligen Arnulf', *Frühmittelalterliche Studien*, 1, pp. 250—364
OLSEN, O. 1966: *Hørg, Hov og Kirke* (København); also issued as *Aarøger for nordisk Oldkyndighed og Historie*, 1965
O'RAHILLY, T. F. 1946: *Early Irish History and Mythology* (Dublin)
Ó RAITHBHEARTAIGH, T. 1932: ed. and trans. *Genealogical Tracts, Vol. 1 (Dublin)*
Ó RÍORDÁIN, B. 1976: 'The High Street Excavations', *Proceedings of the Seventh Viking Congress*, ed. Bo Almqvist and D. Greene, (Dublin), pp. 135—41
OROSIUS, *Historia: Pauli Orosii Historia adversus paganos*, ed. G. Zangemeister (Vienna, 1882)
D'ORS, A. 1956: 'La territorialidad del derecho de los Visigodos', *Settimane Spoleto*, 3, pp. 363—408
PACTUS LEGIS SALICAE: ed. Eckhardt, 1962b
PAGE, R. I. 1965: 'Anglo-Saxon episcopal lists [I—II]', *Nottingham Medieval Studies*, 9, pp. 78—95
— 1966: ed. 'Anglo-Saxon episcopal lists [III]', *Nottingham Medieval Studies*, 10, pp. 2—24
DE PANGE, J. 1951: 'Doutes sur la certitude de cette opinion que le sacre de Pépin est la première époque du sacre des rois de France', *Mélanges Halphen* (Paris), pp. 557—64
DE PAOR, L. 1976: 'The Viking towns of Ireland', *Proceedings of the Seventh Viking Congress*, ed. Bo Almquist and D. Greene (Dublin), pp. 29—37
PARADISI, B. 1971: 'Il Prologo e l'Epilogo dell'Editto di Rotari', *Studi in onore di Eduardo Volterra*, vol. 1 (Milan), pp. 323—56
PARKES, M. B. 1976: 'The Palaeography of the Parker Manuscript of *Chronicle*, Laws and Sedulius, and historiography at Winchester in the late ninth and tenth centuries', *Anglo-Saxon England*, 5, pp. 149—71
PASSIO LEUDEGARII: ed. B. Krusch, *M.G.H.*, S.R.M., vol. 5
PASSIO URSI ET VICTORIS: *Acta Sanctorum*, Sept 30th, vol. 8, pp. 261—93
PAUL THE DEACON: *Historia Langobardorum*, ed. L. Bethmann and G. Waitz, *M.G.H.*, Scriptores Rerum Langobardicarum (1878). Trans. W. D. Foulke, *History of the Lombards* (repr. Philadelphia, 1974)

PENDER, S. 1935: 'A guide to Irish genealogical collections', *Analecta Hibernica*, 7, pp. 1–167
— 1937: ed. *Déssi Genealogies with an appendix of historical references* (Dublin)
— 1951: ed. 'The O Clery Book of Genealogies', *Analecta Hibernica*, 18, pp. ix–xxxv, 1–198
PEREZ PUJOL, E. 1896: *Historia de las instituciones sociales de la España goda* (Madrid)
PETERS, E. 1960: 'The proliferation of segments in the lineage of the Bedouin of Cyrenaica', *Journal of the Royal Anthropological Institute of Great Britain and Ireland*, 90, pp. 29–53
PINELL, J. M. 1965: 'Los Textos de la antiqua liturgia hispanica — fuentes para su estudio', *Estudios sobre la Liturgia Mozarabe*, ed. J. F. Rivera Recio (Toledo), pp. 109–64
PIRENNE, H. 1939: *Mohammed and Charlemagne*, trans. B. Miall
PLUMMER, C. 1896: ed. *Venerabilis Baedae Opera Historica*, 2 vols (Oxford)
— 1899: *Two of the Saxon Chronicles Parallel* (Oxford)
— 1902: *Life and Times of Alfred the Great* (Oxford)
POLLOCK, Sir F. and MAITLAND, F. W. 1968: *History of English Law*, 2nd edn. with new intro. by S. F. C. Milsom (Cambridge)
PRINGSHEIM, F. 1940: 'The Character of Justinian's legislation', *Law Quarterly Review*, 56, pp. 229–46
PROC. BRIT. ACAD.: *Proceedings of the British Academy*
PROCOPIUS: *Procopius, Wars*, ed. and trans. H. Dewing, 5 vols (1914–27)
RATCLIFFE, E. C. 1953: *The coronation service of Queen Elizabeth II* (Cambridge)
RICHARDS, A. I. 1960: 'Social mechanisms for the transfer of political rights in some African tribes', *Journal of the Royal Anthropoligical Institute of Great Britain and Ireland*, 90, pp. 175–90
RICHARDSON, H. G. and SAYLES, G. O. 1963: *The Governance of Medieval England* (Edinburgh)
— 1966: *Law and Legislation in England, from Aethelberht to Magna Carta* (Edinburgh)
RICHÉ, P. 1971: 'L'education à l'époque wisigothique: les *institutionem disciplinae*', *Anales toledanos*, 3, pp. 171–80
VON RICHTHOFEN, K. 1863: *Lex Frisionum*, M.G.H., Leges in folio, vol. 3
— 1875–89: *Lex Saxonum; Lex Thuringorum*, M.G.H., Leges in folio, vol. 5; There is a more convenient edition, with less full annotation by C. von Schwerin, *Leges Saxonum et Lex Thuringorum*, M.G.H. in usum scholarum (1918)
ROBERTSON, E. W. 1872: *Historical essays* (Edinburgh)
ROBERTSON, A. J. 1925: *The Laws of the Kings of England from Edmund to Henry I* (Cambridge)
ROBINSON, J. A. 1918: 'The Coronation Order in the tenth century', *Journal of Theological Studies*, 19, pp. 56–72
ROGER OF WENDOVER: *Chronica sive flores Historiarum*, ed. H. O. Coxe (1841)
ROSS, A. S. C. 1940: *The Terfinnas and Beormas of Ohthere* (Leeds School of English Language Texts and Monographs: 7)

THE RUIN: ed. G. P. Krapp and E. K. Dobbie, *The Exeter Book*, The Anglo-Saxon Poetic Records, 3 (New York, 1936)
DE SALIS, R. 1892: *Leges Burgundionum*, *M.G.H.*, Legum Sectio I, vol. 2, pt. i; trans. Drew, 1972
SALLUST: ed. A. Kurfess (Leipzig, 1954)
SANCHEZ-ALBORNOZ, C. 1962: 'Perviviencia y crisis de la Tradicion juridica Romana en la España goda', *Settimane Spoleto*, 9, pp. 128–99
SAWYER, P. H. 1957: ed. *Textus Roffensis: Rochester Cathedral Library MS. A. 3. 5. Vol. I* (Copenhagen)
— 1965: 'The Wealth of England in the Eleventh Century', *Trans. Roy. Hist. Soc.*, 5th ser., 15, pp. 145–64
— 1968: *Anglo-Saxon Charters: An Annotated List and Bibliography* (London)
SCHMIDT, R. 1961: 'Königsumritt und Huldigung in ottonisch-salischer Zeit', *Vorträge und Forschungen*, 6, ed. T. Mayer, pp. 97–233
SCHNEIDER, R. 1967: 'Zur rechtlichen Bedeutung der Kapitularientexte', *Deutsches Archiv*, 23, pp. 273–94
— 1972: *Königswahl und Königserhebung im Frühmittelalter* (Stuttgart)
SCHRAMM, P. 1968: *Kaiser, Könige und Päpste*, 4 vols (Stuttgart)
SCHULZ, F. 1953: *History of Roman Legal Science*, 2nd edn. (Oxford)
SEMMLER, J. 1960: 'Reichsidee und kirchliche Gesetzgebung', *Zeitschrift für Kirchengeschichte*, 71, pp. 37–65
SETTIMANE SPOLETO: *Settimane di Studio del Centro Italiano di Studi sull'Alto Medioevo*
SIDONIUS, *Carm.*; *Ep.*: *The poems and letters of Sidonius*, ed. W. B. Anderson (Loeb series, 1936, 1965); also ed. and trans. A. Loyen, 3 vols. (Paris, 1969–70)
SISAM: K. 1953: 'Anglo-Saxon Royal Genealogies', *Proc. Brit. Acad.*, 39, pp. 287–348
SPRENGLER, A. 1950–1: 'Die Gebete der Krönungsordines Hinkmars von Reims für Karl den Kahlen als Köning von Lothringen und für Ludwig den Stammler', *Zeitschrift für Kirchengeschichte*, 63, pp. 245–67
STEIN, S. 1926: 'Lex und Capitula; eine kritische Studie', *Mitteilungen des österreichischen Instituts für Geschichtsforschung*, 41, pp. 289–301
— 1941: 'Etude critique des capitulaires francs', *Le Moyen Age*, 51, pp. 1–75
— 1947: 'Lex Salica', *Speculum*, 22, pt. i, pp. 113–34, pt. ii, pp. 395–418
STEIN, E. 1959: *Histoire du Bas-Empire*, vol. 1, French edition by J. R. Palanque (Bruges)
STENGEL, E. E. 1965: *Abhandlungen und Untersuchungen zur Geschichte des Kaisergedankens im Mittelalter* (Köln-Graz)
STENTON, F. M. 1905: Review of Chadwick, 1905, *Folklore*, 16, pp. 122–6
— 1970: ed. D. M. Stenton, *Preparatory to 'Anglo-Saxon England', being the collected papers of Frank Merry Stenton* (Oxford)
— 1971: *Anglo-Saxon England*, 3rd edn. (Oxford)

STJERNA, K. 1909: 'Lund och Birka', *Historisk Tidskrift för Skåneland*, 3, pp. 171−225

STOKES, W. 1890: ed. and trans., *Lives of saints from the Book of Lismore* (Oxford)

STROHEKER, K. F. 1939: 'Leowigild', *Die Welt als Geschichte*, 5, pp. 446−85; repr. in *Germanentum und Spätantike* (Zurich, 1965), pp. 134−91

— 1948: *Der senatorische Adel im spätantiken Gallien* (Tübingen)

STRYPE, J. 1848: *Memorials of Archbishop Cranmer* (Oxford)

STUBBS, W. 1874: ed. *Memorials of St. Dunstan* (Rolls Series)

SWEET, H. 1885: ed. *The Oldest English Texts* (London)

SYME, R. 1964: *Sallust* (Cambridge)

TACITUS, GERMANIA: *Cornelii Taciti De Germania*, ed. M. Hutton (Loeb series, 1914)

TAIT, J. 1916: *The Domesday Survey of Cheshire* (Chetham Soc., new ser. 75)

— 1936: *The Medieval English Borough* (Manchester)

TESSIER, G. 1943: *Recueil des Actes de Charles II le Chauve* (Paris)

THEMISTIUS, Or: *Themistius, Orationes*, ed. P. Schenkl and G. Downey

THEVENIN, M. 1887: *Textes relatifs aux institutions privées et publiques aux époques merovingienne et carolingienne* (Paris)

THOMPSON, E. A. 1965: *The Early Germans* (Oxford)

— 1966: *The Visigoths in the time of Ulfila* (Oxford)

— 1966b: 'Ammianus Marcellinus', *Latin Historians*, ed. T. A. Dorey

— 1969: *The Goths in Spain* (Oxford)

THORPE, L. 1969: *Two Lives of Charlemagne* (Penguin Classics, London)

THURNEYSEN, R. 1931: ed. 'Synchronismen der irischen Könige', *Zeitschrift für celtische Philologie*, 19, pp. 81−99

TOLEDO, COUNCILS OF: ed. J. Vives, *Concilios visigóticos e hispano-romanos* (Barcelona, Madrid, 1965)

TRADITIONEN FREISING: *Die Traditionen des Hochstifts Freising*, ed. T. Bitterauf (München, 1905, 1909)

TRANS. ROY. HIST. SOC.: *Transactions of the Royal Historical Society*

TRAUTMANN, R. T. 1969: 'Length of generation and reign in Ancient India', *Journal of the American Oriental Society*, 89, pp. 564−77

TURNER, D. H. 1971: *The Claudius Pontificals* (Henry Bradshaw Society vol. 97 issued for the year 1964, publ. 1971)

ULLMAN, W. 1963: 'The Bible and Principles of Government in the Middle Ages, *Settimane Spoleto*, 10, pp. 181−227

— 1969: *The Carolingian Renaissance and the Idea of Kingship*

UNWIN, G. 1918: *Finance and Trade Under Edward III* (Manchester)

VANSINA, J. 1965: *Oral tradition. A study in historical methodology* (London)

VERLINDEN, C. 1955: *L'Esclavage dans l'Europe Médiévale*, vol. 1 (Bruges)

VINOGRADOFF, P. 1929: *Roman Law in medieval Europe*, 2nd edn. (Oxford)

VIRGIL, GEORGICS: ed. R. A. B. Mynors (Oxford, 1969)

VISMARA, G. 1967a: *Edictum Theodorici, Ius Romanum Medii Aevi* (Milan), pt. i., 2b aaα
— 1967b: Cristianesimo e legislazione germaniche', *Settimane Spoleto*, 14, pp. 397–467
VITA ANSKARII: *Vita Anskarii auctore Rimberto*, ed. G. Waitz (1884)
VITA FRUTUOSI: ed. M. C. Diaz y Diaz (Braga, 1974)
VITA OSWALDI: ed. J. Raine, *The Historians of the Church of York* (Rolls Series, 1879)
VITA PATRUM JURENSIUM: ed. B. Krusch, *M.G.H.*, S.R.M. (1896); also ed. and trans. Martine, 1968
VITA RUSTICULAE SIVE MARCIAE ABBATISSAE ARELATENSIS: ed. B. Krusch, *M.G.H.*, S.R.M., 4 (1902)
VIVES, J. 1963: ed. *Concilios Visigoticos e Hispano-Romanos* (Barcelona-Madrid)
VOLLRATH-REICHELT, H. 1971: *Königsgedanke und Königtum bei den Angelsachsen* (Köln-Wien)
VOR- UND FRÜHFORMEN DER EUROPÄISCHEN STADT IM MITTELALTER: ed. H. Jankuhn, W. Schlesinger, H. Steuer (Abhandlungen der Akademie der Wissenschaften in Göttingen, phil.-hist. klasse, dritte folge, nr. 83, 1973)
WADE-EVANS, A. W. 1930: trans. 'Beuno Sant', *Archaeologia Cambrensis*, 85, pp. 315–41
— 1944: ed. and trans. *Vitae Sanctorum Britanniae et Genealogiae* (Cardiff)
WADSTEIN, E. 1914: 'Birka och Bjärköarätt', *Namn och Bygd*, 2, pp. 92–7
WALKER, H. E. 1956: 'Bede and the Gewissae — the political evolution of the Heptarchy and its nomenclature', *Cambridge Historical Journal*, 12, pp. 174–86
WALLACE-HADRILL, J. M. 1960: ed. and trans. *The Fourth Book of the Chronicle of Fredegar*
— 1962: *The Long-Haired Kings* (London)
— 1964: 'The *Via Regia* of the Carolingian Age', *Trends in Medieval Political Thought*, ed. B. Smalley (Oxford)
— 1967: *The Barbarian West, 400–1000*, 3rd edn. (London)
— 1971: *Early Germanic Kingship in England and on the Continent* (Oxford)
— 1975: *Early Medieval History* (Oxford)
WALSH, P. 1918: ed. *'Genealogiae Regum et Sanctorum Hiberniae' by the Four Masters, edited from the manuscript of Michél Ó Cléirigh* (Maynooth)
WARD, P. L. 1942: 'An early version of the Anglo-Saxon coronation ceremony', *English Historical Review*, 57, pp. 345–61
WERNER, K. F. 1965: 'Das hochmittelalterliche Imperium im politischen Bewüsstsein Frankreichs (10–12 Jhdts)', *Historische Zeitschrift*, 200, pp. 1–60
WESSÉN, E. 1923: 'Birka och bjärköarätt', *Namn och Bygd*, 11, pp. 135–78
— 1925: 'Till Birca-fragan', *Namn och Bygd*, 13, pp. 39–60

WHITELOCK, D. 1948, 1955b: 'Wulfstan and the laws of Cnut', *English Historical Review*, 63, pp. 433—52; cf. her reply to the criticisms of Jost, *ibid.*, 70, pp. 72—85

— 1955: *English Historical Documents c. 500—1042* (London)

— 1961: et. al., trans. *The Anglo-Saxon Chronicle. A revised translation.* London

— 1973: 'The Appointment of Dunstan as Archbishop of Canterbury', *Otium et Negotium. Studies in Onomatology and Library Science presented to Olof von Feilitzen*, ed. F. Sandgren (Stockholm), pp. 232—47

WIDUKIND, *Res. gest. Sax.*: *Widukindi Res Gestae Saxonum*, ed. G. Waitz, P. Hirsch and H. G. Lohmann, *M.G.H.* in usum scholarum (1935)

WILLIAM OF MALMESBURY, ed. W. Stubbs (Rolls Series, 1887—9)

WILLIAMS, J. E. C. 1971: *The Court Poet in Medieval Ireland* (London); also publ. in *Proc. Brit. Acad.*, 57 (1971)

WINTERSIG, A. 1925: 'Zur Königinnenweihe', *Jahrbuch für liturgiewissenschaft*, 5, pp. 150—3

WOLFRAM, H. 1968: 'Methodische Fragen zur Kritik am "sacralen" Königtum germanischer Stämme', *Festschrift für Otto Höfler*, ed. H. Birkhan and O. Gschwantler (Wien), ii, pp. 473—90

— 1970: 'The shaping of the early medieval kingdom', *Viator*, 1, pp. 1—20

— 1975: 'Athanaric the Visigoth: monarchy or judgeship . . .', *Journal of Medieval History*, 1, pp. 259—78

WORMALD, C. P. 1976: 'The decline of the western Empire and the survival of its aristocracy', *Journal of Roman Studies*, 66, pp. 217—26

— 1977: 'The uses of literacy in Anglo-Saxon England and its neighbours', *Trans. Roy. Hist. Soc.*, 5th ser., 27, pp. 95—114

WRENN, C. L. 1967: *Word and Symbol. Studies in English Language* (London)

WÜRDINGER, H. 1935: 'Einwirkungen des Christentums auf das angelsächsische Recht', *Z.SS.R.G., g.a.*, 55, pp. 105—30

ZEUMER, K. 1898: 'Zur geschichte der westgothischen Gesetzgebung', *Neues Archiv.* 23, pp. 419—516

— 1902: *Leges Visigothorum, M.G.H.*, Legum Sectio I, Vol. 1

— 1902a: 'Die Chronologie der Westgothen könige des Reiches von Toledo', *Neues Archiv der Gessellschaft für ältere deutsche Geschichtskunde*, 27, pp. 411—44

ZIEGLER, A. K. 1930: *Church and State in Visigothic Spain* (Washington)

ZÖLLNER, E. 1951: 'Der Herkunft der Agilulfinger', *Mitteilungen des Instituts für Österreichische Geschichtsforschung*, 59, pp. 245—64

— 1970: *Geschichte der Franken* (München)

ZOSIMUS: *Historia Nova*, ed. L. Mendelssohn (Leipzig, 1897); trans. J. Buchanan and H. Davis (San Antonio, 1967)

Z.SS.R.G., g.a.: *Zeitschrift der Savigny-Stiftung für Rechtsgeschichte, germanistische abteilung*

Index

The following abbreviations are used: gen. genealogy; k. king; m. married; q. queen.

Abbo of Fleury 68
Abingdon 70n
Abrenuntiatio diabolae 78n
Adalgisel, *dux* 12
Adam, in West Saxon gen. 95
Adam of Bremen 149
Adamnan 52
Admonitio Generalis 109–10, 132
adultery 15
Aegae, Cilicia, fair at 146
Aegidius, *magister militum* 24
Ælfric, *Colloquy* 140, 147
Ælfthryth, q. 67n
Æthelbald, k. of Mercia 98
Æthelberg, sister of Eadbald, k. of Kent 80
Æthelberht I, k. of Kent 75, 79n, 85, 89;
  laws of 107, 112, 130–1;
  sister of 91n
Æthelberht II, k. of Kent 20, 89
Æthelfrith, k. of Northumbria 101
Æthelred, k. of Mercia 81
Æthelred II, k. 67, 156
Æthelred, ruler of Mercia 155
Æthelweard 64n, 151
Æthelwold, bishop of Winchester 67, 68, 70n;
  Benedictional of 70
Æthil-, *see* Æthel-
Agali, monastery 36
Agathias 127
Agaune, monastery 22
Agilulfings 16n
Agobard 132
Ahistulf, k. of Lombards, laws of 110
Alamans, 17, 23, 25;
  laws of 108–9, 122
Alaric I, k. of Visigoths 8, 25, 49, 133–4
Alcuin 59
Aldfrith, k. of Lindsey 90
Aldfrith, k. of Northumbria 81
Alethius, *patricius* 14
Alexander III, k. of Scotland 73
Alexandria 141
Alfonso X, *el Sabio* 44

Alfred, k. of Wessex 119, 124, 131, 149, 150;
  laws of 75n, 110, 112, 113, 114, 116, 117, 120, 121, 132, 133, 151
Alhfrith, k. of Deira 19
allegiance, oath of 114
alliteration, in gens. 90;
  of ks. names 98
allod, kingdom as 6, 26–7
Amalric, k. of Visigoths 8
Amalasuntha 9
Amals 8, 9, 27, 96
amber 143, 150
Ambérieux, royal villa 22
Amiens 24, 25n
Ammianus Marcellinus 17, 27, 43
Anastasius, emperor 25
ancestor-worship 97
Angles, settlements of 92
Anglian collection of gens. and k. lists 8, 74, 76–82, 89–93
Anglo-Saxon Chronicle 19, 52, 64, 65n, 66, 74n, 79n, 90, 98n, 121, 132;
  gen. in 74, 134
Anglo-Saxons, gens. of 74–81, 89–94;
  k. lists of 97–102;
  laws of 107, 109, 113, 115;
  Roman influence on 143–4, 148;
  see also kingship
Annales Bertiniani 61
Annales Regni Francorum 58
anointing 2, 34, 41–2, 44–9, 52, 54, 55–63, 66–7, 71;
  see also consecration, ceremonial
Ansegisus, abbot 118, 120, 130
Ansehis, ? for Anschis, Saxon leader 91n
Ansis 8
Anskar, St. Life of 139–40, 152
Ansoald, Lombard notary 118, 128
Ansovald, *dux* 11, 23
anthropology, 3, 14, 50, 71, 85–8, 111, 141, 144–5
Appius Claudius 126
Aquitaine 6, 25, 60

181

arianism 12, 19n, 134n
Aripert, k. of Lombards 18
aristocracy 56;
    Frankish 6, 12−4, 26, 53, 57, 58, 59, 61;
    Germanic 27;
    Roman 7, 25, 26;
    royal 9, 10;
    and sacral kingship 27;
    Viking 27;
    Visigothic 7, 41, 44, 45, 47
Arnulf of Metz 12, 93n
Arquillière, H.X. 61
Arras 24, 25n
Asclepiodatus, referendary 118, 126, 130
association, royal 17−8;
    see also succession, pre-mortem
Athalaric 93
Athanaric, k. (judge) of Visigoths 7, 9n, 137, 138
Athaulf, k. of Visigoths 127
Athelstan, k. 55−6, 65, 66n;
    laws of 110, 118, 145
Augustine, St 131
Augustus 128
Austrasia 12, 53
authentication, of law-codes 118, 119
Auvergne 11
Avitus, bishop of Vienne 2, 18n, 22

Bældæg, son of Woden 79
Balthildis, wife of Clovis II 13
Baltic 142, 149, 150, 151, 152
Balts 8, 9, 28
barter 144−6
basileus 137
Bath 63, 67−70
Bavarians 20;
    laws of 108−9, 115−6, 119, 123, 124, 126, 128, 132
Beauvais 24
Bede, *Historia Ecclesiastica* 7, 19, 52, 74, 77−81, 90−1, 97, 98−101, 121, 125, 131, 151
Beda, Bede, in Lindsey gen. 90
bee, symbolism of 42, 46−7
belagines 137
Belgica Secunda 24, 25, 28
Belisarius 8n, 24
benedictions, regal 53
Benveniste, E. 146
Beornic 80
Beornred, k. of Mercia, as usurper 98
Beornwulf, k. of Mercia 98

Berhtwulf, k. of Mercia 98
Bernicia 19, 81;
    k. list 101;
    royal gen. 77−80, 89, 90
Bernicians 80
Bertetrudis, wife of Chlothar II 14n
Bertrada, q. 63n
Beuno, St, Life of 76
Beyerle, F. 112
Bible 89, 96;
    influence of 1−2, 58, 62, 130−32;
    see also Old Testament
Biddle, M. 152
Binchy, D. A. 145
Birka 140, 151, 152, 153
Bischoff, B. 117
Biscop, in Lindsey gen. 90
bishops, lists of 100;
    Anglo-Saxon 65;
    Frankish 6, 7, 24, 26, 58, 59, 61−3
Bloch, M. 51
Bognetti, G. P. 19n
Boretius, A. 106, 119
Boulogne 24, 25n
Bouman, C. A. 34, 54
Braulio, bishop of Saragossa 32, 36
brehons 143
Bretwalda 80
Brihthelm, archbishop of Canterbury 65−6
Britain 69−70, 143−4, 158
Brodulf, uncle of Charibert II 12
Bromsgrove 147
Brown, Jenny 105n
Brühl, C. -R. 5
Brunichildis, m. (1) Sigibert I, (2) Merovech 11, 12, 13, 16
Brunner, H. 117
Buchner, R. 120
Burgred, k. of Mercia 98
Burgundians 9, 14n, 20−3, 25, 27;
    ks. of 14n, 113, see also Gibichungs;
    k. list 75n;
    laws of 21, 26, 75n, 107, 112, 113, 115, 118, 119, 124, 126, 127, 134
Burgundy 12, 21, 135
burh, 'borough, fortification' 154, 155−6
burial, royal 4, 6, 45
Byzantium 5, 18, 24;
    control of Italy 129

Cadell 104
Cædbæd 90

Caesar 18, 22, 132, 137
calendar, Anglo-Saxon 97
Cambrai 23, 24, 25, 28
Canterbury 65, 117n
capital, *urbs regia* 12, 17–8, 21, 22, 30, 41, 45–6
capitularies 109–11, 118–9, 123, 128–9
Carolingians 3, 56–63, 108, 154;
  gen. of 93n;
  influence on England 114;
  laws of 109–11, 118, 124, 128–9, 135, *see also Lex Salica*;
  links with Merovingians 16
Carouge, royal villa 22
Caser, son of Woden 93n
Cassiodorus 2, 93, 125–6, 127, 137, 144
cattle, trade in 142–3, 145, 157
Cearl, k. of Mercia 100n
Cerdic 8n, 74, 79, 80, 85, 90–1, 92
Ceredig, Ceredigion 82
ceremonial, royal 48
Chadwick, H. M. 19n
Chalon-sur-Saône 22
Chalons-sur-Marne 24
chancery, Frankish 108;
  Germanic 126
chapters, in law-codes 116
Chararic, k. of Franks 23n, 28
Charibert II, k. of Franks 12–3
Charlemagne 57, 59, 68, 108, 111, 114, 116, 118, 119, 120, 124, 128–9
Charles Martel 16
Charles the Bald 3, 55, 59, 60–3, 67, 118, 124, 134n
charters 4, 107, 118, 124–5, 139, 144, 148;
  Anglo-Saxon 70, 122;
  anthropological 85, 97n;
  Italian 121;
  Visigothic 121
Chester 69, 153
Childebert I, k. of Franks 10–1, 15
Childebert II, k. of Franks 11, 13, 15, 16, 23, 108;
  Decretio of 118, 126
Childebert III, k. of Franks, son of Grimoald 16
Childeric I, k. of Franks 7, 23, 24;
  seal-ring of 126
Chilperic I, k. of Burgundians, *patricius Galliae* 20–1
Chilperic II, Gibichung 21
Chilperic I, k. of Franks 11, 16, 129n
Chilperic II (Daniel), k. of Franks 16n

Chilperic, son of Charibert II 12–3
Chindaswinth, k. of Visigoths 18, 47, 49, 117, 133
Chintila, k. of Visigoths 47
chipping, place-name element 143
Chloderic, son of Sigibert the Lame 28
Chlodomer, k. of Franks 6, 10, 23, 26, 28
Chlodovald, son of Chlodomer, monk 10
Chlodovech, son of Chilperic I 14n
Chlothar I, k. of Franks 10–11, 15
Chlothar II, k. of Franks 11, 12, 13, 15, 23, 109, 112
Chlothar III, k. of Franks 13, 53
Chramn, son of Chlothar I 11, 12
Christ, as judge 131;
  in imperial iconography 70
Chrodechildis, wife of Clovis 6, 11, 14n, 21–3, 26, 122
Chrodegang, bishop of Metz 58
Chronica Regum Wisigothorum 48–9
chronicles, and k. lists 101
Chrotechildis, *see* Chrodechildis
Chunibert, bishop of Cologne 12
Church, interest in gens. and k. lists 74–6;
  and law 106–7, 112, 126, 130–2, 134;
  see also kingship
Cinaed (Kenneth) mac Alpine, k. of Scots 69, 73
cities, barbarians and 23–6;
  foundation of 129;
  as *morgengaben* 27
civilitas 127
civitas 23–6;
  as recipient of fines 137, 138
Clanchy, M. 105n
Claudius, a Roman 126
de Clerq, C. 119
Clovis I, k. of Franks 3, 6, 7, 15, 16, 21, 23–6, 28, 56, 108, 122, 129, 131, 133, 134;
  chronology of 10, 24, 25, 28
Clovis II, k. of Franks 13
Cnut. k. of England 124, 134;
  laws of 110, 114, 133
Codex Euricianus 126, 129, 133
coinage 4, 69, 139, 140, 144, 154–6
collatio lustralis 142
Cologne 23, 25, 28
Columba, St 52
Columbanus, St 16
commerce, *see* trade
Comparison of Mosaic and Roman Law 132
compensations, monetary 111;
  see also fines

183

concubinage 14–6, 59
consecration, ceremonial 36, 43, 44, 51, 57;
    see also anointing
consent 10–1, 13, 14, 17, 26
Consilinum, Lucania, fair at 144
Constantine 142
consuls, lists of 100
consulship of Clovis 25, 28
Copley, G. 92
Corbie 117
Corippus, *In Laudem Justini* 43n
Cormac mac Airt 137n
coronation 59, 62, 64;
    feast 54;
    oath 62
de Coulanges, F. 56
court, royal 46
Cranmer, T. 50
Croida, ? k. of Wessex 100n
crown 44, 62
crown-wearing 62, 64, 67
cults 27
Cunedda 82
curiales 126
custom 54, 111, 115, 121, 122, 123, 134, 135
Cwichelm, k. of Wessex 19
Cynegils, k. of Wessex 19, 79–80, 85
Cynric 74, 85, 91, 92

Dagobert I, k. of Franks 12, 13, 16, 57, 108, 109, 112, 126, 128, 133, 135
Dál Cais dynasty 82–3
Dalriada 52
damnatio memoriae 81, 104
Darius 131
David, anointing of 43, 58
death-bed, royal 48
Deira 19, 81;
    k. list 101;
    royal gen. 77, 79–80, 90–1
deman 138
demigods 8
deposition 47
designation of successors 18, 38
Dialogue of the Exchequer 129
Dicineus 137
Digest 114
Dimet, son of Maximus 82
Diocletian 18
Dioscuran twins 17
diplomatic protocols, Roman 118, 126

Dolley, M. 69n, 71n
Domesday Book 147–8, 154
Donatus, grammarian 39
Dorestad 151–2, 153
dower 27, 113
Droitwich 147–8, 155
Dublin 157
Dunod, Dunoding 82
Dunstan, archbishop of Canterbury 54, 64, 66, 67
dux 7, 20, 23–4, 42, 55
Dyfed, royal gen. of 81–2
dynasties, royal 7–17;
    founders of 8n, 73, 91

Ead-, *see also* Ed-
Eadbald, k. of Kent 79
Eadberht, k. of Kent 20
Eadmer, *Vita Dunstani* 67n
Eadred, k. 66n
Eadwig, k. 65, 66n, 67n
Eamer 93
Eardwulf, k. of Kent 20
East Angles 78
East Anglia, royal gen. of 77, 79, 90–1, 92, 93
East Saxons, k. list 97, 98n;
    royal gen. of 78;
    settlements of 92
Ebroin 53
Ecgberht, k. of Wessex and Mercia 100
Ecgferth (Ecgfrith), k. of Mercia 18, 52
Eckhardt, K. A. 16n, 108, 116, 117
Eddana 137
Edgar, k. 5, 55, 56, 63–70, 155;
    laws of 110, 118–9
Edict, *see* Rothari; Theodoric
Edmund, k. 66n, 67n, 68, 114
Edward the Elder, k. 66n;
    laws of 120, 154
Edward the Martyr, k. 67
Edwin, k. of Deira 19, 79–80, 89, 101;
    apostate successors of 97
Egica, k. of Visigoths 18, 33, 38, 42, 49
Einhard 108, 121, 128
Ekwall, E. 92
election, *see* kings
Elizabeth II, coronation of 50
Ely 70n
Emperors, and law-giving 106–7;
    lists of 97, 100, 102n;
    name of 128

Carolingian 129;
Frankish 62;
German 156;
Roman 125; 129, 138; in barbarian idealogy 136; and written law 129; relations with Germanic kings 2
Empire, concept of 5, 68, 69, 70;
and Law 125; *see also* succession;
Byzantine 5, 125;
Frankish 130;
Ottonian 5
England, Carolingian influence in 114;
Irish influence in 103
Ennodius, bishop of Pavia 21–2
enthronement 53, 54, 56, 57, 61–2
Eoganacht dynasty 82–3
Eoppa 101
Epiphanius, bishop of Pavia 21–2
Ermaneric 93
Ermentrude, q. 63
Ervig (Erwig), k. of Visigoths 31, 37, 38, 41, 42, 108, 117, 133
Essex 20, 92
Eugenius I, bishop of Toledo 36
Eugenius II, bishop of Toledo 31, 36
Euric, k. of Visigoths 107, 126
Europe, Northern, as *pays du droit coutumier* 123
Europe, Southern, as *pays du droit écrit* 124
Eusebius 99
Ewig, E. 1n, 11n, 13n
exchange, types of 144–5
Exodus 132

fairs 144–6;
Champagne 157
Felix, *Life of St Guthlac* 90
Felix, bishop of Toledo, *Elogium Sancti Juliani* 36
Fergus mac Erca 73
festkrönung, *see also* crown-wearing
feud, limitation of 111
fili, 'court-poet' 73, 83, 103
fine 113;
payment of 137, 138
Fontaine, J. 49
Fordwich 151, 152
formularies 122;
see also Marculf
Fortes, M. 50, 71
fortifications 153, 155
Franks 28–9;
see also Carolingians; kingship; Merovingians;

k. list 75;
laws of 108–11, 118–20, 126, 128–9, 132, 134, 137; *see also Lex Salica*
Franks Casket 149
Frealaf 90
Freawine 81
Fredegar 13, 16, 135;
continuators of 57–8, 59
Fredegundis, wife of Chilperic I 11, 12, 14n, 15–6
Freeman, E. A. 63–4
Freising 122
Frisia 151–2
Frisians 20, 150, 151–2;
laws of 108, 111, 120, 128, 138
Fulda 116, 117, 137n
Fulrad, abbot of St Denis 58
furs 149, 153

Gaiseric, k. of Vandals 10
Galicia 18
Gallia Narbonensis 17n, 35
Gandersheim Casket 149
Ganshof, F. L. 60, 114, 118, 123
Gapt (Gaut, Geat, Geot) 90, 93, 96
Gascony 12
Gaul, southern distinguished from northern 124, 126
Geat, *see* Gapt
Gelling, Margaret 148
Genealogiae Gentium 78n
genealogies 8n, 72–104;
and biological facts 73–4;
conventions of 73–4, 82;
foreshortening of 86–7;
functions of 72–3, 83–4, 85–9;
keepers of 83, 84, 102–4;
and legislation 74–5;
manipulation of 82–3, 86, 94–5;
owners of 86, 88;
in pre-literate societies 85–9;
as political statements 79–83;
transmission of 87–9
generation, length of 92n
Geneva 21–2
Georgics IV 46–7
Geot, *see* Gapt
Germania Lugdunensis 20, 21n
Gerticos 30, 41, 42, 44
Gewisse 80
Gibbon, E. 57
Gibichungs 9, 14n, 25, 28

gift exchange 140, 141, 149
Gilla in Chomded 83
Gillingham, J. 6n, 71n
gimwali, 'barter' 144—5
Giwis 80
Glanville 123, 124n
Gluckman, M. 14n
Godepert, k. of Lombards 18
Godigisil (Gundegisilus), k. of Burgundians 21
Godomar, Gibichung 21
Goði 27, 96n
Goths, kings of 137;
   see also Ostrogoths, Visigoths
Gotland, law-book of 121
Gregory I, pope 43
Gregory, bishop of Tours 2n, 9, 11, 14, 15, 21, 23, 24, 27, 127
Grierson, P. 140
Grimoald, k. of Lombards, laws of 110
Grimoald, mayor 16
Gudila, deacon 36, 37
Gudja 27
Gunbadingi 107, 134
Gundaharius 9n
Gundegisilus, see Godigisil
Gundioc, k. of Burgundians, *magister militum* 20, 21
Gundiperga, Lombard q., m. (1) Charoald, (2) Rothari 9
Gundoald 16n
Gundobad, k. of Burgundians 21—2, 75n, 107, 127
Gundomarus, k. of Alamans 17
Gundovald, *dux* 11, 23
Gundovald, ? Merovingian 15, 16
Guntram (Guntchramn), k. of Franks 14, 15, 108
Guthlac, O. E. Prose Life 91
Gwynedd 82, 104n
Gwrtheyrn 82, 104

Hamwih 151, 152, 153, 154, 155, 156—7
harbours 156—7;
   see also trading-places, coastal
Harrison, K. 51, 77, 97
Hasdings 8, 9, 28
Hebrews 131
Hedeby 140, 151, 152, 153
Helgö 151
Helladius, bishop of Toledo 36
Hencgest (Hengest) 80, 85, 89, 90, 91n
Hencgestingas 91

Henige, D. 102
Henry I, the Fowler 68
Hereford 155
Hermenegild, son of Leovigild 12, 17
Herstal, Capitulary of 111
Herules 23
Hildeprand, k. of Lombards 18
Hincmar, archbishop of Rheims 3, 55, 61, 62, 63, 105, 119, 130n
Hispana, canonical collection 31
Historia Brittonum 90, 100—2
Historiae Gotlandiae 121
historical time, in anthropology 87
historiography 8, 40, 48;
   classical 43
Höfler, O. 27
Huneric, k. of Vandals 10

Iceland 27, 96, 147
Icil 90, 92, 93
Iclingas 91
iconography, imperial 70
Ida, Northumbrian k. 91, 101
Idalius of Barcelona 37
Ildefonsus, bishop of Toledo 31, 36, 37;
   De Viris Illustribus 36
inauguration ritual 3, 50—71;
   and gen. 73
Ine, k. of Wessex 19, 81;
   laws of 110, 111, 112, 116, 117, 133, 145, 150
Ingitrudis 15
inheritance, laws of 6, 7n, 26—7, see also kingship, heriditary;
   of property 113
interregna 51, 66n;
   Lombard 4, 9, 23;
   Northumbrian 97
Ipswich 151, 152
Ireland 78n, 82—3, 91, 95, 96, 103—4, 142—3, 145, 157;
   gen. in 72—3, 76—7, 82—3, 91, 95, 99;
   k. lists 72, 101;
   kingship in 82—3;
   laws of 115
Isidore, bishop of Seville 31, 32, 36, 47, 49, 130, 132;
   Historia Gothorum 32
Italy 4—5, 23, 25, 124, 125, 142, 144
Iudila, k. of Visigoths 47
ivory 149, 154

Jews, in Spain 33, 36
Johannes, usurper 43
John of Biclar, chronicle of 32
John, E. 64, 65
Jones, A. H. M. 141
Jordanes, 8, 20, 93n, 96, 137
judges 115, 117, 121
judgeship, Visigothic 7, 137
Judith, *Ordo* of 63
Julian, bishop of Toledo 31, 35—49;
  Antikeimenon 37;
  Apologeticum de tribus capitulis 37;
  Ars Grammatica 40, 47;
  De Comprobatione Sextae Aetatis 37;
  Elogium of Ildefonsus 37;
  Historia Wambae 35, 37, 38—48;
  Libellus de divinis iudiciis 37;
  Prognosticum 37
Julian, emperor 43
justice, administration of 114, 121—4
Justin II, emperor 18
Justinian, laws of 113, 114, 130, 134n
Justus, bishop of Toledo 36

Karolina, recension of *Lex Salica* 108, 116, 117
Kaupang 143
Kelleher, J. 94—5, 97
Kenneth, *see* Cinaed
Kent 20;
  k. lists 76n, 97, 98n;
  laws of 106;
  royal gen. 77, 79—80, 85, 90—1, 94
Kern, F. 57, 105
kindred 84, 113
kingdoms, as allods 26—7;
  and Roman cities 23—6;
  territorial division of, Anglo-Saxon 18, 19—20; Burgundian 20—3; Frankish 2n, 6—7, 12—4, 23, 25—6, 28; Visigothic 17—8, 28—9
king lists 65, 72—7, 96—104, 134n;
  confused with gens. 96—7, 101n, 102;
  and conquests 99—100;
  keepers of 81, 97—8, 102—4;
  and legislation 74—5, 97, 134;
  manipulation of 81, 97;
  purpose of 97—8;
  synchronisation of 99
kings: deposition of 38, 40;
  descent of 8, 96;
  designation of 18, 38;
  election of 8, 36, 41—5, 54—7, 65;
  illegitimate 14, 16, 76;
  and legislation 105—38;
  and merchants 139—58;
  peace of 44, 150;
  pictures of 134;
  pre-migration 7—9, 136—8;
  sacrality of 7—8, 59;
  as war-leaders 4, 7, 37—8;
  wergeld of 111n;
  words for 140—1;
  see also anointing, kingdoms, kinship
kingship: hereditary 8—17, 26—7;
  influence of Bible 1—2;
  influence of Church 3, 24—6, 34—5, 45—9, 59;
  influence of Rome 2—3, 23—5, 39—40, 43—4, 68, 129;
  joint or multiple 13, 17—23, 97;
  and law 105, 136—8;
  sacral 7, 27, 54, 71;
  see also anointing, dynasties royal, law
  Alammanic 17;
  Anglo-Saxon 8, 18, 19—20, 52, 55—6, 96;
  Burgundian 9, 14n, 20—3;
  Frankish 6—7, 9—17, 23—7, 53, 56—63, 71;
  Lombard 4, 18—9;
  Ostrogothic 8, 24;
  Vandalic 8;
  Visigothic 7, 8, 12, 17—8, 27, 30, 35, 41—9, 133
Kingston-upon-Thames 68
Kirby, D. 100
Kleinschmidt, H. 71n
Köbler, G. 152
kula, a form of gift-exchange 145

Lammas 145
Landnámabók, gen. in 96n
language, as evidence of trade 140—1, 143;
  of law-codes 115, 128, 130, 134, 135
Lantfrid, Alaman *dux* 109
Lapidge, M. 71n
Latin, in law-codes 115, 128, 130, 134, 135
laudes 58
Law 105—38;
  change of 112—4;
  making of 136—8;
  Divine 132;
  Mosaic 132;
  Roman 112, 124, 126, 127, 130, 133
Law-codes 3, 33, 105—38, 140;
  arrangement of 116—7;
  authentication of 118, 119;

Christian influence in 130—2;
classification of 107—11;
dating of 118, 119;
and gens. 74—5;
innovation in 112—3;
and k. lists 97;
language of 115, 128, 130, 134, 135;
loss of 114;
manuscripts of 115—7, 120, 123, 130, 134;
prologues 105, 107;
publication of 118—9;
purpose of 105—7, 114—5, 133—6;
Roman influence on 125—30;
use of 119—25
Leach, E. 50
Learned Class 81, 102—4
leather 142, 157
Lebor Gabála Erenn 78n
legislatores 138
legitima aetas 10, 60, 111n
legitimacy 15;
of rule 40, 41, 42, 43, 46, 48, 67
Leinster, court-poetry from 73;
k. list 101
Leland, J. 147—8
Leo VI, Byzantine emperor 5
Leo of Narbonne 126
Leovigild (Liuvigild), k. of Visigoths 12, 17, 44, 129;
laws of 75n, 107—8,133
Leth 9, 94
Lething dynasty 9
Leudegarius, bishop of Autun 53, 58
leudes 11, 15, 23
Levison, W. 39, 53
Lewis, I. M. 88
Lex, as custom 122;
as primary legislation 109—10
Lex Ribuaria 108, 112, 116, 128, 133, 134, 137
Lex Romana Visigothorum 133
Lex Salica 106, 109, 110, 112, 126, 127—9, 133, 134, 138;
arrangement of 116, 133;
Christian influence in 131;
cited 6, 26, 113, 122;
evolution of 108;
prologues to 58, 123, 126, 130, 137;
recensions of 108, 116—7;
vernacular glosses 115—6
Lex Saxonum 112, 120, 121, 124
Lex scripta 114—5, 120, 124, 129, 131, 135
Lex Thuringorum 120

Liber Iudiciorum (Leges Visigothorum) 26, 30, 31, 33, 109, 121; *see also* Visigoths, laws of
Liebermann, F. 116, 119
Lindsey, royal gen. of 77, 79, 90
lineages 86—7
liturgy 44, 46, 48, 51, 63;
texts of 31, 32;
see also ordines
Liutprand, k. of Lombards 18;
laws of 110, 122
Liuva I, k. of Visigoths 17
Liuva II, k. of Visigoths 47
Liuvigild, *see* Leovigild
Livy 40
Lóeguire mac Néill 76n
Lombards 4—5, 8—9, 10, 18—9, 23—4, 28—9, 94, 102, 125—6;
capitularies 135;
k. list 75, 94;
laws of 107, 109—10, 113, 114, 115, 117—8, 119, 120, 121, 124, 128, 134;
royal gen. 9, 75, 94
London 143, 151, 152, 155, 156
Lorsch 122;
Annals of 108
Lothar II 60
Lothian 69
Louis of Bavaria 60
Louis the Pious 59, 60, 61, 118
Lughnasa, festival 145
Lycurgus 132
Lynæs, Denmark, boat from 156
Lyons 20, 21, 22

McClure, Judith 30
magister militum 20, 24, 25
Magnacher 14
Magnus Maximus 81—2
maior palatii 16
Maitland, F. W. 113, 125
Malinowski, B. 144—5
manuscripts, legal 115—6, 120, 123, 130;
liturgical 32
Cambridge, C.C.C., **173** 75n; C.C.C., **383** 75n; U.L., **kk.5.16** 100—1;
León, **Archivio Catedralicio 15** 117n
London, B.L., **Add. 23211** 78; **Add. 57337** 70n; **Cotton Claud. A iii** 70n; **Cotton Tib. A xiii** 99—100; **Cotton Tib. B v(1)** 76n; **Cotton Vesp. B vi** 90, 98
Paris, B.N., **Lat. 4404** 116n; **Lat. 4418** 117n; **Lat. 4627** 117n; **Lat. 4628a** 121; **Lat.**

188

12161 117n; **Lat. 10758** 121
Rochester, **Textus Roffensis** 75n
Vatican, **MS. Reg. Christ. Lat. 991** 117n
Marcomer, k. of Franks 9
Marculf's Formulary 121
markets, and kings 139;
　see also fairs, trading-places
marriage, laws of 113
Marseilles 21
matrilinear descent 89
Matthew Paris 64
Mauss, M. 141
megistanes 27
Meirion, Meirionydd 82
merchants, and kings 139—58;
　Roman 141—2, 146;
　royal protection of 150—1, 152—3;
　as strangers 150—51;
　wealth of 141—2;
　words for 143
Mercia 63, 64, 65, 99, 148, 149, 151;
　ks. of 98;
　k. lists 98—100;
　royal gen. 77, 79, 90—1, 92, 93
Mercians 154, 155
Merovech, k. of Franks, eponymous founder of Merovingians 8, 10, 24
Merovech, son of Chilperic I 11—2
Merovech, son of Theuderic II 10n, 13, 14n
Merovingians 3, 4, 6—17, 23—9, 53, 56—9;
　inauguration rituals of 3, 53, 58;
　laws of 108—9, 118, 126, 129, 135, 137;
　as *reges criniti* 23, 56
Metz 12, 13, 93n
migration, effect on kingship 7—9, 138
Milan 4, 18, 19n
Miller, Molly 78
mints, English 154—6
Missale Francorum 58
missi, Frankish 118, 130
mnemonic verse 98
morgengaben 27
Moses 131, 132, 138
Mozarabic chronicles 32, 36
Munderic, ? Merovingian 6n, 14—5
Munster 82

Nantwich 148
Napoleon 114
Narbonne, bishop of 121
negotium, significance of word 146

Neustria 12
Niall Noígiallach 102
Nicholas of Worcester 64, 67n
Northumbria 19, 63, 65, 76, 102;
　k. list 100—2;
　interregna 97;
　Irish influence in 81;
　royal gen. of 77—81, 91;
　see also Bernicia, Deira
Norway 147, 149
Noyon 24, 25n
Numa Pompilius 132

Obthora 94
Ó Corráin, D. 101
Oda, archbishop of Canterbury 65, 66n, 68
Odovacer 25
Odovacrus, *dux* or *rex* 20n
Öland 142
oenach, see fair
Oesa 90, 101
*Oesingas 91
Östergötland 142
Offa, of Angeln 81, 93
Offa, k. of Mercia 18, 19, 52, 81, 92, 93, 98;
　laws of 112n
officials, Roman 20—1, 24, 25, 126—8
Ó Huiginn, Tadhg Dall 84n
oil 71
Oisc 80, 85, 91n
Oiscingas 80, 91
Old Testament 44;
　and Old Testament kingship 43, 44, 58, 62, 67
oral tradition 84, 85—9, 100
ordines 51, 54, 60, 62, 63n, 66;
　frühdeutsch 55
Ordo, second English 66, 70
origin-legends 88, 100n, 101n, 103
Orleans, church council of (511) 6
Orosius 127
Osbern, *Life of Dunstan* 64
Oskytel, archbishop of York 63
Ostrogoths 8, 9, 24, 28;
　dynasty of 96;
　law of 112;
　royal gen. of 8, 93—4, 96
Oswald, k. of Bernicia 79—81
Oswald, St, biographer of 68
Oswine, k. of Deira 19
Oswiu, k. of Northumbria 19, 99
Ottar 149, 150, 154

189

Otto I 3, 5, 54, 55, 68, 124
overlordship, of Edgar 68—70;
    and gen. 77, 79—80;
    Irish 82—3

Pactus, first version of Alaman Law 108—9
Pactus Legis Salicae 26
pagan festivals 145, 148
paganism 96
pagus 17n, 23, 25
Paris, Church of Holy Apostles 6
Patricius Galliae 21
Patrick, St. 131;
    Lives of 76
patrilines 77, 86, 89, 94
patronymics 84
Paul the Deacon 4, 8, 18, 121
Paul, usurper 17, 35, 39, 43, 45, 46, 121
Pavia 4, 18, 19n
Peada, k. of Mercia 99
pedigree-records, *see* genealogies
Penda, k. of Mercia 81, 99, 100
Perctarit, k. of Lombards 18, 19n
Picts, k. lists 72, 97n, 100
Pippin I, mayor 12
Pippin II 16
Pippin III, k. 5, 60, 108, 116, 133;
    anointing of 2, 56—8, 59
Pippin II, of Aquitaine 60
Pirenne, H. 56
plebs 17n
Plectrudis 16
polygamy, *see* concubinage
popes, and inauguration of rulers 56, 58, 59, 62;
    lists of 100
port, 'Harbour, market' 153, 154
portorium, 'toll' 143
Powys 82, 104n
pre-emption 153, 156
pretenders 14—5
Princes Risborough 148
princesses, Merovingian 16
Priscian, grammarian 39
Procopius 23
prologues, of law-codes 135—6
propaganda 83, 93, 97n, 103—4, 136
Pruzzi 149
Pseudo-Isidoran *Institutionum Disciplinae* 40
Pseudo-Sallustian invectives 39
Pybba, father of Penda 100n
Pyrenees 12

Quadripartitus 120
queens 67, 71;
    anointing of 63
Quentovic 151, 152
Quiricus, bishop of Toledo 42

rachinburgii 138
Radbod, *dux* or *rex* 20n
Radegundis, wife of Chlothar I 15
Ragnachar, k. in Cambrai 10, 23, 28
Ralegh Radford, C. A. 70n
Ratchis, k. of Lombards, laws of 110
Ratoldus, *Ordo* of 63n
Rauching, *dux* 15
Ravenna Geographer 91n
Reccared I, k. of Visigoths 17, 33
Reccared II, k. of Visigoths 47
Recceswinth (Reccaswinth), k. of Visigoths 18, 30, 31, 35, 41, 42, 44, 75, 108, 117
Reccopolis 12n
Rechtsschule 105—6, 109, 114, 117
reciprocity, principle of 141
rectores, as authors of *Lex Salica* 137
regalia 41, 44, 45, 54, 59
regalis 9
regnal list, *see* king list
regnal years 55, 65, 81
Regnum Campaniae (Champagne) 15
Regnum Francorum 14
regulus, *see* sub-kings
Reichenau 117, 122
Remigius, bishop of Rheims 6n, 24
Renatus Profuturus Frigeridus 23
rex 9, 11, 15, 18, 20, 22, 23, 45, 55, 137;
    rex dei gratia 56
Rheims 24, 55, 117, 121
Ribe 140, 150, 151, 152
Richardson, H. G. 64, 119
Ricimer, k. of Visigoths 18
Ricula, daughter of Eormenric 91n
Ripuarian Franks 28; *see also Lex Ribuaria*
rites de passage 63
ritual 34—5, 50—71, 136
Roger of Wendover 64, 92n
Roman Empire, commerce in 141—2, 146;
    influence of 2—3, 18, 23, 44—5, 68, 110, 118—9, 125—6, 129—30, 142—3;
    see also kingship; Law, Roman; officials, Roman
romanitas 93
Romans, attitude to barbarians 126—7;
    as subjects of barbarians 133

Rome 65–6
Rothari, k. of Lombards 133;
  Edict of 26, 75, 94, 102, 107, 110, 111, 112, 115, 117–8, 128, 129;
  gen. of 94;
  k. list 121
royal touch 71
royal villae 30, 31;
  see also Ambérieux, Carouge, Gerticos
rulers, supreme 7, 17;
  see also overlordship

sacrality, of kings 7–8, 59;
  of leaders 7
Sagittarius, bishop of Embrun 14, 16
St Denis, monastery 57, 59, 121
St Gallen 117, 122
S. Juan de Baños, Visigothic church 30
St Médard (Soissons), monastery 58
saints, gens. of 76;
  lives of 52–3, 54, 68, 76, 139;
  and prophecy 76
Salamanca 30, 41
Salian Franks 28
Sallust 39–40
salt, distribution of 147–8;
  toll on 153
Saltwic, see Droitwich
Sapaudia 22n
satrap 7
Satzung 112, 135
Saul, anointing of 43, 58
Savigny 114
Saxnot 78
Saxons, continental 7;
  laws of 108, 111–2, 128
Sayles, G. O. 64, 119
Scandinavia 121, 137, 142–3, 149–54;
  laws of 115
sceptre 44
Schramm, P. 51
scop 102n
Scota, eponym of the Scotti 73
Scotland 52, 73
Scyld Scefing 95
seampending 147, 155
Seaxburh, q. 52n
Seaxnet, in East Saxon gen. 78, 96
Sebbi, k. of Wessex 20
senators, Roman 126
Senchas Mor 131

Senlis 24
Septimania 17
Servatus Lupus 116, 137n
ships 22, 156
shire, West Saxon 19
Sidonius Apollinaris 20, 126
Sighere, k. of Wessex 20
Sigibert the Lame, k. of Ripuarian Franks 23, 28
Sigibert I, k. of Franks 11, 15
Sigibert II, k. of Franks 13
Sigibert III, k. of Franks 12–3
Sigired, k. of Kent 20
Sigismund, k. of Burgundians 22;
  daughter of 14n
Sigivald, ? Merovingian 6n, 15
siliquaticum 141
Singidunum, in Dacia 23
Sisam K. 74, 78, 89
Sisbert, bishop of Toledo 36, 38
Sisebut, k. of Visigoths 47
Sisenand, k. of Visigoths 47
skald 102
Skuldelev, Denmark, boats from 156
slaves, in Spain 33;
  trade in 143, 151, 157
Soemil 90
*Soemlingas 91
Soissons 24
Solon 126, 132
Southampton 157;
  see also Hamwih
Spain 2, 4, 17n, 117, 124, 133, 142;
  evidence for 30–4, see also Julian;
  see also Visigoths
Stein, S. 119
Stenton, F. M. 67
Stephen II, pope 59
strangers, royal protection of 157–8
Suavegotha 14n
subkingdoms 19
subkings 9n, 12, 19, 59, 60, 62, 69
succession 13–7, 25, 42, 51, 59;
  agnatic 10n;
  disputed 18–9;
  elective 42, 44;
  hereditary 8–17, 84;
  imperial 18;
  pre-mortem 52, 60;
  see also association, royal
Suetonius 128
Sulpicius Alexander 9, 23

191

Sunno, k. of Franks 9
Sussex, royal dynasty of 78
Sutton Hoo 4, 140
Sweden 142
Swinthila, k. of Visigoths 18, 32, 47
Syagrius, *Romanorum rex* 24, 126
synchronisms 99

Tacitus 111, 136
Tailtiu, Teltown, fair at 145, 157
Tait, J. 155–6
tanistry 10n
Tara, ks. of 102, 137, 145
Teilreiche 16
Ten Commandments 132
textkritik 116
Theodoric, k. of Ostrogoths 22, 25, 93, 129;
  Edict of 125
Theodoric II, k. of Visigoths 20
Theodosian Code 108, 112, 131
Thérouanne 24, 25, 28
Theudebert I, k. of Franks 2, 6, 11, 13, 23, 129n
Theudebert II, k. of Franks 13, 15, 16
Theudelinda (Theodesinda), wife of Godigisel 21
Theudelinda, Bavarian (Lething) princess, wife of (1) Authari, (2) Agilulf 4, 9, 16n
Theuderic I, k. of Franks 6, 11, 15, 26, 109, 129n
Theuderic II, k. of Franks 13, 16
Theuderic IV, k. of Franks 16n
thing, 27
Thompson, E. A. 27
Thor 78
Thuringians, Law of 108, 111, 128
Tiberius II, emperor 18
titles, in Anglo-Saxon charters 70
Toledo, Church of 31, 35, 38, 44, 48;
  St Leocadia 44, 45;
  SS. Peter and Paul 41, 44, 46, 49;
  city of 30, 31, 36, 37, 40, 44, 45, 46, 48;
  councils of 26, 31, 33, 37, 38, 47
tolls 140, 142–4, 147–8, 153, 156
toponymics, and gens. 83–4
Tournai 4, 7, 23, 24, 25n
Tours 117
towns, in Ireland 157;
  planned 155–6;
  see also trading-places
trade: alternatives to 140;
  commodities of 149–51, 156;
  linguistic evidence for 140–1, 146;
  local and long-distance 146, 154;
  regulation of 139;
  Roman 141–2, 146;
  types of 146;
  see also exchange, merchants
traders, see merchants
trading-places, coastal 151–6;
  and kings 152–3;
  regulation of 139, 142;
  see also *burh*, port, towns, *wic*
treason, law on 112
treasure, royal 11, 15, 23
Trobriand Islands 141, 144–5
Troyes, Council of 121
Tulga, k. of Visigoths 47
Tuy 18
Twelve Tables 130
Tyttla, k. of East Angles 92n

Uecta 79
Uí Néill dynasty 102
Ullmann, W. 1, 71n
unction 34, 41, 44–9;
  see also anointing of kings
usurpation 15, 47, 98
usurpers 45, 74;
  see also Beornred; Johannis; Paul

Vadomarus, k. of Alamans 17
Västergötland 142
Valentinian III, emperor 142
Vandals 8, 28
vava, a form of barter 145
verbum regis 118, 123–4, 135
Vergil 40, 46–7
vernacular, in law-codes 115
Vienne 21
Vikings 27, 60, 69, 151, 155, 157
Vinogradoff, P. 124
Visigoths 7, 8, 9, 27, 28–9, 30–49;
  judgeship of 7, 137;
  k. lists 48–9, 75;
  laws of 31, 107–8, 112–5, 117, 119–21, 124, 127, 129, 130, 133–4;
  see also aristocracy; kingship
Voltaire 57
Vortigern 104
Vouillé 23, 28
Vulgar Law, Roman, see Law, Roman

192

Wægdæg, son of Woden 79
wægnscilling 147, 155
Wærmund 93
Wales, absence of k. lists 96—7;
　gens. in 72, 77, 81—2, 91, 95, 103;
　laws of 144
Wallace-Hadrill, J. M. 1, 16n, 27, 93, 106, 112, 125, 128
walrus tusks 149, 154
Wamba (Bamba), *see Gerticos*
Wamba, k. of Visigoths 35, 38, 39, 40, 41—6, 49, 121
war, leadership in 7
warfare, royal 48
wasi, a form of gift-exchange 145
Wehha 90, 92
Wehhingas 91
Weistum 112
wergild, -geld 111, 112n, 113
Wessex 19, 92, 151;
　burhs in 155;
　dynasty of 92, 102;
　k. list 75n, 78, 101—2;
　royal consecration rites 66—70;
　royal gen. 74, 75n, 77—81, 85, 90—1, 93, 95, 135
West Saxons 78, 80;
　law of 110
westworks 70
whale-bone 149
Whitelock, Dorothy 65n, 71n
wic, place-name element 148, 152
wicgerefa 152

Wickham, C. J. 4n, 19n, 122n
Widukind 5, 54, 55, 68, 121
Wig 81
Wigford, near Lincoln 152
Wiglaf, k. of Mercia 100
Wihtgils, or Witta 80
Wihtlæg 93
Wihtred, k. of Kent 20
William I, k. of England 129
William of Malmesbury 64
Winchester 70, 117n, 155
Winta 90
witan, in law-making 138
Witiza, k. of Visigoths 18
Witta, *see* Wihtgils
Witteric, k. of Visigoths 47
Wittigis, k. of Ostrogoths 8n
Woden, ancestors of 90;
　in royal gens. 8, 77—9, 82, 90, 96
Worcester 70n, 117n, 153, 155—6
Wuffa 92
Wuffingas 91
Wuldetrada 16n
Wulfhere, k. of Mercia 99n
Wulfstan, I, archbishop of York 65
Wulfstan II, archbishop of York 117n, 119, 130

York 117n, 150, 151, 152, 155

Zacharias, pope 56, 58
Zülpich 23